THE WINES OF
ITALY

David Gleave M.W.

Consultant Editor
Joanna Simon

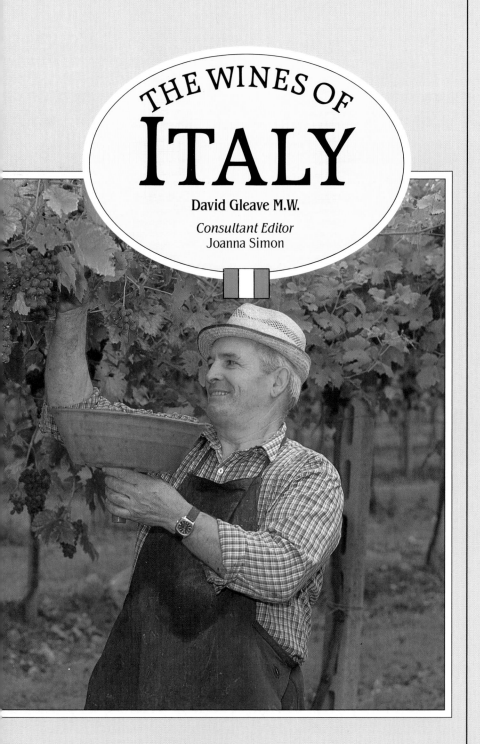

THE WINES OF
ITALY

David Gleave M.W.

Consultant Editor
Joanna Simon

a Salamander book

Published by Salamander Books Limited
LONDON • NEW YORK

A Salamander Book

Published by Salamander Books Ltd,
52 Bedford Row,
London WC1R 4LR,
United Kingdom

© Salamander Books Ltd 1989

ISBN 0 86101 372 7

Distributed in the UK by
Hodder & Stoughton Services,
P.O. Box 6,
Mill Road, Dunton Green, Sevenoaks,
Kent TN3 2XX

Credits

Editor:
Philip de Ste. Croix

Editorial assistant:
Roseanne Eckart

Designer:
Roger Hyde

Maps:
Sebastian Quigley
© Salamander Books Ltd

Index:
Jill Ford

Filmset:
SX Composing Ltd, England

Colour and monochrome reproduction:
Kentscan Ltd, England

Printed in Italy

DEDICATION
For Charlotte

AUTHOR

David Gleave was born and educated in Toronto, Canada. His family moved to
Vancouver in 1976, where he briefly attended the University of British Columbia.
He took time off from his studies to travel to Europe in 1978, but, after hitch-
hiking through France, Germany and Italy to Greece and Israel, he returned to
London to live. He worked at a variety of jobs, mostly related to catering, before
moving to Dublin in 1980. He spent two and a half years there, and first
developed his interest in wines while working in a bar in Dublin.

He returned to London in 1983, and has lived there ever since. He passed the
Master of Wine examination in 1986, and is today recognised as one of the
foremost authorities on Italian wine in the British trade. He is the Wine Buyer for
Winecellars and The Market chain of shops in London, the UK's leading specialists
in quality Italian wines. He writes widely on the subject for magazines like *Wine &
Spirit, WINE,* and *Decanter,* and he lectures to Diploma students for the Wine and
Spirit Education Trust.

CONSULTANT EDITOR

Joanna Simon has edited two of the foremost journals in the English language:
Wine & Spirit magazine, which she joined as assistant editor in 1981, becoming
editor in 1984, and *WINE,* which she edited between October 1986 and December
1987. She has travelled extensively in Europe and Australia, has tasted for a
number of wine magazines, as well as *The Financial Times,* and has written for a
wide range of trade and consumer publications on wine-related subjects. She is
currently wine correspondent for *The Sunday Times,* and Contributing Editor of
WINE and *Wine & Spirit.*

ACKNOWLEDGEMENTS

This book could never have been written unless a great number of people had selflessly provided me with time, help and advice over the years. Amongst these, I owe my parents a special debt of gratitude for instilling in me an interest in both wine and the written word. Nicolas Belfrage, as boss, teacher and friend, has provided immense help, as have his fellow directors, Colin Loxley and James Pickford, whose understanding view of the idiosyncratic approach I take to my job has provided me with the freedom to research this book. And among my other colleagues, both Ilona Doyle and Paul Nugent provided invaluable support.

I have been given great help by numerous people in the London wine trade, but in relation to Italian wines, Maureen Ashley, Luciana Lynch and Renato Trestini have provided both general and specific advice. Paul Merritt and Michael Garner are due a special vote of thanks for all their help, but especially that on the wines of Alba. In Italy, many people have been exceptionally generous, but none more so than Tom O'Toole.

While writing this book, Joanna Simon and Philip de Ste. Croix were patient, encouraging and full of advice. And Fiona Wild and Roseanne Eckart, by reading the finished text, ensured that most errors were removed; all that remain are my own.

As a wine merchant, I have built up a special relationship with many producers, but, not unsurprisingly, particularly with those whose wines we import. These producers will be found in these pages, not only because I know their wines well, but also, just as we import them because we have such regard for their quality, because they deserve to be. To declare my interest, they are: Giuseppe Mascarello, Giacomo Ascheri, Mario Pasolini, Alois Lageder, Isole e Olena, Selvapiana, Fattoria Felsina, Capezzana, Altesino, Villa di Vetrice, Teruzzi e Puthod, Anselmi, Colli di Catone and Marco De Bartoli.

CONTENTS

FOREWORD

The first bottle of wine that I drank at my parents' table was Italian. It was a Chianti Classico, bought for a special occasion, and the flavours, rich and distinctive, made a lasting impression upon me. Perhaps it was the importance of the occasion, or the significance of my first glass of wine, but the memory of the majesty of that wine remains clear to this day.

Years later, when the mysteries of wine had lured me to the subject, I went in search of that taste again. But whenever I attempted to enter the world of Italian wine, I would find myself rebuffed, mostly by my own ignorance of the vast range that was on offer. With French wines, I found the key with greater ease. The books available had built upon a long tradition of scholarship to present a lucid and cogent view of their subject, while the wines that served as introductions to the taste of France were easily found.

But that memory of the Chianti, now enhanced by a trip to Italy, lingered persistently. I searched for books that would unlock the doors I was trying to enter, but most of what was available was of little help. And then I came across Burton Anderson's *Vino*, which, for the first time, presented the human face of Italian wine. It went behind the tangled web of bureaucracy that choked much of the Italian wine world, and conveyed the beauty of the places, the tastes of the wines and, most of all, the philosophies that motivated the winemakers. *Vino* illuminated a small patch of the great expanse of darkness that had been Italian wines. Several years later, Nicolas Belfrage's *Life Beyond Lambrusco*, which adopted quite a different approach, served to broaden the circumference of the circle of light.

Both books, however, require a certain level of knowledge on the part of the reader before they can be approached. This makes them difficult for the person coming to Italian wines for the first time. Italy and her wines remain a confusing subject, but in writing this book I have tried to present the subject as clearly as possible. In an attempt to create a little order out of the glorious confusion, I have arbitrarily imposed a structure of sorts on Italy. Rather than view it region by region, and wine by wine, I have carved it up into zones that, while not political boundaries, more closely approximate

Metric/Imperial Equivalents

The Italian wine industry uses metric measurements to express volumes, weights, dimensions, etc. This book, therefore, also uses metric units for such measurements. For those readers unfamiliar with the metric system, or who are more comfortable thinking in Imperial units, listed below are the necessary conversion factors.

1 metre (m) = 3.281 ft
1 kilometre (km) = 0.6214 miles
1 hectolitre (hl) = 100 litres = 22 UK gallons or 26.4 US gallons
1 hectare (ha) = 10,000m^2 = 2.471 acres
1 kilogramme (kg) = 2.205lb
1 tonne = 1,000kg = 2,205lb

vinous boundaries. And within these zones, I have divided the subject not by wines, but by grape varieties, which is, I feel, much less confusing.

These zones have been mapped out throughout the book. In drawing up these maps, we have not tried to show the de-limited zone for every Italian wine, which would be more confusing than enlightening in a book of this size, but have tried to con-centrate on what I consider to be the more important DOC areas, and to convey a general sense of the geography of the parti-cular zone. In adopting this system, I have drawn from both Renato Ratti, whose Oen-ological Map first conceived of Italy in such a way, and from Nicolas Belfrage, who adapted it to suit his own purposes. My tinkering with both, and the approach I have taken, will, I hope, clear up some of the confusion sur-rounding Italian wines, while enabling me to convey their essential excitement.

Key to map
1 Valle d'Aosta.
2 Piemonte.
3 Liguria.
4 Lombardy.
5 Trentino-Alto Adige.
6 Veneto.
7 Friuli-Venezia Giulia.
8 Emilia-Romagna.
9 Tuscany.
10 Umbria.
11 The Marches.
12 Lazio.
13 Abruzzi.
14 Molise.
15 Campania.
16 Puglia.
17 Basilicata.
18 Calabria.
19 Sardinia.
20 Sicily.

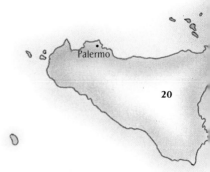

"*T*he problem with Italian wines is that they taste so Italian."

"Perhaps that is because they *are* Italian."

"Yes, but they taste so different from French wines."

This is not an unusual conversation. To someone raised on French wines, neither Australia nor California, Chile nor New Zealand pose any problems. But Italy does. Italian wines generally have a taste and character all their own, something attributable to Italy's different grape varieties, soils and climatic conditions, as well as to the various unique production techniques that have evolved since the Greeks first brought the vine to Italy almost 3,000 years ago.

The vine thrives on Italy's mountainous slopes, rich plains and gently rolling hills. Italy can probably claim the longest, unbroken tradition of viticulture of any country. Italy, or her various regions, have forged this tradition over the millennia, and today she

offers, to those willing to explore, a whole spectrum of tastes and styles that no other wine producing country, not even France, can match. In an age where diversity of taste, culture and style are disappearing, surely Italian wine, with its startling individuality, should be treasured.

Just as there are those who find Shostakovich too strident and demanding, prefer-

Above: *These Nebbiolo grapes, harvested by hand in Barolo, produce one of Italy's most traditional and individual wines.*

While the French tradition prides itself on its pre-eminence, the Italian, in the last quarter of a century, has undergone more changes than it had in the previous thousand years. This is, to a large extent, a reflection of the changes that have occurred in Italian society. From the depression and chaos of the war years has emerged a dynamic, affluent country that, if still slightly chaotic, indulges itself, and the visitor, with its love of life. The creative skill of the Italians, allied to their ardent individuality, has been fused to a tradition that stretches back thousands of years, giving a country rich in history yet instilled with a youthful enthusiasm for life.

These same elements make Italian wines such an exciting subject. On its strong foundation of tradition has been built a structure at once modern and timeless, one that satisfies the tastes of today while evoking memories of the Medici, Dante, the Romans and the Greeks. Italian winemakers have travelled abroad for the first time, to places like France, California and Australia, and have brought back with them new ideas and skills.

This great ferment of activity, with the most modern of ideas being used alongside others that date back to the Greeks, makes Italy the most exciting country in the world of wine today. But it also makes it more than a little confusing. There are those who feel that the structure erected by Italy's winemakers is nothing more than a vinous Tower of Babel, a hopeless jumble of styles that confuses more than it actually achieves.

This is unfair. Using old or new grape varieties, Italy's winemakers have created something called "Italian Wine" that the country can be immensely proud of. In the last couple of generations, these winemakers have established, within their tradition of viniculture, a tradition of quality. Italy's wines, once bought and sold in bulk, and regarded as little more than something to drink only with food, are now, thanks to new skills and equipment, but most of all to a new philosophy, capable of standing beside the best that the rest of the world has to offer.

In the pages that follow, I hope to convey something of the flavour of these traditions and changes, and the people and philosophies behind them. I have tried to chisel away at some of the baroque ornamentation in order to present a clearer view of Italy's wines. In places, I may have cut away too much for some tastes. I apologise in advance for such temerity. But this is an attempt to introduce people to the great glory of Italian wines, and to impart some of what I find endlessly fascinating about the country and her wines, her food and her people.

This is not, and nor have I tried to make it, a definitive tome. For those who get to the end and feel their appetite whetted, I recommend other books, notably Burton Anderson's *Vino* and Nicolas Belfrage's *Life Beyond Lambrusco*. Better still, why not visit Italy itself? But for those starting out, and still uncertain, come, let us begin.

ring instead the mellifluous genius of Mozart, so are there those, grown accustomed to the cedary scent and velvety texture of mature claret, who cannot come to terms with the tannic clout that is retained by even a mature Barolo. But as music accommodates both Shostakovich and Mozart, so should wine rejoice that its two diverse traditions can co-exist in comparative harmony.

*T*he Greeks called Italy "Enotria Tellus", the land of vines. This was not because they found the peninsula carpeted with vines when they arrived, but more because of the great affinity that the vine displayed for the sun and soil of Italy, and the superior quality of wine that the new colony produced. Today's visitor to Italy, unaware of this ancient title, could easily come to the conclusion that Italy should be called the "land of vines" because of the way in which, in most parts of the peninsula, from the outskirts of Milan and Turin, down the craggy Apennine spine to the volcanic slopes of Sicily's Mt Etna, the vine has taken root.

But while the Greeks can take credit for introducing the vine to the South, the Etruscans, about whom much less is known, brought it to most of northern and central Italy. This has given her two distinct viticultural traditions, both of which have spawned different practices in the vineyard, and both of which have bequeathed to Italy an unrivalled diversity of vine varieties.

What both the Greeks and Etruscans found was not only a climate that was well-suited to the vine, but also a mountainous country. Pliny observed that the vine loves an open hill, but what he probably meant was that he preferred the wine from such vines. The vine, grown on hillsides, produces lower yields, and hence better grapes, than those grown on plains. And, in places, the altitude will compensate for the latitude, meaning that even in hotter parts of the country, a hilly site can provide a particularly cool microclimate. This, allied with the length of Italy (Palermo is further from Milan than London is), ensures a country with a varied climate, which in turn makes generalisations about vintages extremely difficult.

This varied climate might help to explain the great diversity of Italy's grape varieties. It is impossible to pinpoint the exact number of vine varieties planted in Italy today, but a rough estimate of 900-1,000 would probably be close to the mark. These range from well-known natives like the Nebbiolo (the only grape of Barolo and Barbaresco) and Sangiovese (the major constituent of Chianti) to famous imports such as the Cabernet Sauvignon and Chardonnay, with a host of obscure varieties in between, some of which may be found only in one region or, in some cases, solely in a single vineyard.

In addition to the climate, the reason for this bewildering profusion of vine varieties, from the great and noble to the base and plebeian, lies in Italy's history. The strongly regional nature of Italy meant that many varieties were given local names, while others, planted and propagated in several diverse areas, became, due to mutation and local conditions, virtually different varieties. And trading, not only between regions, but also between, say, the Medici of Florence and the French, meant that many varieties were brought to regions where they came, after several generations, to be viewed as native.

An example of this confusion lies in a

Above: *Vineyards in San Severo in northern Puglia. The vines are now trained higher. This gives them a better balance of sugar and acid, though it can also lead to excessive yields.*

curiosity of a white vine called the Pagadebit. Found in both Friuli and Romagna, it is easy to conjecture that the name, meaning "pay a debt", simply refers to a hardy local vine that would yield prolifically even in poor years, and that the two varieties are unrelated. Yet the Cagnina, a rare red Romagnolan grape, is said to be Friuli's Terrano, a clone of Refosco. This would seem to indicate that there was once a certain amount of trade in vines between the two regions, which in turn means that the Pagadebit could, in fact, be the same vine in each region.

Another source of confusion is the Italian habit of giving different vines, planted in separate regions, the same name. The Trebbiano, Italy's most widely planted white grape, is a case in point. As the Trebbiano Toscano, it is rightly damned by the critics because of the large quantities of dull, neutral wine it produces. Yet other varieties like the Trebbiano di Soave, Trebbiano di Lugana and Trebbiano d'Abruzzo, are, despite the fact that they produce distinctly different and quite characterful wines, subject to the same sweeping denunciation as the Tuscan variety simply because they have a name in common. They may be distinct clones, or different varieties, but they are certainly not the Trebbiano Toscano.

To understand this glorious confusion, it is necessary only to drive down a gravel track in Tuscany, or the Via Emilia, and stop the car beside a field in which the vine is planted alongside olive and fruit trees and even, in some cases, wheat. This system of *"coltura promiscua"*, or mixed culture, as distinct from specialised culture, where the vines are planted in splendid isolation, was prevalent

Above: *Harvesting grapes near Brindisi in Puglia. The hot climate and different soil combine to produce wines that are unique to their region, and as different from those of the North as they can be.*

Above: *Breaking the ground by hand above Tito, near Potenza, in the region of Basilicata. Such a "low tech" approach to agriculture can still be glimpsed in various parts of Italy.*

in much of Italy until as recently as the fifties. To the small tenant farmer and the local landowner, both operating under a medieval system of agriculture, the vine was simply another crop. And its product, wine, was never really accorded any special status, but was rather viewed as an agricultural product and an integral part of everyday life.

In areas like Piemonte, once part of the Kingdom of Savoy, the French influence has meant that there has been a greater preponderance of specialised vineyards for several centuries, but in the rest of Italy, the vine was viewed as merely another ingredient in the agricultural mix. This began to change after World War II, and through the fifties, when many of those who had been traditionally dependent upon working the land for scraping a living found that the industrial regeneration of the cities offered the possibility of work with far greater rewards.

By the beginning of the sixties, most farmers were unable to rely on the great pool of cheap labour that had previously been available, and were forced to reorganise their fields in order to work them more efficiently. This meant both mechanisation and specialisation. The vines were given their own plot of land, while olive trees and wheat were given another.

The sixties was a period of widespread replanting in which the face of Italian viticulture was changed forever. Until then, it was still possible, as the famous Piemontese winemaker Renato Ratti pointed out, to trace the systems of training that existed in the vineyards back to their Greek and Etruscan origins. In those regions where the Greeks had been responsible for introducing the

vine, most notably in the South, the vine was densely planted and trained low, without support, while in those like the North and Centre, in which the Etruscan influence could still be glimpsed, the vine was trained high, up trees or poles, with fewer plants per hectare under cultivation.

Today, the systems of training the vine vary widely from region to region, and have less to do with tradition and more to do with the contemporary wisdom that prevailed when the vineyard was planted. It is still possible to see the Etruscan influence in the North, especially in the Veneto and Friuli, where vines are trained high, but a growing number of producers are switching to lower systems of training, with a greater number of plants per hectare, in pursuit of higher levels of quality.

In the South, where the vines were traditionally trained, in the "*alberello*" system, in a bush, low and without support, higher systems are now being employed. The old system was more expensive, not only because of greater labour, but also because of lower yields, which in turn gave wines deep in colour, high in alcohol and low in acid. This made them much sought after for use in blending, as a dollop of strong, concentrated southern wine would go a long way towards fleshing out a more anaemic example from the North.

With the vines trained higher today, in the *tendone* system, yields have increased, and the wines are less concentrated. This makes

Above: *The high training methods used for these vines in Valpolicella would not have been unfamiliar to the Etruscans, who introduced them into Italy.*

Right: *Tying up of Barbera shoots, near Casorzo in Piemonte, where the vines are trained low, along wire supports.*

them less suited for use in blending, but their high yield makes them too dilute to be considered as good quality. True, higher training can be a handy way of retaining acid in the grapes under the hot southern sun, but this is only ever useful if yields are kept low.

Vineyard Terms

Alberello Free standing, bush-style training used extensively in the South.

Guyot Low style of training, along wires. Widely used in Piemonte.

Pergola High system of training, usually up posts and over wires to form an arbour.

Quintale 100kg of grapes, used to express the yield. A yield of 80 quintali and a *resa* of 70 per cent would give 56 hectolitres/hectare.

Spalliera Trained low, along wires.

Tendone Trained high, up poles and along wires. Used in the South.

Above: *In Piemonte's Langhe hills, the Nebbiolo is trained low, along wires. This reflects Greek and French influence, and also the needs of the vine.*

In some regions, the system of training that has developed can be attributed to natural factors, rather than to tradition. In the flatlands of Emilia, for instance, the humid soil would cause rot if the grapes were hanging close to it, so it has always been necessary to train the Lambrusco vine high, either up trees or poles. In Piemonte's Langhe hills, on the other hand, where the Nebbiolo holds sway, lower systems of training, most notably the Guyot, prevail. Though the Greeks are said to have introduced the vine to Piemonte, the French influence, which favours low training, is strong here. But the Nebbiolo, with its infertile bud at the base of each cane, needs to be trained along wires in order to produce fruit, and the Guyot system would seem most suitable.

The wholesale replanting of the sixties saw not only great changes with regard to systems of training, but also to what was planted in the vineyard. Not since phylloxera had there been replanting on such a scale, and many minor varieties, often despised by the poor farmer because of niggardly yields, disappeared.

At the time, given the low price of much Italian wine, high yields were an economic necessity. It was felt necessary to increase yields rather than quality, so it was recommended that high yielding clones be planted. And the cost of reshaping the vineyards was reduced by planting at a lower density of, say 1,500-3,000 vines per hectare.

Since then, in the last quarter of a century, the market for quality Italian wines has grown at as fast a rate as the realisation of the mistakes that were made during replanting. Today's growers realise that quality wine is made in the vineyard, and that high yields are incompatible with the level of quality they are seeking. This search for quality has led them to make changes in the vineyard.

Most vineyards now replanted by producers whose aim is quality are cultivated at a much higher plant density than they were in the sixties. Today, there will be as many as 5,000-8,000 vines per hectare. The theory is that this gives less quantity per vine, but better quality. But the producers are also keen to reduce yields per hectare. This can be done by using less fertiliser, especially nitrogen, but also by severe pruning. Many of Italy's top producers now pass through the vineyard at the end of June, once flowering has taken place, in order to thin their crop. This reduction in quantity leads to better grapes which, if a similar dedication to quality is employed in the cellar, will lead to better wine.

Today, high yields are the greatest cause of poor quality wine in Italy. The authorities, at the behest of greedy, lazy growers, have systematically increased yields over the past decade. This is a great folly, undermining the straitened path of quality that is increasingly being pursued by Italy's best growers.

This pursuit of quality begins, but does not end, with low yields. Research is being stepped up in various parts of Italy in attempts to increase the quality of grapes produced. In some regions, traditional grape varieties, prized and retained after phylloxera or during the sixties because of their vigour and high yields, are now being replaced by other varieties, often imported. With other varieties, work is being done to find the best clones, those best suited to specific soils or microclimates.

This is an exciting – indeed, revolutionary – time for Italian viticulture. The revolution is being fought on various fronts – mechanisation, clonal selection, the classification of vineyards, reduction of yields – but the aim is to produce the best quality grapes. For today, Italy's winemakers are at long last realising that great wine is made not only in the cellar, but also in the vineyard.

*I*taly's wineries are a diverse bunch. Some offer a glimpse of the future, with their high-tech gadgetry and technical wizardry, while others afford a rare view of the past, of how wine was made centuries, and even millennia, ago. But most have been transformed beyond all recognition in the last quarter of a century, as new ideas have swept out the dustiest corners of the old "cantine", leaving them lively and glistening and, most important, better able to turn their best grapes into wines that are capable of matching the finest that the rest of the world has to offer.

Remnants of Italy's vinous history can still be found in the odd cellar, but the number of these artefacts is diminishing rapidly. By contrast, at the end of World War II, many wines were still made in a fashion that would not have seemed at all unusual to the Romans. True, wood had replaced clay amphorae to become not only an ideal vessel for transportation, but also a means for producing and storing wines. The style of the wine produced – strong, concentrated and robust – varied little from that which the Romans had drunk. They diluted its strength with water, of course.

But more has changed in the last forty years than had changed in the previous two thousand, and the key element in this dramatic transformation has been the increase in the amount of control exerted by the winemaker. Wine is, after all, an intermediate phase between sweet grape juice and vinegar, and it is up to the winemaker to ensure that this is a stable phase.

In the past, the same *laissez-faire* philosophy that reigned in the vineyards was to be found in the winery. Heat and oxygen had always been present in the *cantina,* so they were regarded as constant factors in the

---

Below: *The control panel at Villa Banfi's "high tech" cellars in Montalcino. Such equipment, modern as any to be found in countries like Australia, has radically changed Italy's wines since the war.*

winemaking equation. It is only since the fifties that many of the previously unknown quantities in this equation have become known to Italian producers, and the hand of man has come to play more of a guiding rôle in the production of wine.

This is perhaps most true of white wines. It is often said that while red wines are made in the vineyard, white wines are made in the cellar. Though this axiom is currently under siege, it was widely held to be true in the Italy of the sixties and seventies. The white wines of the past, crushed roughly with little regard to the amount of harmful, bitter elements extracted, fermented at temperatures that soared to 30°C in some years, and stored in large oak vats called "*botte*" until they were sold, usually in demijohns to local clients, were not up to the standard required if Italy was going to challenge the export markets.

The move away from wine that was used solely as a beverage for local consumption as an integral part of the meal, towards a product that could successfully be exported, forced producers to look to and learn from

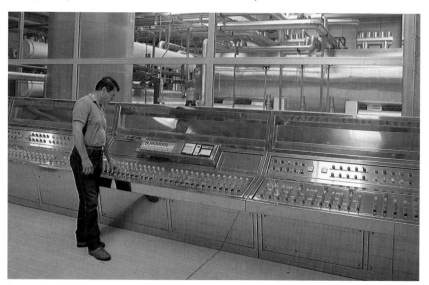

Above: *Demijohns – large bottles in wicker cases as seen here – are still widely used in Italy. Many people will get their weekly supply of wine by going to a local producer and buying a demijohn of his (sometimes) excess production.*

the outside world. Equipment, techniques and ideas were imported, and the old style, oxidised white wine was urged along the road to extinction.

Initially, the use of materials such as stainless steel, cement or fibreglass, that enabled the winemaker to control temperature during fermentation and to protect the wine from oxidation, was an important advance. Temperature control during the early,

Below: *Stainless steel fermentation tanks at a co-operative in Basilicata. This expensive equipment is essential in the production of sound wines, as they permit proper temperature control.*

tumultuous stages of fermentation enabled the winemaker to preserve the perfume or character of the grape variety, rather than helplessly watch it boil away, as had previously been the case. And once this phase had been successfully negotiated, the new materials provided the producer with a storage vessel that protected the wine from oxygen, another element which can have a destructive influence on the aromas of a young wine.

There are, according to most winemakers, two basic aromas found in wine: the primary, which consist of those of the grape and the production process; and the secondary, which the wine acquires as it ages. The ability to control temperature and to protect the wine from oxygen ensured that these primary aromas were captured. In the early days, though, they were often subsequently lost at bottling, either by the action of heat (wines were either pasteurised or bottled at a high temperature to render them stable) or sulphur dioxide, a necessary preservative that, when used in excessive quantities, can flatten and mask the wine's perfume.

Above: Barriques *such as these are favoured by many of Italy's modern winemakers for the flattering scent and texture they impart to the wine.*

Over the years, various technological advances have remedied these problems. A greater degree of hygiene in the cellar has led to a reduction in the use of sulphur, as has an increased understanding of its properties, while most white wines are now bottled at cool temperatures in sterile conditions.

If there is such a thing as a typical dry white wine in Italy, its production method would follow a not too dissimilar path to this: the grapes arrive at the winery and are gently crushed so that only the best juice is extracted; this juice is then chilled, and may or may not be kept in contact with the skins for anything from six to 24 hours to extract more flavour. After this, it is cleaned up, either by cold precipitation, centrifugation or vacuum filtration, to enable the wine-maker to exert greater control over the fermentation. Fermentation takes place in any one of a great variety of vessels, from small, new French *barriques* and large, old oak *botti* to cement, glass-lined or stainless steel vats. Whatever the material, it is vital that it be clean, and essential that the producer can control the temperature.

Fermentation proceeds at anything from 15-23°C, but more likely at about 16-18°C. Once finished, the wine is racked from its lees (the detritus of fermentation) and stored in its container until it is ready to be bottled. If it has been fermented in *barrique,* the wine may rest there a little longer to pick up the vanilla flavour of the oak; if it has been fermented in stainless steel, it may be transferred to *barrique* to acquire an oaky sheen prior to bottling, or it may simply be stored in cement or stainless steel until it is bottled in the April or May following the vintage.

Above: *Francesco Gravner, one of Italy's great white wine producers, has little wood in his cellar, and he now regrets having replaced it several years ago.*

The malolactic fermentation, during which the appley malic acid is transformed into the softer lactic acid, will, if all the conditions are right, take place in the Spring. The winemaker can either encourage it to give a softer, more complex wine, or inhibit it in order to retain a decent bite of acidity. Today, many producers are making wines where 50 per cent of the blend has undergone the malolactic, while the other half has not, giving the wine a certain complexity but also a sufficient level of acidity.

At bottling, a small amount of carbon dioxide may be retained in the wine. This not only enhances the flavour, but also protects the wine from oxygen, and accounts for the slight prickle on the tip of the tongue that one experiences when tasting many modern Italian dry white wines.

Above: A number of small producers, unable to afford the cost of installing their own bottling line, use mobile ones like that pictured above.

This march of technology continues, with new techniques being developed in attempts to increase quality. One of the most beneficial of these is the deliberate oxidation of the must prior to fermentation. This method is being used for non-aromatic grapes like Chardonnay, and serves to precipitate oxidative substances in the wine, thus rendering it more stable at a later stage. As the oxidation is reversed during fermentation, there is, claim the adherents of this system, no discernible difference in quality, except that a wine produced in this way would have lower levels of sulphur. This is because no sulphur is added before fermentation, when in any case it becomes bound and ineffective, but only after fermentation and at bottling, when it remains in a free state, and is most effective. This is propelling Italian white wines ever further down the road to lower sulphur levels, a fact that will please those of us who are particularly sensitive to it.

New technology, judiciously applied, has undoubtedly increased quality, but it has also, in some cases, conspired to rob many

wines of character. A pale colour and a neutral taste are now seen by most producers, and many Italian consumers, as virtues. The must is cleaned up to too great a degree, and this, combined with excessive yields, results in wines that are anonymous, and at the opposite end of the spectrum to the old-style, alcoholic and oxidised white wine. In recent years, the pendulum has begun to swing back, and producers are discovering that less technology can actually be a better way of achieving greater character.

For red wines, the situation has changed at a more gradual pace, but with no less dramatic results. Once again, temperature control has been one of the most important factors in this transformation, enabling winemakers to produce healthier wines capable of longer ageing in both cask and bottle.

Most producers will de-stem the grapes once they arrive at the winery in order to reduce the level of tannin. After crushing, the must will be macerated on the skins for anything from two to three to 30 (or in some cases, even 60) days, depending on the style of wine required. But whereas in the past, the skins would float to the top, forming a hard cap that, despite attempts to punch it down and break it up, was a fertile breeding ground for bacteria and volatile acidity (the first step on the road to vinegar), today, the winemaker will pump the must over the cap, keeping it moist and extracting colour. This gives wines with good colour and fruit, and thankfully lacking the austere tannic grip that was so evident in the past.

Some producers take the opportunity at this point to make a better red wine by producing a *rosato*. After macerating the must on the skins for anything from 12 to 24 hours, they will drain some of it off, the exact quantity depending on the quality of the grapes. This gives a higher proportion of grape skins to juice, meaning that more colour, tannin and flavour will be given to the wine. The juice that has been drained off will be fermented to dryness, and will usually turn out as a delicious *rosato*. This procedure is particularly prominent in Tuscany.

Following fermentation, the wine is racked off its lees. This is done several times in its first year so that the wine does not pick up any off-flavours, or run the risk of bacterial spoilage. In the past, many wines were ruined by being left in contact with their lees for too long, but today, increased racking has led to cleaner, healthier wines.

After the malolactic fermentation in the Spring, something always encouraged for red wines, the wine will be transferred to its

Above: The grape skins, after crushing, and once the winemaker is satisfied that they have been macerated in the fermenting must for a sufficient length of time, are removed from the tanks.

appropriate ageing vessel. In the case of light red wines, they will, like white wines, be bottled early in order to preserve their essential charm, the primary fruit aromas.

The next stage is one of maturation. Today, the extent and method of maturation depends very much on the style of wine required. This is a great step forward from the days when wines were kept in *botte* until they were sold, when storage and maturation were virtually synonymous. Unlike the French, particularly the Bordelais, who shipped their wines to England in small, 225-litre oak barrels called *barriques*, where they were bottled early by London merchants, the Italians sold their wine in demi-johns, but seldom, if ever, for the purpose of bottling.

The wines of Bordeaux acquired their great reputation for longevity largely because they were bottled early. The time they spent in oak gave them a distinctive character, and early bottling enabled the wine to develop its secondary flavours in bottle, over a long period of time.

Italian wines, though, were not bottled until they were ready for drinking, if they were bottled at all. And as their wines did not reach the market that the Bordelais had, obviating the need for shipping and storing the wines in small oak *barriques*, Italian producers found it easier to store them in large, oak barrels.

Wines mature differently in small oak from the way they develop in large oak. Smaller

Above: Barriques *in Ratti's cellars at La Morra must be kept topped up to protect the wine from oxygen and bacteria.*

Above: *These large, Slovenian oak casks, called "botti", are the traditional vessels for storage and maturation in much of Italy. Wines age more slowly in these large casks.*

oak imparts greater flavour to the wine, as well as softer tannins, and ages the wine at a faster rate, while large oak vats permit a gentle oxygenation of the wine, without imparting a distinctively oaky flavour.

Unlike that of their French counterparts, the maturation of Italian wines took place in contact with oxygen, rather than in bottle. As a result, they did not develop in bottle, so were outside the "classical" French tradition of quality. The long spell in *botte* often led to unacceptable levels of oxidation and volatile acidity, but this was due more to sloppy cellar work than to any intrinsic defect in such a system of ageing.

Today, this system of ageing is changing. Italy's winemakers are determined that the health of the wine they have nurtured from its conception in the vineyard through its first tentative steps in the cellar should not be endangered by neglect during maturation. New methods of ageing the wine call for diverse sizes of vessels made of any different number of materials to be used to store wines for the varying lengths of maturation time.

The old system is still in use, but greater care is being taken to keep the casks topped up, and to prevent the ingress of oxygen, thus ensuring that healthier wines are produced. But in the last decade or so, there has been a great increase in the use of *barriques* in the cellars of Italy. The distinctive polish they add to a wine is much sought after by producers of both white and red wines, and this fusion of French and New World techniques with Italian grapes has produced some stunning results.

Italy's winemakers now view maturation as a distinct and important stage in the production of a wine. No longer do wines spend an indeterminate length of time in *botte*. Instead, great thought is given to the most beneficial way in which to treat the wine from the end of fermentation to bottling. The wine may be aged in *barrique*, or in *botte*, or have a short spell in each, but the aim of Italy's winemakers is to put into bottle something that will continue to age slowly, in the Bordeaux tradition, for a number of years. This, as much as anything, has changed the face of Italian wines.

*T*he Italians have long produced some of the world's greatest sweet wines, and have led the rest of us in the amount of sparkling wine they consume. Occasionally, these predilections converge, most notably in the shape of Asti Spumante, but more often their unique sweet wines and useful sparklers stand apart.

Sweet wines are made either by retaining a certain amount of the grape's natural sugar, or by adding a specially prepared sweetener to a fully fermented, dry wine. While the Germans are particularly adept in the use of the latter method, almost all Italian sweet wines, with the exception of branded commercial concoctions, are made by stopping the fermentation before all the sugar has been transformed to alcohol.

The fermentation will either stop naturally, when the alcohol has reached a level where the yeasts are no longer able to function, or will be stopped by the intervention of the winemaker. Of wines made by the latter method, Moscato d'Asti is perhaps the best known. After crushing, the must is stored at a low temperature until the producer needs to bottle more wine. Fermentation is started by raising the temperature, and proceeds until the wine reaches the required strength, usually around 5-6° of alcohol. At this point, the producer will stun the yeasts by dropping the temperature back to about 0°C, and remove them by filtration. The naturally sweet wine is then ready to be bottled and sold.

The other great method of producing sweet wines is to start with grapes that have a naturally high level of sugar. While those used in the production of Moscato d'Asti will seldom have a potential alcohol of more than 12°, the grapes used for Vin Santo or Recioto della Valpolicella will have a much higher degree of natural sweetness and thus potential alcohol.

Below: *Drying the grapes for use in Amarone and Recioto della Valpolicella wines. The grapes are picked slightly earlier, and are laid out to dry until about the end of January. At the end of this period (known as the "appassimento") the grapes are shrivelled and rich in sugar. This technique is widely used for making sweet wines.*

Left: *These bottles of* "Méthode Champenoise" *sparkling wine are tilted to work sediment towards the neck.*

though, are distinctly Italian and widely produced. These "*passito*" wines are made by laying the grapes on racks, or by hanging them from rafters, or even by laying them out under the sun, in order to dry them before crushing.

Whatever the method, the concentration of sugar that occurs during this period of drying, the "*appassimento*", gives a sweet must in which the yeasts have difficulty working. Whether all the sugar is transformed into alcohol, as in Recioto della Valpolicella Amarone, or whether a certain proportion remains after the yeasts have ceased working, as in Recioto Amabile, depends on a number of factors, not least of which is the style desired by the producer. In the case of Valpolicella, the provenance of the grapes also contributes greatly to the final style, as those from certain soils within the Classico zone will not be able to provide a sufficient level of nutrients for the yeasts to carry on working once the alcohol reaches a level of 13.5-14°.

While sweet wines are produced in every corner of Italy, and from a staggering number of different grapes, the production of sparkling wines is centred more in the north. The Italian penchant for "*spumante*" wines ensures a ready market for the vast amount produced across the northern regions, from Piemonte through Lombardy and Trentino to the Veneto.

There is little that is uniquely Italian in much of what is produced. The grapes are either native (Prosecco) or, more likely, foreign (Pinot Bianco, Pinot Nero and Chardonnay), while the production process, depending on the style required, is either *Cuve Close* or *Méthode Champenoise*. The former is the least expensive method, and involves capturing the carbon dioxide given off while the wine undergoes a secondary fermentation in a large, hermetically sealed vat called an "*autoclave*". The latter, as its name implies, is the same as that employed in Champagne. Called "*metodo classico*" in Italy, it produces a finer (and more expensive) wine than *Cuve Close* through a secondary fermentation in bottle.

The production process used in Asti Spumante (described on page 48) is the only uniquely Italian method of making fully fledged sparkling wines. *Frizzante* wines, however (those with about one third to a half of the pressure found in sparkling wines), are distinctly native, and are widely produced. Frothing and bubbling, and best when slightly sweet, they are usually made in sealed, stainless vats called *autoclavi*, and pander to the sweet tooth that most Italians have, as well as to their predilection for a hint of a sparkle in their wines. And, of course, along with the fully sparkling and great sweet wines, they add to the great diversity and richness of Italian wines.

Production Terms

Abboccato Medium sweet, but usually light bodied.
Amabile Sweeter and fuller than *abboccato*.
Appassimento The period of drying for grapes destined for the production of *passito* wines.
Dolce Sweet.
Frizzante Semi-sparkling wine, usually made sparkling by a partial secondary fermentation in the tank.
Metodo Classico Term used for the Méthode Champenoise system of producing sparkling wines.
Passito Made from dried grapes
Spumante Sparkling.

This can be achieved either by leaving the grapes to shrivel on the vine after they have been attacked by *botrytis cinerea* (noble rot), as with French Sauternes, or by drying them after harvesting, but before crushing. In both cases, the result is an increase in sugar and a decrease in liquid, but the results are markedly different.

Few wines are made from botrytised grapes in Italy. A notable exception is Orvieto Abboccato, where producers like Decugnano dei Barbi and Barberani (whose Calcaia is outstanding) produce stylish and elegant versions. Sweet wines from dried grapes,

*I*talians approach the law in a characteristically individual way. There is a great concern for the human element, and a belief that the abstractions of the law should not override its humanity. As a result, most Italians regard the law as something that is open to interpretation, and if this means breaking or bending it, so be it.

This approach can be both a positive and negative force in the vineyard and the cellar. One producer may choose to ignore too restrictive a law because he has no interest in quality, while another will sidestep the law in order to make a better wine. In each case, the fault lies largely with the way the laws were originally framed.

Italy's wine laws evolved out of the chaos of the 1950s, and were modelled on the French system of Appellation Côntrollée. In 1963, the Italian government implemented a system of *"denominazione di origine"*, or denomination of origin, where the area, name, vines, yields and production practices are all controlled in order that a wine with a particular name, say Chianti, should in fact come from the stipulated area, and should be made within the guidelines laid down by law so that it will have the characteristic colour and taste.

There are, basically, three categories of the law. The *"Denominazione di Origine Controllata"* (DOC) aims to control the denomination of origin by laying down laws for the producers to follow, while the more exclusive *"Denominazione di Origine Controllata e Garantita"* (DOCG) attempts both to control and guarantee the wine's origin and quality. The third category, *vino da tavola*, applies to wines that do not have a DOC, either because they are produced in an area where one does not exist, or because the producer has followed practices other than those stipulated by the DOC.

In order to be granted a DOC, the growers of a particular zone must make an application to the National Committee for DOC, proving that their request is for a wine with an established tradition in their particular zone. This is where the laws have failed. Established practices were often those that

Red wine label

Vintage — 1982

Commune — MONFORTE

Site of vineyard — BUSSIA

DOCG zone — BAROLO
DENOMINAZIONE DI ORIGINE CONTROLLATA E GARANTITA

Indication of quality (in this case, DOCG)

Registration number of the bottler — R.I.V 2015/Cn

BRICCO BUSSIA
VIGNA COLONNELLO

Hill of Bussia

Name of the vineyard, or "cru"

Number of bottles produced in 1982 — Di questa annata sono state imbottigliate N. 4123 bottiglie
e N. 170 Magnum   Bottiglia N.

IMBOTTIGLIATO DAL VITICOLTORE NELL'AZIENDA AGRICOLA

Bottled by the grower

Farm — PODERI
ALDO CONTERNO

Name of grower

Volume in bottle — 75cl. e   PIEMONTE MONFORTE ITALIA   13,5% VOL.

Alcoholic strength

Wine Laws

DOC – *Denominazione di Origine Controllata* DOC regulations stipulate the vine varieties that may be used; where they may be grown; maximum yields; minimum alcohol, acidity and extract; permitted blending; a characteristic taste (known as *"tipicita"*). There are now nearly 250 DOCs, with more on the way. Sadly, excessive yields, rigid restrictions and permitted blending with wines from outside the zone (often from the South) diminish the efficacy of many DOCs.

DOCG – *Denominazione di Origine Controllata e Garantita* The same stipulations apply as for DOC, but they are stricter. In addition, the wine must be analysed and tasted by a special panel before being granted its coveted seal. The first four DOCGs (Vino Nobile di Montepulciano, Brunello di Montalcino, Barbaresco and Barolo) were joined by Chianti in 1984 and, most recently, by Albana di Romagna. The manner in which quality was compromised in the former, and the very selection of the latter, has done much to tarnish the lustre of DOCG.

Vino da Tavola Can be a simple "table wine" or a table wine with some indication of its origin eg. Nebbiolo delle Langhe. Because some producers choose to work outside the law, or simply because they are disillusioned with it, some of Italy's greatest wines carry the humble *vino da tavola* designation. This is especially true in Tuscany.

Vini Tipici A proposed category that would be roughly equivalent to the French *Vin de Pays*. It will take time to establish, but if it is as successful as the French system, it will be worth pursuing. The name, though, is likely to be changed at some point along the way.

had sprung up in the chaos of the thirties, forties and fifties, and consequently they had little to do with quality, but everything to do with quantity. The law, by enshrining what *was* happening rather than what *should* have been happening, lost its opportunity to promote quality, and became unwieldy and, in some zones, discredited.

It is easy to make this criticism from the distance of a quarter of a century. Some form of control was badly needed. Luigi Veronelli, the author of the *Catologo dei Vini* and one of Italy's leading authorities on food and wine, had been campaigning for controls in the early sixties, but became disillusioned when he saw the shape that they ultimately took. There is no doubt that, despite its shortcomings, DOC has improved the situation markedly, but if it had been framed more with an eye to quality, and with less of a view to political considerations, it could have done considerably more to improve both the quality and the image of Italian wines.

As it is, it has been left to individual growers to perform this task. The best producers have interpreted the law to suit their own needs, and have either bent or broken it in their pursuit of quality. In Chianti, for instance, there was widespread relief when the rules for DOCG greatly diminished the proportion of white grapes that was supposed to be added to the blend, as it was a stipulation that the best producers had been ignoring for years. But there was also a great deal of incredulity at the fact that DOCG only recognised the remedy for past inadequacies, and took no note of the direction in which the better producers were moving. As a result, it has lost much of its credibility among these same producers.

Whether it be DOC, DOCG, or the humble *vino da tavola* designation that appears on the label, it can only ever indicate that some attempt has been made to *control* quality. The only thing that can ever *guarantee* quality is the name of the producer, especially those who are forging ahead into the area that DOC and DOCG will one day, given time and unanimity of purpose on the part of grower and legislator alike, occupy.

White wine label

Producer

Grape variety

Town and DOC zone

Indication of quality (in this case, DOC)

Volume in bottle

Bottled by the producer

Alcoholic strength

Name of Italian distributor

Label Language

Annata The year of the vintage.

Azienda An estate or farm. An *azienda agricola* is a farm where only their own grapes are used in production, while an *azienda vinicola* buys in grapes.

Bianco White.

Cantina A winery. A Cantina Sociale is a co-operative.

Casa Vinicola A house that buys in grapes or wine.

Cascina A farm.

Cerasuolo Rosé. *Chiaretto* is also used, usually for slightly darker rosés.

Classico The traditional zone of production.

Commerciante Merchant houses.

Consorzio A consortium of growers, usually one that sets and administers production regulations.

Etichetta Label.

Fattoria A farm.

Imbottigliato Bottled.

Invecchiato Aged.

Liquoroso A high strength wine, usually fortified.

Podere A small farm.

Produttore Producer.

Riserva A reserve wine, usually a special selection that has been aged for longer than usual.

Ronco A hill. Usually used to designate a *cru*.

Rosato Rosé.

Rosso Red.

Secco Dry.

Superiore Usually denotes a DOC wine with extra alcohol, though can indicate a different *uvaggio* or favoured zone.

Tenuta Farm.

Uvaggio Grape mix.

Vecchio Old.

Vendemmia The vintage.

Vigna Means vineyard, and is used to indicate a *cru*. Vigneto is also applied.

Vignaiolo Grape grower.

Italy offers the wine buyer greater choice than any other country. This choice, born out of the great wealth of grape varieties, terrains and production techniques, can be exhilarating and challenging, but it can also be confusing and, at times, frustrating.

Over the years that I have been buying and selling Italian wines, I have noticed this reaction in both consumers and professionals. Some, their pride hurt, fail to return. This is foolish. It is rather like throwing down *Ulysses* because James Joyce seems impenetrable, instead of persevering and watching as a faintly flickering light slowly begins to illuminate the magical prose. And as you proceed, the majesty and genius of the work becomes evident, making it more enjoyable, if no less difficult, to read.

The appreciation of Italian wines, it must be said, requires less intellectual vigour than *Ulysses*, but at least as much perseverance. For the palate new to wine, their flavours can often be too assertive, their tannin content and acid levels too high, while the palate trained in France will find them – well, different. And the diversity of styles and stubbornly regional character of much Italian wine can, to some, appear to be an elaborate artifice, full of false trails and deceitful clues, erected to hide the few gems it has to offer.

Above: *An "enoteca" or wine shop in Orvieto. Many "enoteche" carry a good selection of local wines.*

But buying Italian wine is no more difficult than buying French, German, Spanish or even Australian wine, once you learn to follow a few, well-tried rules. The first, of course, is to find a decent place to buy them. This can take the form of a supermarket, a wine merchant, a restaurant or, if you are in Italy, a producer, but you should satisfy yourself that their conception of quality and good taste converges with your own.

One of the most important questions to pose before buying is whether you are trying to suit your wallet or palate. Italian wines, even in Italy, are not necessarily inexpensive. Though Italy's wines once had the image of being, at best, cheap and cheerful, today, because of inflation and increases in quality, they are more often medium priced. Where the price is related to quality, they can offer remarkable value for money, but where the wines have been caught up in the cycle of fashion or the spiral of investment, then they are sold at ludicrous prices that bear little relation to the quality of the wine. These, like similar wines from other countries, should be

Above: *These bottles of 1958 Chianti Rufina have been well-stored in a cool cellar. Such bottles are unhappily rare.*

avoided by all but those with more money than sense.

Buying wine is not a simple decision. Factors like style, vintage, producer and cost all need to be considered before you can make a fair assessment of what the contents of a bottle are likely to taste like. Vintages are of crucial importance throughout Italy, while the name of the producer can often make the difference between a great and an indifferent bottle. For this reason, I have listed, in boxes under the relevant regional sections, a selection of the leading producers.

Having bought the wine, the knowledge brought to bear in making the decision can be negated simply by serving it on the wrong occasion, too young or too old, too warm or too cold, or with the wrong food. Some wines, both white and red, should be drunk young, while others need to be aged for a number of years before they reach their peak. The factors influencing the length of ageing range from the grape variety and the vintage to the producer.

In Italy today, the tyranny of fashion dictates that white wines should be drunk as young as possible. This means that any wine more than two years old is regarded by most restaurateurs as lacking in freshness. This is idiotic. Many of the best white wines, whether a Pinot Grigio or Tocai from Friuli or a Tuscan Chardonnay, need at least a year to shrug off their youthful awkwardness and to begin to develop some interesting secondary flavours in bottle.

Many of the red wines are also drunk too young. Some, like several of the Super Tuscans, are produced to be drunk young, in restaurants, within three to five years of the vintage, but many others are made to last. Only through experience, or by talking to the person selling the wine, can you hope to distinguish between those wines that are more forward, or those from a lighter vintage, and others that should be tucked away to shed their burly, youthful character.

I, for one, seldom have the patience to wait for the decade or more that these latter wines need. My curiosity gets the better of me, and I like to tackle the powerful fruit to see how it is developing in bottle. In these situations, it is often wise to attempt to accelerate their development once the cork has been drawn. With a young Barolo, for instance, the wine should be opened for a while prior to drinking, anything from four to six or even ten hours, depending on vintage, producer and your preference, and decanted. Decanting wine not only enhances its aesthetic appeal, but also aerates it, allowing it to develop flavours that have been suppressed during its time in bottle. Indeed, I have heard people argue that all wine should be decanted before serving because you, too, would need a little time to show off your best if you had been in a bottle for years.

All this preparation will go amiss, however, if the wine is served at the wrong temperature. Too often, even in the best restaurant, red wines are served too warm and white wines too cold. The temperature at which a wine should be served varies greatly, and depends upon its style and age. All Chianti, for instance, should not be served at the same temperature: a young *"normale"* can be quaffed cool, at a temperature that enhances its fresh, lively fruit; a more mature "*riserva*", on the other hand, needs to be served at a slightly higher temperature, but not so warm that it becomes soupy and volatile. Quite often, it is necessary to plunge a bottle of red wine into an ice bucket to chill it down, all because of some mistaken interpretation of what constitutes room temperature. In these days of central heating, red wines are often ruined if they are served at actual "*room temperature*".

If red wines are served too warm, whites are too often chilled beyond all recognition. Light, perfumed wines, like a Moscato d'Asti, should be chilled, but an oaky Chardonnay should seldom be served cooler than a young Chianti. Exact temperatures are impossible to define as they depend not only on where you are and how you feel, but also on what you are eating with the wine.

The character of many Italian wines can be radically altered if served alongside different foods. Italian wines need food to be fully appreciated, but they need the right food. For instance, the neutrality of some whites can actually be enhanced by food, while the acid and tannin of certain reds, like Barolo, can be subdued by the right dish.

To Italians, wine has always been a part of the meal. I have often arrived at a farm in Italy to visit and taste the wine, only to find that a meal had been prepared. To them, the thought of tasting wines without food, outside the context in which they are produced to be enjoyed, is absurd. After politely protesting, I usually manage to taste the wines twice, once prior to the meal and again, much to the detriment of my waistline, during the meal. The difference is often quite remarkable. A wine that seems indifferent without food, like a pleasant enough Soave, can, beside a seafood *risotto*, reveal its personality and taste brilliantly.

Italy's cooking, like its wine, is essentially regional. To match the *cuisine* of the Veneto with wines of Piemonte would be to do both a great disservice. The wines of a particular region cannot really be understood without being drunk with the dishes native to that region. A dry Lambrusco as a foil to rich, Emilian cooking is just as valid as a Barolo partnered with hare. Each wine comes into its own alongside such dishes.

The problem, even in Italy, is to find an opportunity, outside the home, where quality wines can be matched with real Italian cooking. No matter how many "*trattorie*" you come across, each advertising "*cucina casalinga*", the only time you are likely to find real home cooking is at someone's table. Take advantage of it to see how the wines of the region partner the food. If the flavours of the food are complex and rich, then the wine should be simple and direct; if, however, the food is simple, then it should be served with a wine of complexity, a wine whose lustre will, when set against a plain background, shine all the more brilliantly.

To match wines with specific dishes is always difficult. The English, given a plate of spaghetti, will always say "Now all we need is a bottle of Chianti". Maybe, but so much depends on the sauce. A rich sauce may prove too much for a younger Chianti to compete with; a Dolcetto is likely to be just the thing. The wine for other pasta depends to a great extent on the texture, filling and, of course, the sauce. Generalisations, other than the one that Italian wines need the right food, are difficult to make.

Above: *Wine for sale at the Val Biferno co-operative in Molise. Many producers sell direct to the public – the* "vendita diretta" *sign is the one to watch for.*

Right: *Matching local wines with dishes in Italy's restaurants can be a great experience. If both are of a high quality, they complement each other perfectly.*

Wine and Food: A Few General Hints

Aperitifs Something light and white, either still or sparkling. Prosecco is ideal in the latter category, while wine like Soave, Favorita, Verdicchio all make admirable dry aperitifs. If your preference is for something sweet, a good Moscato d'Asti, with its dry finish, is ideal. A dry Marsala Vergine or one of the aged, oxidised specialities of the South can be splendid.

Antipasti If seafood or vegetables, a light white, like Vernaccia di San Gimignano, Arneis or something non-oaked from the North-East, like a Tocai or Pinot Bianco. If *prosciutto* or salami, or "*crostini*" with *funghi* or liver, a young Chianti *normale* is just the thing.

I Primi The wine to accompany pasta depends upon the sauce, filling and texture, while that to accompany *risotto* depends upon the latter's ingredients. Pasta, whether with a meaty sauce or simply with butter and parmesan, should be accompanied by something fairly simple, to set the stage for the great wine that will partner "*il secondo*". In Piemonte, it would be a Dolcetto or Barbera, in the North-East, a young Valpolicella or Refosco, while in Tuscany, a young Chianti would grace the table. If "*il primo*" consists of seafood, a decent, crisp dry white, depending on the sauce and the type of fish.

Il Secondo In the summer, at the seaside, a chilled dry white. The finer and more complex the fish, the simpler the nature of the wine should be, but something with a stronger flavour, and a firmer flesh, like swordfish, needs a fuller type of wine. Red wine can, and often does, accompany fish very well; not, perhaps, Barolo, but other simpler and fruitier reds.

The great beefsteaks of Tuscany call for a fine Chianti *riserva* from a top estate and vintage, while the richer braised beef, "*Stracotto al Barolo*", is ideal with a mature Barolo. Once again, the finer the wine, the simpler the dish.

Formaggi Contrary to popular belief, cheese and wine are difficult to match well. A strong *pecorino* or *provolone* will often overpower even the most robust of red wines. Quite often, either a Marsala Vergine, or a Vernaccia di Oristano, dry and piquant, are better bets, though something sweet, like a Moscato Passito, Vin Santo or Recioto della Valpolicella, are wonderful when sipped along with a small piece of strong, crumbling cheese.

I Dolci e La Frutta Chocolate is very difficult with wine, so steer well clear of it if you want to show a particularly fine bottle. The best way to end an Italian meal is with a simple dessert or a bowl of fruit and a refreshing glass of Moscato d'Asti. If you are feeling more reflective, a glass of Vin Santo, with almond biscuits, "*cantucci*", or a splendid Amarone, a "*vino da meditazione*", is a wonderful digestif. With *panettone*, or similar Italian cakes, Moscato d'Asti is sheer perfection; with roast chestnuts, Lambrusco or Cagnina.

THE NORTH-WEST

Morgex
Aosta
VALLE D'AOSTA
Lago Maggiore
Lago di Como
Varese
Como
LOMBARDY
Bergamo
NOVARA
MILAN (MILANO)
Vercelli
Po
Ticino
Lambro
Adda
Pavia
TURIN (TORINO)
Chieri
Casale Monferrato
Asti
Tanaro
Alessandria
PIEMONTE
Bra
Alba
Dogliani
Ovada
Gavi
Cuneo
Mondovi
LIGURIA
GENOA (GENOVA)
Savona
Imperia
La Spezia
1
2
3
4
5
6
7
8
9
10
11
12
13
14
15
16
17
18
19
20
21
22
23
24
25
26
27
28

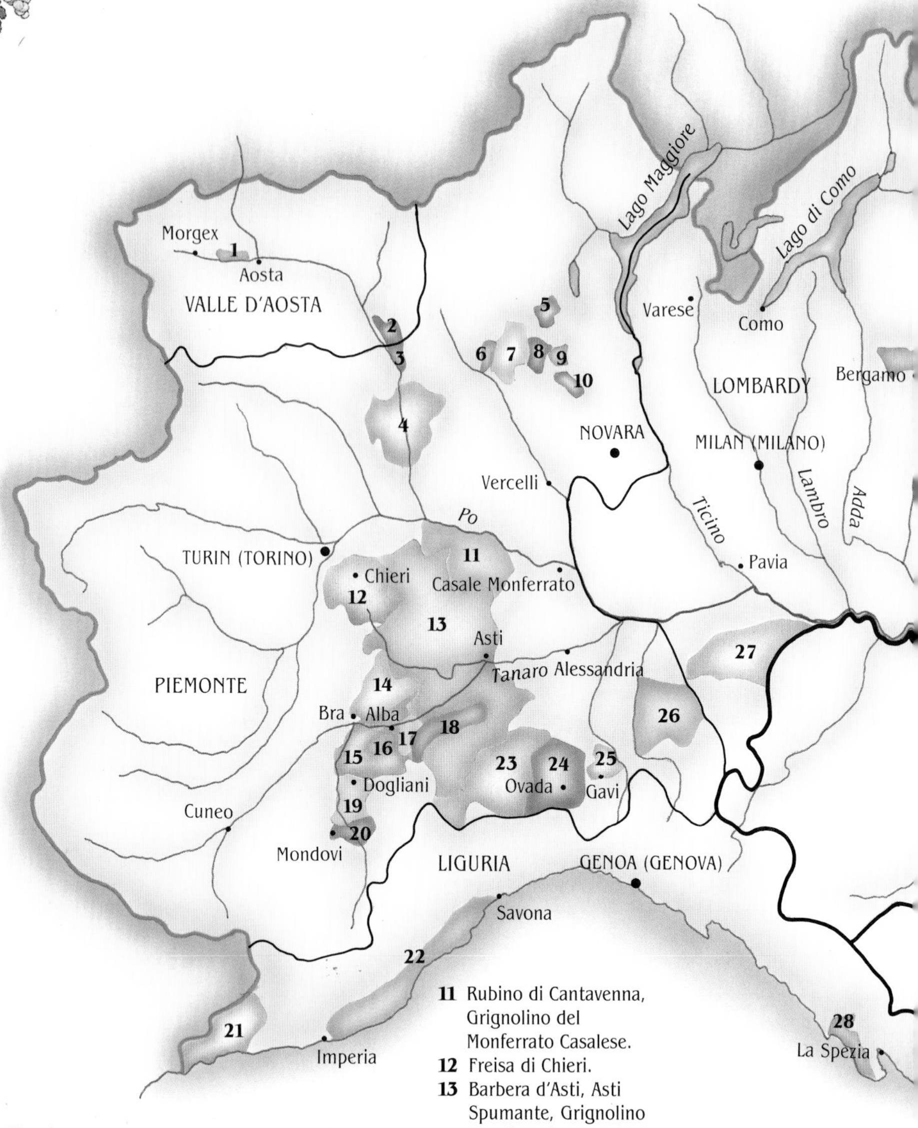

Key to map

1 Enfer d'Arvier.
2 Donnaz.
3 Carema.
4 Erbaluce di Caluso.
5 Boca.
6 Lessona.
7 Bramaterra.
8 Gattinara.
9 Ghemme.
10 Fara.
11 Rubino di Cantavenna, Grignolino del Monferrato Casalese.
12 Freisa di Chieri.
13 Barbera d'Asti, Asti Spumante, Grignolino d'Asti, Freisa d'Asti, Moscato d'Asti, Barbera del Monferrato, Malvasia di Castelnuovo Don Bosco.
14 Roero.

This is a largely green and ruggedly mountainous zone, with seams of sand and flatland here and there, that consists of four regions: the Valle d'Aosta, Piemonte, Lombardy and Liguria. Its people are as diverse as its topography. They are distinctly non-Italian in parts, identifying more strongly with their region (or city) than with the rest of Italy.

The North-West boasts two of Italy's most powerful cities: Turin, a bustling, business-like city that is the centre of the Fiat organisation; and Milan, a modern, hustling and enormously wealthy fashion centre. It is often said that while political power resides in Rome, financial power rests in Milan. The truth of the latter part of this axiom was illustrated by an article in *The Economist* early in 1988, which suggested that if Milan and its environs were hived off to form a separate state, the result would be a country richer than Switzerland.

Though Lombardy is to an extent financially dominated by Milan, it also sustains a thriving agricultural economy. The fertile valley on the northern bank of the Po supports various cereal crops, while the flatlands in the west of the region, running over into Piemonte as far as Novara, are the source for much of the rice that has made this part of Italy famous for its *risotto.*

This agricultural economy includes three major wine zones. The gentle hills in the south-western part of the region, where the borders of Emilia-Romagna, Piemonte and Lombardy converge, the Oltrepò Pavese,

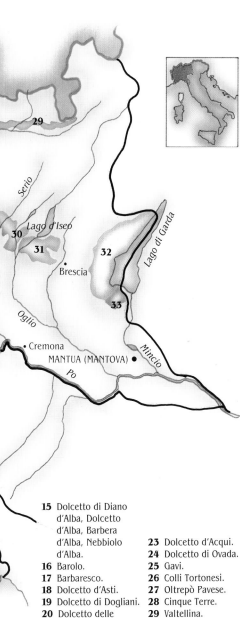

15 Dolcetto di Diano d'Alba, Dolcetto d'Alba, Barbera d'Alba, Nebbiolo d'Alba.
16 Barolo.
17 Barbaresco.
18 Dolcetto d'Asti.
19 Dolcetto di Dogliani.
20 Dolcetto delle Langhe Monregalesi.
21 Dolceacqua.
22 Riviera Ligure di Ponente.
23 Dolcetto d'Acqui.
24 Dolcetto di Ovada.
25 Gavi.
26 Colli Tortonesi.
27 Oltrepò Pavese.
28 Cinque Terre.
29 Valtellina.
30 Valcalepio.
31 Franciacorta.
32 Riviera del Garda.
33 Lugana.

Above: *Flowers soften the face of this typical Piemontese vineyard in the hilly country around Monforte d'Alba.*

probably have the most potential, while the Alpine valleys of the Valtelline, abutting the Swiss border, are without doubt the most beautiful. To the east, on the western shores of Lake Garda, a wide range of grapes are grown, and quality is rising at a rapid rate.

Entering Italy from the north, through the Mont Blanc tunnel, you would expect the French influence to recede rapidly. But it remains strong in the Valle d'Aosta, Italy's smallest region, where French is the first language. An autonomous region, it also has the lowest wine production of any in Italy, hardly surprising given the difficulty the vine has finding space to grow amidst the mountains and Alpine resorts.

Liguria also borders France, but here you leave behind Provence and the French Riviera and drive along a road that is miraculously squeezed between a crescent-shaped strip of beach and Liguria's forbidding but beautiful mountains. Little of Liguria's wine is exported as most is drunk by the tourists who flock to the Italian Riviera during the summer, but her most famous exports, fine olive oil and the exquisite pesto genovese (a basil and oil paste), thankfully escape the attention of many of the summer visitors.

Between Liguria and Valle d'Aosta, which are two of Italy's smaller regions, lies Piemonte, the second largest after Sicily. Its name, meaning foot of the mountain, is derived from the foothills that swing, in an arc, from Lake Maggiore in the north-east round its western border with France to the Ligurian border and the Apennines in the south.

This mountainous border seems to have endowed the Piemontese with an inner reserve and the strength to lead life at their own pace that other Italians, ever conscious of the need to follow fashion, view as a distant arrogance. This strength is nowhere more evident, and nowhere more needed, than in the Langhe hills south of Alba. For here, despite the French influence (the dialect veers strongly towards French), the greatest and most quintessential of Italian wines are produced from native grapes like the Nebbiolo, Dolcetto and Barbera.

The strength is needed to persevere in the production of these wines, for the best of them demand as much of the drinker as they do of the producer, making them resolutely unfashionable in this age of instant gratification. But the perseverance of the grower should be matched in equal measure by that of the wine drinker, for these are some of the world's finest wines. If the struggle becomes too much at times, retreat for a glass of the delightfully frivolous wines produced further east in the Monferrato hills, around Asti, from the Moscato grape. Surrender, though, should never be countenanced, for where these wines are found, our journey to the heart of fine Italian wine begins.

Although the Pinot Noir gives it a good run for its money, the Nebbiolo is probably one of the most difficult grapes in the world. Not only is it obstinate in the vineyard, but it remains a puzzle to many an experienced taster. Its styles range from the relatively light and fruity, as accessible as one of William Blake's early poems, to the great wines of the Langhe hills, Barolo and Barbaresco, as subtle and demanding of attention as Blake's later poems.

Despite the heights that it attains in north-western Italy, the Nebbiolo has resisted attempts to transplant it elsewhere. True, Mas de Daumas Gassac, the brilliant estate in L'Hérault in the south of France, has a tiny proportion in its blend, and several Italian expatriate producers in Australia are experimenting with it, but most moves to establish it abroad have met with the failure that was experienced in Oregon several years back.

Although its origins would seem to be in the Langhe hills of southern Piemonte, where its presence can be traced back as far as 1268, it was widely planted across northern Italy by the middle of the nineteenth century. But after phylloxera and the financial devastation that ensued, it was replaced by more vigorous and less demanding varieties in

many areas. Its domain receded, so that today, with the exception of the odd grower here and there, it is to be found primarily in the sub-alpine landscapes of Piemonte and, to a lesser extent, Lombardy.

Its name is thought to be derived from "*nebbia*", the Italian word for fog. A late ripening variety, it is usually harvested at the end of October, and sometimes well into November, when the Langhe hills are wreathed in a thick, eerie fog. It is a low yielding variety, usually trained in the *Guyot* system, and is very sensitive to the terrain in which it is grown.

This sensitivity makes it prone to mutation, and has resulted in a number of sub-varieties and a plethora of local synonyms. The three recognised sub-varieties for Barolo and Barbaresco are the Lampia, which yields well and gives good colour and body and a fine perfume; the Michet, a niggardly bearer that is difficult to grow but which gives structure to the wines, and is generally regarded as the best of the three; and the Rosé, simi-

Below: *Terraces of vines in Autumn in Serralunga d'Alba. This commune is known for the long-lived, densely structured style of Barolo it produces.*

larly low yielding but giving wines that are rather light in body with a distinctive and powerful perfume.

In the rest of the north-west, the vine goes under a variety of names, though its wines are almost always named after the commune or area in which it is grown. This, say some authorities, reflects the way in which it adapts to variations in soil and climate. In northern Lombardy, near the Swiss border on the steep inclines of Valtellina, it is called the Chiavennasca, while further west, on the equally precipitous slopes of Carema, it is known as either the Pugnet or Picotener. In the Novara-Vercelli hills of eastern Piemonte, it is called Spanna, as are the wines that are partially or wholly made from it.

The Nebbiolo excels in northerly, hillside sites. With the snow-capped Alps forming a dramatic backdrop, the hills provide the Nebbiolo with the long growing season it needs to achieve full ripeness, and to soften its high natural acidity. But to endure the damp, foggy mornings of late October, it also needs a thick, tough skin, and in this skin reside the tannins that characterise the wines of the Nebbiolo, making them tough when young but capable of great longevity.

The extent of this tannic toughness varies, depending on where it is grown and how it is handled by the winemaker. The wines of the Nebbiolo are seldom deep in colour, having more of a violet-tinged ruby that fades to garnet with age. There is a widespread myth of deep coloured, almost black, Nebbiolo wines, but true Nebbiolo, unblended with other grapes or wines from more southerly climes, never, in my experience, achieves such a depth of colour.

Above: *Gianni Voerzio, brother of Roberto, – a well established winemaker in his own right – is one of Barolo's most promising young producers. He is shown here with bunches of ripe, thick-skinned, Nebbiolo grapes just prior to the harvest.*

Its perfume is exquisite. It ranges from black cherries and raspberries in the younger wines, like Spanna or Roero, through the subtle hint of violets that is found in Carema to the unsurpassed complexity of Barolo and Barbaresco, where mint, liquorice, truffles and myriad other aromas commingle to create a perfume of memorable dimensions. It is doubtful whether any grape, even the Pinot Noir, is capable of expressing such a dramatic range of flavours.

But it is on the palate that many tasters run into trouble with the Nebbiolo. Even the lighter wines have what many people regard as an unacceptable level of tannin and acidity. The novice, approaching a Barolo for the first time, is likely to find his gums coated with a hard, unyielding tannin, and the back of his palate pierced by a searing acidity. But repeated acquaintance will show that in this tannic shell there is a rich, succulent kernel of fruit that will emerge with either age or aeration, or both.

These are not wines to be drunk on their own, or even to be judged, while young, in shows, like an Australian Cabernet would be. They only really come into their own with age and with food. The hearty Piemontese *cuisine*, especially the game that is so abundant in the Autumn, is the perfect foil to these wines.

*N*ebbiolo's greatest wines are found around the small, provincial town of Alba, south-east of Turin. Alba rests on the banks of the Tanaro river, and is home to Barolo, Barbaresco and, in Autumn, the great white truffles. Searched out in the Langhe hills by farmers and their dogs, they are prohibitively expensive, but wonderfully scented. They are grated over pasta and risotto in every restaurant during the Autumn, their scent setting off to perfection the wine accompanying the meal. This is the season to visit Alba.

For the wine-lover, it is an ideal time, as it coincides with the harvest in Barolo and Barbaresco. The zone for Barbaresco lies in the hills to the north of Alba, while Barolo is found to the south, but many producers and merchants make both, either owning land or buying grapes in each region. They are often called the King and Queen of Italian wines, for the depth and power of Barolo is felt to be masculine, while the lighter Barbaresco is held to be more elegant and feminine.

Barbaresco, with just over 500 hectares under vine, is the smaller of the two zones. Because the terrain is gentler, the hills being gradual slopes rather than precipitous inclines, and the soil less varied, there is not as great a difference between communes in Barbaresco as there is in Barolo. They are, though, distinct from each other, with Neive producing chunky, densely textured wines and Treiso fine, elegant wines, while those from Barbaresco itself are generally reckoned to be of medium weight but with good tannin and a fine scent.

The soil, though similar, is lighter in Barbaresco than in Barolo. In both areas, on the right bank of the Tanaro, it is of alluvial marine origin, and is fairly heavy, with more chalk and clay than is to be found on the left

Key to map
1 Barbaresco.
2 Barolo.

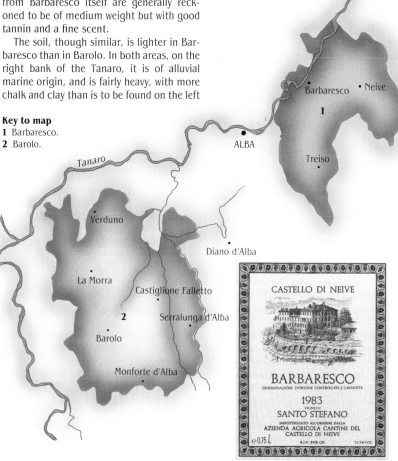

Above: *Aldo Conterno scrutinising Nebbiolo grapes as they arrive at his cantina in Monforte d'Alba. Careful selection is the key to quality.*

Above: *The lighter soil of Barbaresco gives a wine that is generally less heavy than that from neighbouring Barolo.*

bank. The combination of lighter soil and gentler slopes gives, generally, a slightly lighter wine in Barbaresco, and one with a lower level of alcohol (the minimum required by law is 12°, while in Barolo it is 13°). For this reason, the ageing requirements in the DOCG discipline differ. Barbaresco must be aged for two years (one of which is in cask) before release, while Barolo has to spend three years (two in cask) in the cellar before it can be sold.

Despite their depiction as masculine and feminine, though helpful as a general rule, not even an experienced taster can regularly tell the two apart. Barolo, though, has always overshadowed Barbaresco, and today it remains commercially more significant.

It was the first wine of the Langhe hills to be made dry. At the beginning of the nineteenth century, the Marchesa Falletti di Barolo, being of French origin, decided that she wanted a fellow countryman to run the family winery. Accordingly, she drafted in Monsieur Oudart, who transformed Barolo from a sweet, slightly *frizzante* wine (there are Freisas and Barberas still made in this fashion today) into a dry, tannic wine capable of long ageing.

The delimited area for Barolo was mapped out toward the end of the nineteenth century, and was officially charted in 1909. Today, it consists of about 1,200 hectares of vines, which are divided up between just over 1,200 owners. There are many small-holdings, and some of the great vineyards, like Cannubi or Boschis, are split, as in Burgundy, between many "*contadini*", or farmers.

Barolo consists of two valleys. On the one side, taking in the communes of La Morra and Barolo, is the Valley of Barolo. The soil here is a calcareous marl of Tortonian origin, and tends to be lighter than the soil in the Serralunga Valley, which is of Helvetian origin, and contains a higher content of lime and iron. This includes the communes of Monforte and Serralunga, while the fifth major commune, Castiglione Falletto, straddles the two valleys.

The wines of each valley vary markedly. Those from Serralunga and Monforte tend to be fuller and more tannic, and are felt to have the greatest ageing potential, while those from La Morra and Barolo are, as a rule, lighter and more perfumed, and will usually mature earlier. Castiglione Falletto, straddling the two valleys as it does, combines the elegance of Barolo with the power of Serralunga.

Some producers feel that only by blending wines from, say, La Morra and Monforte, can you combine all the elements to produce a top Barolo. Each commune, they maintain, will lend a particular attribute to the wine, and the overall effect will far exceed the sum total of the individual constituents. It is understandable that the merchants, given their reliance on buying in grapes, should take this stance, but even some of the old-timers, great winemakers like Violante Sobrero and Bartolo Mascarello, blend together wines from their various holdings.

This is, perhaps, a more practical course, given the fragmented nature of the vineyards here. A grower with half a hectare in La Morra, and an even smaller parcel in Serralunga, is unlikely to bother to go to the trouble of vinifying and bottling them separately. Yet the

Above: *Following the death of Renato Ratti in September 1988, his nephew, Massimo Martinelli, shown here, will continue to run the* cantina.

oldest bottles still in existence, dating back to the middle of the eighteenth century, are labelled with the name of the vineyard, indicating that the concept of "cru" wines is hardly new.

In recent years, beginning in the early sixties, many producers started, once again, to indicate on their labels the vineyard from which the wine came. It is now possible to have three bottles from a producer like Prunotto or Vietti, all from the same vintage and all called Barolo, but each displaying the distinctive style of the vineyard.

Unless you carry about a pocket map of Barolo, this is, without doubt, confusing. But so is Burgundy, with its various villages and, even within a village like Nuits St-Georges, the numerous vineyards. Great grapes like the Nebbiolo and the Pinot Noir express the "terroir" in which they are grown, and this is what the producers are trying to capture by specifying the particular sites. We grumble about it in Burgundy, but have come to accept it; we will, no doubt, reach the same point with Barolo and Barbaresco one day.

But there is another reason why these producers have moved back to the concept of the "cru". This can be traced back to a time when the Nebbiolo grape used to fetch several times the price of Dolcetto and Barbera. The growers, seeing a way to increase their income, set about planting Nebbiolo on sites that had never previously been used for the grape, and to which it was unsuited. This resulted in poor grapes, and led to Barolo that was, at best, of indifferent quality.

This, more than anything, has led to a devaluation of Barolo's image. At the turn of the century, and right up to the years follow-

Above: *The old and the new,* botti *and* barriques, *happily co-exist in Ratti's cellars at Annunziata, where "modern" Barolo was first made.*

fortnight, after which the wine would be aged in cask for a year or two. It was then put into demi-johns, and placed outside in the winter, or in the attic in the summer, the extremes of temperature serving to accelerate its maturation. After this, it was bottled, and was capable of ageing for a long period.

This would have been the method used at the turn of the century. Towards the end of the 1930s, however, another style of vinification evolved, says Ratti. This involved the fermenting must being kept in contact with the skins for as long as 60 days, by means of submerging the "cap" (the skins float to the top of the fermenting vat, forming a cap). This was seen as a technological advance, but the result was austere, tannic wines that required anything from four to eight years in cask, and a short spell in demi-john, before they were sufficiently supple to be bottled.

This practice naturally led to a different style of Barolo. The extended period of ageing meant that the major part of the wine's evolution occurred in cask rather than in bottle. During the time it spent in cask, the oxygen it picked up would, in most cases, render the wines incapable of developing further in bottle. Barolo and Barbaresco became, then, wines that were aged in an "oxidative" rather than a "reductive" (in the absence of oxygen) manner.

The period in cask also left the wine open to attack by bacteria. Unless it was carefully tended, with the vats being constantly topped up to ensure that there was no space left inside in which oxygen and bacteria could attack the wine, then deterioration would set in. To many people, a Barolo from this period is characterised by excessive levels of volatile acidity (acetic acid, an indication that the wine is well on the way to becoming vinegar) and evident oxidation.

The late sixties and early seventies saw a younger generation come on the scene. They were dissatisfied by the wines their fathers had been making, and were seeking ways to transform them. At this point, Emile Peynaud, the celebrated oenologist from Bordeaux, visited Alba and tasted a range of wines. There is some dispute as to what the wines were, with some people insisting that they were Barbera d'Asti, and they should know because they were there, while others are equally adamant that they were present to see the great man taste a range of Barolo. Either way, both camps agree that he pronounced the wines oxidised. This hurt the proud Piemontese, and gave fuel to a move to produce wines that would not need to be aged in cask for years before they shed their tannic clout, wines that could be bottled earlier, before they had become oxidised, and given a chance to develop over a longer period of time.

ing the Second World War, only the traditional sites, those that enabled the Nebbiolo to reach full ripeness, were planted. Yields were low, selection was rigorous and great wines were produced. If only the best sites were used, there was no need to stipulate the vineyard, and these were the wines that established the reputation of Barolo.

During the 1960s, in the period preceding and following the granting of DOC in 1966, optimism for the future of these wines led to widespread plantings on new sites. Today, much of what is planted with Nebbiolo (more so in Barolo than in Barbaresco) is unsuited to the production of top quality grapes. Unfortunately, these grapes are used to make Barolo. It is little wonder, then, that the best producers are keen to specify vineyards and distance themselves from these other wines, which are little more than travesties of a great name.

The vineyard, though, will only be of value if the name of the producer is of high repute. People like Pio Cesare do not believe in *"cru"* wines, yet their Barolo and Barbaresco are always good bets, simply because they aim for quality. And the producer, through his handling of the grapes, will influence the style of wine produced.

The approach to winemaking in Barolo and Barbaresco has been going through something of a revolution in the last decade or so. And, like the transformation in style engineered by M. Oudart almost two centuries ago, this one was also helped on its way by a Frenchman. According to Renato Ratti, one of the leading producers of Barolo, as well as being its historian, the post-Oudart method of vinification involved pressing followed by maceration on the skins for about a

The ensuing revolution has led to producers being divided into "traditionalist" and "modernist" camps. The latter macerate on the skins for anything from four or five days to a fortnight, and ferment in stainless steel vats at a controlled temperature. Their aim is to preserve the fruit aromas of the Nebbiolo grape, which, they feel, will develop and be refined during the long bottle ageing that the wine will undergo. To this end, after the completion of the malolactic fermentation in the Spring following the vintage, they put the wine in barrels, the large Slovenian oak "*botte*", for a year or so. They may supplement this with a short spell in *barrique* (an oak cask of 225-litre capacity), but are keen to ensure that the wine does not lose any of its fruit through protracted contact with oxygen. The wine will be bottled after about two years, ready, the producer feels, to develop the refined bouquet that ageing in bottle, in the absence of oxygen, permits. The modernist credo could be summarised as "less cask and more bottle".

The producers classified as "traditionalists" adopt a different approach. They also ferment at a controlled temperature, ranging from 25°-32°, but will macerate for about 20-30 days depending on the nature of the vintage. Their wines will be put in *botte* in the Spring, after the malolactic fermentation has been completed, and will remain there for anything from the minimum of two years required by law (one year in Barbaresco) to three, five or even 10 years. The length of their tenure in cask will depend on the vintage and the provenance of the grapes. Those wines from good vintages, like 1982 and 1985, will spend longer in cask, as will those from older vines or vineyards in Serralunga or Monforte.

For these producers, the use of *barrique* is out of the question. Bruno Giacosa feels that they are unsuited to Albese wines, while Mauro Mascarello, of Giuseppe Mascarello e Figlio, has experimented with them but was dissatisfied with the results. Aldo Conterno uses it for his Nebbiolo delle Langhe, but does not believe in it for Barolo. It is not a part of the tradition, he says.

Angelo Gaja, one of Barbaresco's great producers, is a firm believer in *barrique* ageing. The natural astringency of the Nebbiolo grape is better tempered by ageing in *barrique* than in *botte*, he maintains, because the former replaces the hard grape tannins with softer, sweeter ones from the oak. With ageing in *botte*, the tannins are softened less by the wood and more by oxidation, and this is something he is keen to avoid.

Yet there are no finer producers than Gaja and Conterno. And Giovanni Conterno, elder brother of Aldo, of the firm of Giacomo Conterno, ages his wines in cask, especially his outstanding Monfortino, for anything up to 13 years. So where lies the truth?

As with any revolution, many minor issues get blown up out of all proportion, and come to dwarf those of greater importance. With the Albese revolution, the issues of cask ageing and maceration have taken centre stage, while those of temperature control during fermentation and the use of grapes from the best sites, though of greater significance in the long term, have been relegated to secondary rôles.

Above: *Angelo Gaja, one of the greatest producers in Barbaresco, bought into Barolo in 1988. Often labelled a modernist, Gaja himself disputes such neat distinctions.*

These are the key changes. The ability to control temperature means that the producer is able to make a wine with a higher degree of alcohol, and one that is healthier, with better ageing potential. And the use of the best grapes, especially with a wine as temperamental as Nebbiolo, allied with a controlled fermentation, means that the producer can, if he wishes, put his wine in *botte* for three to five years, and still have, at the end of this period (as long as vats are topped up and the contents tended carefully), a wine that will continue to age and develop in bottle.

In a sense, this is a return to tradition, aided by the use of modern technology. The best producers, whether "modernist" or "traditionalist", are those who obtain the lowest yields from vines grown in the best sites, and who take care to ensure that these are transformed into wines that will continue to express the character of both the grape and the vineyard over a long period of time. Whether macerated for one week or a month, or aged in cask for one year or five, the best wines are now, more than ever, worthy of being placed in the finest cellars, and being allowed to develop, alongside the greatest

Barolo and Barbaresco Vintages

1988 Following a long, hot summer, the grapes were in perfect condition at the end of the first week of October. A great vintage seemed in prospect. A large part of the harvest had been gathered in Barbaresco when rain came on 10 October, and stayed for a whole week. This washed away hopes of greatness in Barolo, but those who picked in Barbaresco will have made some fine wines. Quality in Barolo will be inferior to 1982 and 1985, but better than 1983, 1986 and 1987.

1987 Rain at the vintage marred what looked like being a splendid year. Early indications are that quality will be good, the wines being medium weight and having fair ageing potential.

1986 Hail in Barolo led to a reduction in quantity (some producers made no wine at all), but some good, well-defined wines have been produced. Several people in Barbaresco are now, somewhat surprisingly, rating this vintage higher than 1985.

1985 A long, hot summer and autumn produced wines of memorable proportions. From cask, they have great colour, a remarkable scent and a ripe, full fruit on the palate that is already bursting with a tremendous range of flavours. Seems to be one of the greatest vintages.

1984 Very patchy. The cool, wet summer that produced lean, dilute Dolcetto and Barbera gave way to a long, warm autumn that saved the late ripening Nebbiolo. Quality varies markedly between commune and producer, with some people making better wines than in 1983. Mascarello's Monprivato, for instance, is excellent, but Aldo Conterno produced no Barolo at all. The best wines have good definition, tannin and acid, and should age well.

1983 Another vintage in which a long autumn seemed at first to have saved the vintage. The wines, initially lauded, are maturing rapidly. They are light in colour and low in acid and tannin, and have a distinctive and rather coarse, vegetal perfume. Should be drunk while the 1982s negotiate the awkward road to maturity. Aldo Conterno's is one of the best.

1982 A dream year. The wines are consistently good, thanks largely to a flawless summer and a fine autumn. They have good colour, a fine but restrained perfume and an intense, fleshy fruit that masks a good level of tannin. Their only fault seems to be a low acidity, which casts doubt on their ageing potential. At the moment, though, it ranks with 1985, 1971 and 1958 as one of the great post-war vintages.

1981 Autumn rains resulted in rather dilute wines that lack charm. By careful selection, some producers have made decent wines that are at their peak now.

1980 A large vintage of medium weight, medium quality wines that are drinking well at the moment, and should continue to do so for a few years yet. While lacking concentration and power, the best have good perfume, low tannin and an appealing and accessible character. A Vigna Colonello from Aldo Conterno, tasted in mid-1988, had wonderful balance, and showed signs of being able to age for quite a few years yet.

1979 Another large vintage, lacking the depth of 1978 but with more grip and structure than 1980, if less charm at the top level. Drinking well now and into the early nineties. Giovanni Conterno feels his Monfortino was better in 1979 than in 1978.

1978 A splendid autumn reversed the adverse effects of a poor, wet summer, giving a small crop of wines that was originally hailed as one of the decade's great vintages. Initial praise seems, on recent evidence, to have been misplaced. The ripe, intense fruit they had in the early and mid-eighties seems to have evolved rapidly – but they may just be going through a difficult stage in bottle. The best, like Gaja's wines, should last for years.

1977, 1976 and **1975** All poor, and only the rare bottle is likely to be drinkable today.

1974 Wines of good depth and structure, though not quite up to the standard of 1971. They have matured well and are at their peak now.

1973 Dismal.

1972 A complete washout.

1971 A superb vintage. Wines are intensely flavoured, with a great balance of tannin and acidity. They have developed well in bottle, and most are at their peak now. A few, like Giovanni Conterno's superb Monfortino, will go on for years yet.

1970 A fine vintage, overshadowed by the 1971s. The wines are lighter and lacking the concentration of their successor. They are elegant and well-defined, and, though most are at their peak now, the best should carry on for a few years yet.

Of the older vintages, 1967, 1964, 1962, 1961, 1958, 1952, 1947 and 1931 were all very good.

growths of Bordeaux and Burgundy, into wines of dazzling quality.

There are a growing number of producers like this, but there are many more who, despite the DOCG, continue to sell wines that simply are not worthy of the name of Barolo or Barbaresco. With the advent of DOCG in 1980, the authorities missed their chance, not only to tighten up on quality, but also to differentiate between a basic Barolo and a great "cru". It is as though a wine from the Domaine de la Romanée-Conti was labelled Bourgogne Rouge, cru La Tâche. What is needed is greater distinction, so that a wine can be called La Morra "Vigneto La Conca" in

the same way that a Burgundy is labelled Volnay "Les Caillerets".

This system, or something similar, will come one day. For now, it is enough to know that the best wines of Barolo and Barbaresco have never been better. There are a number of young producers coming along, people like Altare and Voerzio in Barolo and Pasquero and Mauro Bianco in Barbaresco, who, allied with the greatest of the older generation, the Conterno brothers and Mauro Mascarello, Bruno Giacosa and Angelo Gaja, are restoring these wines to their deserved position of pre-eminence, alongside the best that the rest of the world can offer.

The Langhe form an area which has, arguably, a greater concentration of fine producers than any other wine region in the world. It is full of staunch individualists, colourful characters and family rivalries, all dynamic enough to fill a sprawling Russian novel. The best producers infuse their wines with a tremendous character, of the grape, the commune and themselves. As such, any list of top producers is bound to be, yes, enjoyable to compose, but also highly subjective. Rather like a person's list of their favourite composers or writers, it will reveal more about the person compiling it than anything else. Baring my soul then, there follows my selection (in alphabetical order) of some of the best producers currently at work in Barolo and Barbaresco.

Elio Altare A perfectionist who falls uneasily between the modern and traditional camps. Though he adheres to the modernist doctrine on maceration and ageing, his wines are hard and tough in their youth. Beside his excellent Barolo, he also produces an outstanding, *barrique*-aged Nebbiolo (Vigna Arborina) and Barbera (Vigna Larigi), as well as one of the best Dolcetto. Anything bottled under the Altare name is worth a try.

Ceretto Winemaker Marcello Ceretto is in the van of the modernist movement. His wines are elegant and restrained, and both from Barbaresco (Bricco Asili) and Barolo (Zonchera, Brunate and Bricco Rocche). Brother Bruno uses his great energy and garrulousness to promote and sell the wines. At best, the wines are a delicious embodiment of the modern style, but prices, I feel, are too high. Others, though, rate them at the very top.

Aldo Conterno This quietly spoken, modest man produces some of the greatest of Barolos from his Bricco Bussia vineyard. The wines are made to last (long maceration, three to four years in cask), being almost unapproachable in their youth but unfolding with age into subtle, expressive Barolos of the highest order. Only his finest Nebbiolo grapes go into his Barolo; the rest go into his Nebbiolo delle Langhe, Il Favot. His *normale* is called Bussia Soprana, while his first *cru*, made from a particularly favoured vineyard on the hill of Bussia, is Vigna Colonello. His greatest wine, though, is Gran Bussia, a selection of the finest grapes made only in the best years like 1985, 1982, 1978 and 1971. His Freisa and *barrique*-aged Barbera are both excellent. There is nobody making better wine in the Langhe at present.

Giacomo Conterno Giovanni Conterno, elder brother of Aldo, is the great guardian of the traditional doctrine. Sadly, the two brothers have not spoken for over 20 years. Giovanni's wines are big, strapping and powerful, reflecting both the style of the commune, Serralunga, where his Cascina Francia holdings are, and the low yields he gets in the vineyard (he has been known to leave more grapes on the vine than he harvests, even in a fine vintage). He ages his wines in cask for anything up to 14 years, bottling them when he feels, intuitively, that

Below: *Aldo Conterno, one of the finest producers in the Langhe, is seen here checking on the progress of one of his Barolo from the great 1985 vintage, which is scheduled for bottling in the middle of 1989. His wines are made to last.*

they are ready. His Monfortino, a special selection, is outstanding, arguably the finest single Barolo produced. His Dolcetto and Barbera are both densely packed with fruit, and are outstanding. While they occasionally disappoint, when his wines are on form, they are immensely exciting.

Angelo Gaja Gaja is the great modernist and innovator of the Langhe. His wines are thoroughly modern, and more international than any others in Alba, with their sleek, refined fruit and judiciously applied oak. He makes a Dolcetto that, though good, lacks

---

Barolo: Best of the Rest

Top Rank Clerico, Cogno-Marcarini, Prunotto, Giuseppe Rinaldi, Alfonso Scavino, Paolo Scavino, Sobrero (sold his vineyards in 1985 – 1983 was the last vintage produced), Vietti, Roberto Voerzio.

Very Good Accomasso, Barale, Cavallotto, Pio Cesare, Cordero di Montezemolo, Einaudi, R. Fenocchio, Grasso, E. Pira (Luigi Pira, the last producer to crush the grapes by foot, died in 1980. 1975 was the last vintage that he bottled. The wines are now made by Chiara Boschis of Giacomo Borgogno), Francesco Rinaldi, Gigi Rosso, Luciano Sandrone, Scarpa, Sebaste Vajra, G. Voerzio.

Above Average Ascheri, Azelia, Bersano, S. & B. Borgogno, Giacomo Borgogno, Bovio, Brezza, Brovia, Cappellano, Carnevale, Casetta, Castello di Verduno, Coluè, Rocche Costamagna, Duca d'Asti, Fantino Conterno, Franco Fiorina, Fontanafredda, Gemma, Fratelli Giacosa, Marchesi di Barolo, Molino, Oberto, Fratelli Oddero, Ponte Rocca, Porta Rossa, Rocche dei Manzoni, Settimo Aurelio, Terre del Barolo, Tenuta Carretta, Tenuta Cerequio, Tenuta Montanello, Accademia Torregiorgi, Veglio, Vignolo Lutati, Zunino.

Barbaresco: Best of the Rest

Top Rank Castello di Neive, Secondo Pasquero-Elia, Produttori del Barbaresco, Prunotto, Vietti.

Very Good Luigi Bianco, Mauro Bianco, Barale, Carlo Boffa, Bordino, Pio Cesare, Cigliuti, Marchesi di Gresy, G. Cortese, Anfosso De Fornville, Glicine, Giovannini-Moresco, I Paglieri (Roagna), Francesco Rinaldi, Rizzi, Scarpa, Accademia Torregiorgi.

Above Average Bersano, Ca'Rome, Confratelli di San Michele, R. Cortese, Contratto, Duca d'Asti, Franco Fiorina, Gemma, Fratelli Giacosa, Meinardi, Fratelli Oddero, Parroco di Neive, Pelissero, La Spinona, Traversa, Vezza, Vignaioli (Elvio Pertinace).

---

charm, and a Barbera (Vignarey) that is outstanding, as well as a Chardonnay and a Cabernet. These are dwarfed, however, by the stature of his Barbarescos. His *normale* elegant and classy, would be enough to put him in the top rank, even without the help of his three outstanding *crus*. Costa Russi matures earliest, being soft and supple and seeming, at times, to lack a little backbone. Sorì Tildin is firmer and more structured, needing time to develop, while Sorì San Lorenzo, the greatest of the three, combines charm and finesse with a muscular, intense fruit that unfolds slowly over a number of years. Though prohibitively expensive, the quality of the wines is such that an attempt can at least be made to justify the high prices. In July 1988, Gaja bought some vineyards in Serralunga, over 20 years after he left Barolo to concentrate his efforts on Barbaresco. This latest move has sent a murmur of excitement echoing through the Langhe.

Bruno Giacosa Owns a small vineyard in Serralunga, but buys all other grapes to meet his requirements for Barolo, Barbaresco, Dolcetto, Barbera and Arneis. Giacosa is a reticent man who, when you ask him how he makes his wines, shrugs his shoulders and mutters that he is a traditionalist. If you ask him how long his Barolo and Barbaresco remain in the cask, he says "until they are ready to be bottled. A good wine can stand up to years of barrel ageing," he insists. Though he

may not want to articulate his credo, the wines say it all: they are outstanding, rich and concentrated yet restrained and elegant.

Giuseppe Mascarello Mauro Mascarello took over the family *cantina* in 1967, experimented with modern ways and returned, in the early seventies, to a more traditional approach to winemaking. He makes an outstanding Dolcetto (Gagliassi) and Barbera (Ginestra), as well as a Barbaresco from the Marcarini vineyard. In good years, he buys more grapes than he would in lesser years. He makes Barolo from several different *crus*, including Dardi in Monforte, but his greatest wine is undoubtedly from his own Monprivato vineyard in Castiglione Falletto. It is certainly one of the most complete and harmonious wines in Alba.

Renato Ratti Ratti was, until his death in September 1988, many things to Barolo: historian, producer, innovator and assiduous promoter. He articulated, better than most, the principles of the modern movement, both in writing and in his wine. His nephew, Massimo Martinelli, has made the wine for a number of years, and will now carry on running the *cantina*. All his Barolo is from the Marcenasco vineyard in La Morra, the greatest *cru* of which is La Conca. The wines are perfumed and exciting, with the type of tannic grip on the palate that, to some, belies their modern credentials, but it gives to them the structure to develop superbly.

While Nebbiolo reaches its peak in Barolo and Barbaresco, there are many other wines of note in the north-west that are based on this grape. Some, like those of the Novara-Vercelli hills, were held in higher esteem than the great pair a century or so ago, while others, rather obscure until now, show signs of reaching a wider audience.

Nebbiolo d'Alba covers the area north and south of the Tanaro River, excluding the Barolo and Barbaresco zones. A Nebbiolo d'Alba from the heavier soil south of the Tanaro will be fuller and more austere than one from the north, grown in the sandier, more porous soil of the Roeri hills. This area was granted a separate Roero DOC in 1985, although producers retain the option to call it Nebbiolo d'Alba. Some of the Roero wines, though, have already shown just how attractive young, fresh Nebbiolo can be. Lightened by anything from two to 5 per cent of Arneis, the wines are at their fragrant best about two to three years after the vintage.

Nebbiolo grown in the Barolo or Barbaresco zone can, for a number of reasons, be declassified to Nebbiolo delle Langhe. It may be that it is a wine made from grapes that the producer felt were not fit for use in his Barolo, as is the case with Aldo Conterno's Il Favot. Here though, the raw material is better than many people's Barolo. Conterno ages it in *barrique*, as does Elio Altare with his magnificent and experimental Vigna Arborina, rich yet silky and refined. Others, like Valentino Migliorini, blend a proportion of Barbera with their Nebbiolo. His Bricco Manzoni, polished by a spell in *barrique*, delights those who usually find Nebbiolo too austere.

In north-western Piemonte, on the border with the Valle d'Aosta, Nebbiolo is grown on the steep, terraced slopes of Carema. Here, the steepness of the incline means that vine and vineyard worker struggle in equal measures, but the resulting wine is worth all the effort. Carema can be one of the most elegant and highly perfumed of all Nebbiolo-based wines. From a producer like Luigi Ferrando, the wines are light in colour with a fine scent of liquorice and violets and a silky, subtle texture in the mouth. Ferrando's white label should be drunk younger than his black label *riserva*, which, from certain vintages, can attain great heights.

Over the border in the Valle d'Aosta, a small amount of Nebbiolo is planted among the Alps and the tourist resorts. It is the sole constituent of Donnaz, a wine that, like Carema, can be finely perfumed, but it never quite has the style or class of its neighbour.

Nebbiolo is the mainstay of a number of DOC wines in the Novara and Vercelli hills of eastern Piemonte. Almost all are blended, to a lesser or greater extent, with Vespolina or Bonarda or both. The style here tends toward the robust and rustic with, in some cases, hints of faded glory.

At one point, in the middle of the last century, wines from Lessona had a more ex-

alted reputation than Barolo or Barbaresco. Now, though, it is a source of pleasant, everyday wines that make you wonder what all the fuss was about. But Paolo de Marchi of the Isole e Olena estate in Chianti Classico has vowed to re-plant his family property in this area with Nebbiolo, and he is quite convinced that he can produce an exciting wine.

Today, Gattinara has the greatest reputation of these wines. Made from a minimum of 90 per cent Nebbiolo with up to 10 per cent Bonarda, some people place it next to Barolo and Barbaresco in terms of quality. From producers like Dessilani, Ferrando and Vallana, it can indeed be good, but those prepared to consider it in the same breath as the other two reveal a preference for the lighter, less complex style of Nebbiolo. Ghemme, on the other hand, from a producer like Antichi Vigneti di Cantalupo, can be more impressive than its more famous neighbour, but it still never matches either of the Albese giants.

Of the other wines of these hills, Fara and

Above: *On the steep slopes of the Valtellina in northern Lombardy, the Nebbiolo, here called the Chiavennasca, produces a lighter, more approachable style of wine than it does in Piemonte. The exception is Sfursat, a strapping red made from semi-dried grapes.*

Boca can both be fine, but little is seen outside the zone, while Bramaterra, a recent DOC, shows promise as a full, slightly graceless red. The wine usually seen up here, though, is often sold simply as Spanna. The local name for Nebbiolo, Spanna is often a blend, sometimes with sturdier wines from the south that serve to round off some of Nebbiolo's harsher edges. They can age remarkably well (Vallana's wines particularly so) and are, from people like Dessilani, a fine introduction to Nebbiolo.

Nebbiolo's domain extends eastward into Lombardy where, in the shadow of the Alps in the Valtellina, close to the Swiss border, a lighter, more delicate style is produced. This style is attributed to the steep slopes and northerly latitude, and that the grapes ripen at all here is due to the towering mountains trapping heat in the tiny valley. The exception to the delicate style is Sfursat, made from semi-dried grapes and reaching a minimum of 14.5° alcohol. It is full and intense, becoming velvety and nuanced after five years or so.

Some people rank Sfursat as the finest of the Valtellina wines, while others prefer the more elegant Valtellina Superiore. The four wines of this zone, Inferno, Sassella, Grumello and Valgella, are defined by specific delimited areas, and must be made from at least 95 per cent Nebbiolo. Here, the producer is often a greater arbiter of style than the zone. In certain vintages, these wines, though lacking in the power of much of Piemonte's Nebbiolo, are noted for their finesse and complexity. A 1971 Inferno from Enologica Valtellinese, with a fine truffley perfume and rich, silky fruit, was my first encounter with the splendours of Nebbiolo. At the time, I found Barolo too imposing, and the Inferno much more accessible. These wines are a great introduction to Nebbiolo, and lead to the grandeur of Barolo, just as Blake's early lyrical poems, like "The Lamb", are at the beginning of the route to his great, late poems like "Milton".

*N*ebbiolo, the genius of Piemontese viticulture, cannot be drunk with the same ease as either Barbera or Dolcetto, and, as a result, the latter pair play a central part in Piemontese life, accompanying to perfection much of the local cuisine. Neither is as temperamental as the Nebbiolo, and both ripen earlier, and so can be planted on sites unsuited to ripening the great grape.

Dolcetto is the first to ripen, often a full four weeks before the Nebbiolo. Its name, which means "little sweet one", refers not to the sweetness of the wines but to the high degree of natural ripeness it achieves on the vine. It is thought to be a native of the Monferrato hills, but has not strayed beyond the borders of Piemonte.

As well as being made into a soft, everyday quaffing wine as Dolcetto del Piemonte, it is DOC in seven zones (see box). The styles range from the fresh and gulpable through the softly fruity to the chocolatey rich and plummy wines that some producers in Alba, Ovada and Dogliani produce. It is usually deep in colour with a low acidity and a ripe and wonderfully seamless type of fruit that smacks of just-crushed grapes. Because of its fairly low acidity, it is not generally reckoned to be a candidate for ageing, although some of the more intense versions, from producers like Chionetti, Giacomo Conterno and Giuseppe Mascarello, often benefit from several years in bottle. The overall quality of Dolcetto is very high indeed. And with the technological advances of recent years, which allow the producer to retain the grape's appealing fruit flavours, the Dolcetto should be a candidate for greater popularity.

Dolcetto Zones

Dolcetto d'Acqui The lightest of the Dolcetto DOCs made for early drinking in the area around Acqui Terme, south of Asti and Alessandria. Though attractive, the raspberryish fruit lacks the class of the better zones. Better producers include C.S. di Cassine, Spinola, Villa Banfi-Argusto.

Dolcetto d'Alba Grown around Alba, Barolo and Barbaresco, and generally reckoned to be the best zone for Dolcetto, with, surprisingly, the highest permitted yields of any of the seven DOC zones. Styles vary according to producer, but the wines tend to be deep purple in colour with a scent of plums and chocolate and a rich, soft and round fruit in the mouth. Most are best drunk within two years of the vintage, though from certain vineyards and producers (G. Mascarello, G. Conterno), they can last for several years longer. Single vineyard versions often have an extra depth of fruit, and are usually worth the higher price charged for them. Accomasso, Altare, Ascheri, Mauro Bianco, Bovio, Brovia, Castello di Neive, Clerico, Cogno-Marcarini, Aldo Conterno, Giacomo Conterno, Cordero di Montezemolo, Deltetto, R. Fenocchio, Gaja, Bruno Giacosa, Grasso, Giuseppe Mascarello, Molino, Oberto, Oddero, Prunotto, Ratti, Sandrone, Paolo Scavino, Vajra, Viberti, Vietti, Roberto Voerzio.

Dolcetto d'Asti The Monferrato hills around Asti seem better suited to the production of Barbera than to Dolcetto, which is generally light, artisanal and quaffable, though lacking in distinction. Brema, Carnevale, Cossetti, La Gosa and Ronco are some of the names worth looking for.

Dolcetto delle Langhe Monregalesi A small zone south of Alba, between Dogliani and Mondovi, with the lowest yields of all the DOC zones (49hl/ha). Seldom seen, but reckoned to be the most distinctively perfumed of Dolcetto. One producer of repute, La Meridiana.

Dolcetto di Diano d'Alba The area around the village of Diano d'Alba, south of Alba, is highly regarded for the texture and scent of its Dolcetto. Casavecchia, Coluè, Fontanafredda, Porta Rossa, Rosso, Savigliano, Veglio.

Dolcetto di Dogliani This zone is centred on the village of Dogliani, located in the Langhe, south of Alba. The wines have good depth, being plump and scented, and are less robust but more elegant than those from Alba. They quite often have a rather high acidity in their youth, and need about a year to settle down. Boschis, Chionetti, C.S. di Dogliani, Devalle, Einaudi, Gillardi, Schellino.

Dolcetto di Ovada From the hills around Ovada, south of Alessandria between Gavi and Acqui Terme. The wines are chunky with a bitter chocolate type of fruit, and often surpass the Albese version for structure and depth, if not for class. From producers like Poggio (who recently died – 1985 was his last vintage), the wines need three to four years to be at their best. Cascina Scarsi Olive, I Pola, Poggio, Ratto, Savoia, Scazzola, Tenuta Cannona, Tre Castelli, Valmosè.

Above: *Some of the best Dolcetto and Barbera is made around Alba.*

Barbera, like Dolcetto, probably originated in the Monferrato hills, and is also a firm local favourite. But there the similarities end. Barbera is by far the most populous vine in the north-west, and it tops Sangiovese for this dubious privilege on a national scale. This popularity derives from its ability to thrive in sites where other vines fail, and in its prolific yields.

Because of its vigour and adaptability, it is Barbera that we often see in large bottles selling for a pittance per litre on supermarket shelves in Italy. It was this type of wine that was at the centre of the methanol scandal in 1986 that left 22 people dead and countless others injured, and further debased the image of Barbera. Yet given the right site and the cool, long growing season provided by the Langhe and Monferrato hills or the Oltrepò Pavese, Barbera can produce wines of astonishingly high quality. It is in these wines that the post-methanol future of Barbera lies, for the Italians are, thankfully, turning away from the downmarket jugs and upgrading the quality of the wine they drink.

Due to its ubiquitous presence, the local producers have created a startling range of styles. Barbera can be light and fruity, rich and meaty, oaked or non-oaked, sweet, dry, *frizzante* or even white and sparkling. In Piemonte, it gives of its best in Alba and Asti, the only DOCs where it is 100 per cent varietal. When young, it has a deep and sometimes frothing purple colour with a scent of plums or, in some cases, the farmyard, while on the palate it may have a slight prickle of gas. It usually has a vibrant, mouthfilling and damsony type of fruit that is cut by a sharp bite of acidity on the finish.

In the Monferrato hills around Asti, where the Nebbiolo is not such a consideration, Barbera gets better sites and shows just what it is capable of. Producers like Scarpa make fat, well-rounded wines in the traditional style, while Giacomo Bologna uses *barrique* on two of his wines, Bricco dell'Uccellone (seminal and long established, but less impressive in recent years) and the newly released and outstanding Bricco della Bigotta. He also makes a delicious, slightly sweet and *frizzante* wine called La Monella which is bursting with ripe, grapey fruit.

Elsewhere in Piemonte, such as under the Monferrato and Rubino di Cantavenna DOCs, the addition of other grapes, like Freisa and Grignolino, gives a suppler, softer style of wine that is best drunk young. Over the border, though, in the Oltrepò Pavese, it produces some wines, firm and robust, that rank with the best of Alba and Asti. And here, as with the best Piemontese versions, Barbera's high acidity frequently enables it to age surprisingly successfully.

Pick of Barbera

Barbera d'Alba Altare, Ascheri, Barale, Brovia, Castello di Neive, Pio Cesare, Cogno-Marcarini, Aldo Conterno, Giacomo Conterno, Bruno Giacosa, Fratelli Giacosa, Giuseppe Mascarello, R. Fenocchio, Gaja, Prunotto, Ratti, Vajra, Vietti.

Barbera d'Asti Amilcare, Bava, Bertelli, Braida (Giacomo Bologna), Carnevale, Cascina La Spinetta, Castello di Gabiano, Contratto, Spinola, Podere Borlotto, Rabezzana, G. Ratti, Ronco, Scarpa, Tenuta dei Rei, Viarengo.

Barbera del Monferrato Bava, Brema, Calvo, C.S. del Monferrato, Castello di Gabiano, Duca d'Asti, Gaudio, Nuova Cappelletta, G. Ratti, Ronco, Valmosè.

A lthough Barbera and Dolcetto are currently the most popular and noble of
the north-west's plebeian varieties, a
host of others swell the ranks and seem
poised, when fashion swings in their direction, to be raised alongside their erstwhile
superiors. Some, like Freisa and Grignolino,
were once popular and are now striving to
adapt to modern tastes, while others, like
Ruchè (or Rouchet), once seemingly irre-
trievably obscure, are slowly growing in
popularity.

Grignolino, in the middle of the last
century, was treated with greater deference
than the Nebbiolo. Its light colour, fine perfume and delicate, fragile flavour was the
perfect foil to the heartier, robust style of
other Piemontese red wines. Its popularity
waned, however, largely because of low
yields, and today it is confined almost solely
to the Monferrato hills, where it is DOC in Asti
and Monferrato Casalese. Without food, it
can seem wan, pinched and austere, but

these qualities enable it to cut through and
survive some of the richer Piemontese
dishes, especially *bagna caôda*, the oil, garlic and anchovy fondue distinct to the region.

Freisa, made in a variety of styles, is more
attuned to modern tastes. Once made sweet
and *frizzante*, its star waned while dry wines
were in vogue, but, over the past 20 years or
so, people like Aldo Conterno have
engineered a revival in its fortunes. It is now
more often dry, sometimes slightly frothing,
with a raspberryish scent, and from some
producers, a ''sweet and sour'' type fruit on
the palate that puts me in mind of nothing
more than a good Vouvray. The best Freisa
that I have tasted, though, is Aldo Vajra's dry,
intensely flavoured and silky rich version,
which spends about two years in *botte* before
bottling. It is quite outstanding, approaching some Nebbiolo in terms of structure and
complexity.

A grape that deserves wider popularity is
the Brachetto, which makes grapey, scented
and bubbling wines in the hills around Acqui.
The American giant, Villa Banfi, latched on to
this appeal, seeing an opportunity to re-
create their success with Lambrusco. True
similarities do exist, but once the Lambrusco
fad has passed, Brachetto will remain, producing wines that, in the hands of people like
Giacomo Bologna, have something of the
charm and vibrancy of a good Moscato d'Asti.
A superb dry version, with a perfume of
crushed rose petals and a light but luxuriantly textured fruit, comes from Scarpa, a

house based at Nizza Monferrato specialising in native Piemontese varietals.

Until recently, Scarpa were one of the few people left who produced Ruchè in anything approaching commercial quantities. A rare native variety, said to have been brought to Piemonte from Burgundy in the eighteenth century, its survival was ensured by the DOC it was granted in the Castagnole Monferrato zone in 1987. Other young producers like Antonio Deltetto at Canale have taken it up, and it should prove increasingly successful, if not on a commercial basis then from the point of view of interest. Its wines tend to be deep coloured, with a truffley, peculiarly Piemontese scent and a rich, alluring but tannic structure on the palate that bears more than a passing resemblance to Nebbiolo.

A variety set for greater things is the Bonarda. According to Jancis Robinson, there are, rather confusingly, two Bonardas which, though related, are distinctly individual. The Piemontese variety is the lighter of the two and is used, along with Vespolina, to soften the austerity of the Nebbiolo in the Novarese wines like Ghemme, Lessona and Fara. The other is a strain of Croatina, and is found over the border in Lombardy's Oltrepò Pavese. Soft and bitter-rich with a Dolcetto-like colour and fruit, it often has a slight fizz to enhance its lively character and quaffability. It is also used in a blend with Barbera in the Oltrepò Rosso DOC, whose sub-denominations include the colourfully named Sangue di Giuda, Buttafuoco and Barbacarlo.

Above: A tractor moving between the rows of vines near Castelnuovo Don Bosco, spraying the grapes in order to ensure they are healthy at harvest.

Although a great deal of both has previously slaked Milan's thirst, a small amount is now being exported and, from producers such as Castello di Luzzano, is worth seeking out.

From the point of view of popularity, eastern Lombardy is dominated by the Marzemino grape. Also known as the Berzamino, it is found in several DOCs, the most widely seen of which is Riviera del Garda. Here it is blended with Groppello, a highly rated local variety that produces fairly robust wines for youthful drinking. Marzemino reaches its greatest heights on the steep slopes of Mario Pasolini's farm overlooking Brescia. His Ronco di Mompiano is made from 70 per cent Marzemino and 30 per cent Merlot, the colour, perfume and race of the former being lent a certain flesh by the richness of the latter, giving a delicious and wholly individual wine of great distinction.

As we descend further down the list of rare varieties found in the north-west, three deserve to be plucked from obscurity. The Malvasia Nera, also found in Puglia, produces sweet red wines in Piemonte, being DOC in Casorzo d'Asti and Castelnuovo Don Bosco, north-west of the town of Asti. Rare, perfumed and individual, they are seldom seen outside the region.

In Italy's smallest and north-westernmost region, the Valle d'Aosta, the French influence is evident in the name of its indigenous local grape, the Petit Rouge, which is found in Chambave Rosso, Enfer d'Arvier and Torrette. Little finds its way further than the tables of the local restaurants, busy all year round with tourists who come for the skiing in the winter and the stunning Alpine beauty in the summer.

The same situation exists with the Rossese grape, Liguria's major red variety. DOC in Riviera Ligure di Ponente and Dolceacqua, it produces attractively perfumed and vibrantly fruity wines of great appeal. Its historical claim to fame rests on Napoleon's preference for it, something the local people have seen fit to promote rather than to forget.

Given the diversity and quality of the native red grapes, it will surprise few to learn that the French varieties have not made significant inroads into the north-west, especially in Piemonte. Well, it may surprise the French, but the Italians who view the Piemontese as a reserved, slightly arrogant lot, will take for granted their vinous chauvinism.

With the mighty Nebbiolo holding sway, supported by its loyal lieutenants Dolcetto

Above: *The Alps provide a stunning backdrop to Petit Rouge vines grown at Arvier in the Valle d'Aosta. Most of the wine is drunk locally.*

and Barbera, there would seem to be little room (or need, some would say) for grapes like the Cabernet Sauvignon or the Pinot Noir. In the case of the latter, little is found in Piemonte. Fontanafredda have a small amount on their estate at Serralunga, but much of this goes into their fine *Méthode Champenoise* sparkler, Contessa Rosa, while Cascina del Drago produce an attractively perfumed and supple version in the Langhe.

While there is talk of a great deal of experimentation with Pinot Nero in Piemonte, especially in the Langhe, and though it is DOC in the Valle d'Aosta, Lombardy is home to Italy's largest plantings of this difficult Burgundian grape. It has achieved a certain degree of success there, with some fine non-oaked versions capturing the grape's alluring perfume, while others, notably Ca' del Bosco, have produced stylised Burgundian look-alikes that are almost too good to be true. It is DOC in the Oltrepò Pavese, where it can be

Above: *Lorenzo Tablino of Fontanafredda in his quality control laboratory. Best noted for their Barolo, they also make a sparkler called Contessa Rosa.*

red, pink or white, though much of what is planted is used as a base for the vast amounts of *spumante* produced in the north-west. A great deal of this is grown in Lombardy but transported to Piemonte to be blended with Pinot Grigio and, in some cases Chardonnay, and to be transformed into *spumante* of varying degrees of distinction.

The Cabernet Sauvignon plays very much a secondary rôle in the north-west, both in terms of quality and quantity. Once again, it is being experimented with in the Langhe, but so far only Angelo Gaja has produced anything that, though inferior to, can at least be considered alongside the best Tuscan versions. Called Darmagi (supposedly his father's response when Angelo told him he had planted Cabernet on a particularly favoured site in Barbaresco, it means, in Piemontese dialect, "what a pity!"), it is a state-of-the-art Cabernet, all oak and blackcurrants, but lacking the exciting originality and sheer genius of his Barbaresco. Given Gaja's undoubted mastery of the Nebbiolo, however, it may be that he needs time to come up with a Cabernet-based wine that will have all the breed and nuance we expect.

This he may do, as the Bordelais have done, by blending it with Merlot. Certainly, Gaja's friend and fellow modernist, Maurizio Zanella of Ca' del Bosco, has gone this way, producing a refined wine of great class (and expense) which he very modestly named after himself.

Cabernet Sauvignon is also blended with Merlot in the Valcalepio DOC, north of Bergamo, but here it takes on much less of Zanella's *cru classé* character, instead being more of a Bordeaux Rouge type wine. The

Merlot is used more in blends in the north-west, though some varietal table wines are made in Lombardy. On the whole, however, it lacks the importance here that it acquires in the north-east.

This is also the case with the Cabernet Franc. While few varietals are made, it is the major component in the unusual blend used for Franciacorta Rosso. Barbera, Nebbiolo and Merlot make up the rest of the blend, which, from producers like Contessa Maggi and Longhi-de-Carli can be fragrant and herbaceous, with the French grapes providing the perfume and the Italians the depth, while others, notably Ca' del Bosco, aim for more richness and complexity. My preference is for the former style, which is best drunk young while the Cabernet Franc retains the appealing grassiness that a good Chinon or Bourgueil should have, but combines this with more depth and less acidity than the Loire reds often have.

While the north-west's native red grapes, Nebbiolo in particular, can be difficult to come to terms with, the most widely planted and greatest of the native white grapes, the Moscato, produces wines as accessible and enjoyable as any can ever hope to be. And its most popular wines, Asti Spumante and Moscato d'Asti, are the finest example of the Piemontese penchant for sweet, scented and sparkling wines.

Indeed, their scent is incomparable. Fresh and delicate with hints of peaches and elderflowers, it is derived from the fact that it is the Moscato Bianco grape that is planted here, which, as Jancis Robinson points out in her excellent book *Vines, Grapes and Wines*, produces the best and most fragrant of Muscat wines.

The Moscato is Piemonte's oldest known grape variety. Its most famous wine is Asti Spumante. Production is huge, having risen from 2 million bottles in 1950 to 23 million in 1970 to, in 1984, an incredible 75 million bottles. This increase in production reflects the great demand for Asti. The ease with which it has sold has resulted in some wine of dubious quality being released on the market. This in turn has led to the wine acquiring the pejorative sobriquet of "nasty Asti".

At its best, Asti is anything but nasty; it is, rather, delicious. Its production zone, covering almost 10,000 hectares, is centred on the Langhe and Monferrato hills, and consists of six sub-zones. Quality has improved markedly as the Consorzio, which now controls about 85 per cent of total production, has grown in importance.

Unlike other sparkling wines, which often undergo a secondary fermentation, either in tank or in bottle, and then acquire their character from a degree of bottle ageing, Asti undergoes a single fermentation, and often seems not to be wine, but rather partly fermented grape juice that has been made sparkling. The unique production process aims to capture the fresh, primary fruit aromas of the grape.

After the juice from the crushed grapes is cleaned up by filtration and centrifugation, it is prevented from fermenting by chilling it to 0°C, a temperature at which the yeasts cannot work. It is then stored at this temperature until it is needed by the producer. At this point, the temperature is allowed to rise and the wine begins to ferment. Once it reaches about 5°C, it is transferred to sealed containers for 30 days, during which time the fermentation continues but the carbon dioxide gas is retained and dissolved in the wine. Before all the sugar has been fermented into alcohol, the temperature is once again lowered to 0°C and, at the end of the 30 day period, officials of the Consorzio will break the seal to stop the fermentation; and the wine (which retains some sweetness and relatively low alcohol) can be bottled. There are individual variations on this theme, but the aim of the best producers, people like Fontanafredda, Martini, Contratto and La Brenta d'Oro, is to capture that essential grapiness

of the Moscato in the bottle. This combination of low alcohol, a heavenly scent and a light, grapey fruit makes it wonderful both as an aperitif and a digestif.

It may surprise some readers to realise that the best Moscato grapes go into Moscato d'Asti rather than Asti Spumante. It is, in theory, the base wine for Asti Spumante. With only 5-6° of alcohol and a slight sparkle, it has a superb perfume and a wonderfully grapey and lively fruit on the palate that finishes dry. This light, lively character makes a glass an essential component of any Piemontese meal. Following Dolcetto, Barbera and Barolo, each of which is likely to have accompanied a hearty dish of impressive proportions, a sip of Moscato d'Asti will once again enliven the proceedings, and enable you to leave the table feeling sated rather than stuffed.

In the easternmost part of the Asti zone, around the village of Strevi, the Moscato produces fine and intensely perfumed wines that are distinctive enough to warrant their own DOC. They are felt to have a greater richness and class than the wines produced in the other sub-zones. By far the greatest wine in this area is Domenico Ivaldi's Moscato Passito from his Casarito vineyard. Intensely

Right: State-of-the-art stainless steel tanks that are used at Fontanafredda in the production of one of the best Asti Spumante.

Moscato Grape: DOC Zones and Best Producers

Piemonte

Asti Spumante Do not scorn its popularity – enjoy its sparkling grapiness and scented, peachy character. Bera, Brenta d'Oro, Cinzano, Contratto, Fontanafredda, Gancia, Guasti, Martini & Rossi, Vignaioli di Santo Stefano.

Moscato d'Asti With little more than 5-6° of alcohol, it is light and scented with a delicate sweetness that is enhanced by a slight spritz. The best Moscato grapes of Asti are used in this wine. Arione, Ascheri, Bera, Braida (Giacomo Bologna), Carnevale, Il Cascinone, Duca d'Asti, Dogliotti, Dolcetto e Moscato, Fontanafredda, Gomba, Marenco, Mo, Rivetti, Saracco, Traversa, Valmosè, Vignaioli di Santo Stefano, R. Voerzio.

Moscato di Strevi Grown in the hills around Strevi in the eastern part of the Asti zone, this Moscato, usually slightly *frizzante*, is richer and finer than those from the west of the zone. Bruni, Mangiarotti and Villa Banfi all produce good versions, but they are dwarfed by Ivaldi, especially his Passito from the Casarito vineyard.

Lombardy

Moscato di Scanzo Though not DOC, this celebrated dark Moscato is noted as much for its rarity as for its fine perfume and great complexity, despite having up to 18° alcohol. Collinetta, La Cornasella, La Meridiana, Valbona.

Oltrepò Pavese The lighter style is usually *frizzante* and fragrant, similar to, but higher in alcohol than, Moscato d'Asti. The *liquoroso*, fortified and either medium sweet or luscious, is a new addition to the DOC. Better producers include Bagnasco, Contardi, Padroggi and Torti.

Valle d'Aosta

Valle d'Aosta Chambave Moscato can be either light and dry or, when made from semi-dried grapes (called Passito or Flétri), rich, perfumed, luscious and noted for its longevity. La Crotta di Vegneron is a noted co-operative producer, while Ezio Voyat is the best private producer.

flavoured yet delicately nuanced and capable of great longevity, it is one of Italy's – and the world's – great sweet wines.

Moscato d'Asti and Asti Spumante, both made solely with Moscato grapes, should not be confused with Moscato Spumante. Though the latter can be a pleasantly commercial concoction, it never matches the quality of either of the former pair. Quite often, it is merely a base wine from Puglia or the Veneto with a hint of sweetness to mask its defects, a good dash of sparkle to enhance its freshness and a splash of Moscato for perfume. The best are sound and pleasant, but the worst are vile, industrial blends. As it is usually cheap, some people mistakenly feel that they are getting a bargain, but it should always be distinguished from the real Moscato wines of the north-west.

Lombardy boasts several Moscato-based wines that are worthy of note. It is DOC in the Oltrepò Pavese, both in a light and frothing version and in a rich, fortified style, known as *Moscato liquoroso*. The former is of such quality that very little from Asti can better it, proof once again of the promise long threatened but seldom fulfilled by this zone.

Other than a small amount of DOC Moscato in the Valle d'Aosta, grown near Chambave, where both a scented, dry version of fair quality and a Passito (or "Flétri") of substantially greater renown are produced, little else is made that can match what is made around Asti, both in terms of commercial significance and sheer enjoyment.

The rest of the native white grapes have been, until recently, of little significance. But technological advances that allow producers to exercise greater control over fermentation, enabling them both to capture and to retain the character of the grape, have led to an increased awareness of the potential and the intrinsic qualities of some of these previously ignored varieties.

The best of these dry whites are emerging from the Roeri hills. The Roeri have always been viewed as something of a poor relation to the Langhe. While the hills south of the Tanaro had a great reputation for their Barolo, Barbaresco and "*tartufi bianchi*", those on the northern side were more noted for the fruit, honey and small amount of Nebbiolo d'Alba and Arneis they produced. But the lighter, sandier soil of the Roeri has, in recent years, begun to fulfil its potential for the production of light and dry white wines.

Foremost among these are those from the Arneis grape. Though native to the region, by the early seventies it had been virtually abandoned by growers because of its low yields and high mortality rate (its name, in dialect, means "little difficult one"). Bruno Giacosa and La Cornarea were among the first producers to renew producing it on a commercial basis, and today its future seems assured by the number of young producers making versions of great quality. This was recognised by the authorities when, with the 1988 vintage, they granted a DOC for it in the Roero zone north of the Tanaro river.

Below: *A perfectly formed bunch of Moscato grapes, grown in the Monferrato hills around Asti, where it produces delicately scented and charming wines.*

It produces wines with a distinctive and unforgettable character. They have hints of pears, apples and nuts on the nose, and combine power and delicacy on the palate in such a way that they seem to resemble nothing more than a good French Condrieu. And like Condrieu, the wines do not age well, being at their best in the first year or two following the vintage. This short life-span can be attributed to the grape's low level of natural acidity, which, as it softens in bottle, leaves the wine flabby and lacking in definition. The best version is probably that from Barbaresco specialists, Castello di Neive, though Bruno Giacosa is also highly rated, and Roberto Voerzio's seems to get better each year, an indication that he could soon be challenging for the top position.

Until the recent rise of Arneis, the Cortese was widely viewed as the prime grape for dry whites in the north-west. Although DOC in the Colli Tortonesi and the Alto Monferrato, as well as in the Oltrepò, where it performs well, it is most renowned as the grape of DOC Gavi. This wine, from the hills around the town of Gavi in south-eastern Piemonte, has become extremely fashionable in Italy in recent years. Dry, neutral and acid, with a

Above: *Lombardy's Oltrepò Pavese could become a force in Italian wines should its producers waken from the slumber its gently rolling hills seem to evoke.*

slightly oily texture cut by a hint of limes, it is, at best, a decent, fresh white wine. Yet such is the force of fashion in Italy that the wines, especially the one from La Scolca, established in the early sixties as one of Italy's first modern dry whites, fetch prices that rival that of a good Barolo.

The reputation and price of Gavi are greatly inflated. Both Arneis and Favorita produce better wines. The latter's upturn in fortunes has been so sudden that even as recently as 1985, Nicolas Belfrage, in *Life Beyond Lambrusco*, could find little better to say about it than that it was best suited as "a cutting wine for lightening Barbera". But thanks to the attentions of several young producers, the grape has been rescued from the anonymity of blends and is now making delicately scented, racy dry whites with a nice twist of acidity on the finish. Although I have come across a couple that are ineffably boring, several others that I have encountered

have such style and interest as to infuse me with great optimism for this grape's future.

The two finest that I have tasted are from Malvirà (Fratelli Damonte) and Carlo Deltetto. The former has a little more weight and penetration on the palate, but the latter, made by Antonio Deltetto, who recently took over from his father, is delicately perfumed with a vibrant and delicious fruit in the mouth. Both producers, incidentally, also turn out a fine Arneis.

According to Carlo Deltetto, the Favorita seems to be related to Liguria's Vermentino. If this is true, it was probably brought to Piemonte by traders from the Ligurian coast, who travelled north to sell their goods. Their constant criss-crossing of the region accounts not only for the Favorita, but also for the presence of anchovies in landlocked Piemonte's famous dish, "*bagna caôda*".

The Vermentino is Liguria's most widely seen dry white, being DOC in Riviera di Ponente as well as making a number of attractive table wines. Light and crisp, they are best drunk young, and accompany to perfection the seafood found along the coast. The Ligurian Vermentino is not thought to be related to the Sardinian grape of the same name, which is, in fact, the Malvasia.

Ligurian dishes that are too robust for the light Vermentino are best matched with the Pigato, which is noted for its rich and rather alcoholic dry whites. DOC under Riviera di

Above: *Blanc de Morgex vines in the Valle d'Aosta, trained in pergolas in a scene that evokes Switzerland more than Italy. The resulting dry and perfumed white wine from such vineyards is seldom seen outside its native region.*

wines, rich and luscious but with a firm acidity on the finish. Luigi Ferrando of Carema fame produces minute quantities of a late harvested, *barrique*-aged Erbaluce called Solativo that is exquisite.

Lombardy, apart from being home to some fine Moscato, has little in the way of fine native white grapes. The Oltrepò Pavese produces some good Riesling Italico, but nothing to match the best versions we will come across in the north-east. Most of the best whites here are made from foreign grapes, the beginning of a trend that intensifies as we move east.

The true Riesling, Riesling Renano, competes in the Oltrepò Pavese with its spurious namesake. It produces light, dry and perfumed wines that are, at best, charming, but always lacking in the substance and classical varietal expression of the wines made from this grape in the Alto Adige and Collio.

Another grape of German origin that excels in the north-east, the Müller-Thurgau (a cross of Riesling and Sylvaner), makes its first appearance here. It is, though, very much of a cameo appearance before it assumes larger rôles in Trentino, the South Tyrol and Friuli. Though not DOC, some good *Vini da Tavola* are produced in the Oltrepò Pavese. Light, perfumed and directly varietal, they are best drunk young.

The Pinot Grigio also makes its presence felt here, but not nearly to the same extent as in the north-east. It is DOC in the Oltrepò Pavese, where it makes still dry whites that are sound, nutty and fresh. Occasionally, though, depending on the producer, its wines are *frizzante* or, sometimes, a coppery colour. This *ramato* (copper coloured) style, uniquely Italian, is derived from macerating the must on the reddish tinged skins of the Pinot Grigio for anything from six to 24 hours. This gives the wine not only its distinctive colour, but also a fuller, broader flavour. This style, though slightly out of favour at the moment, what with the fashion for pale, crystal clear wines, is more prevalent in the north-east.

Ponente, its wines prove more than a match for the heartiest of seafood or pasta dishes.

Another variety that, like the Pigato, is seldom seen outside of its own neighbourhood, is the Valle d'Aosta's Blanc de Morgex. It yields scented and crisp dry white wines that are, in the hands of some producers, of a certain interest. Of wider renown are the wines of the Erbaluce grape, grown around Caluso, north-east of Turin. It makes a decent dry white, but the real stars here are the Passito

---

Other North-Western Whites

Arneis DOC in Roero. Dry, rich and nutty, can be one of Italy's finest dry whites. Best drunk young. Almondo, Bel Colle, Carretta, Castello di Neive, Cornarea, Deltetto, Bruno Giacosa, Malvirà, Pezzuto-Malot, Rabezzana, Rabino, R. Voerzio.

Favorita Dry on the palate and subtly restrained on both nose and palate. Its delicacy is a treat in an age of overblown white wines. Drink young. Bel Colle, Cavallotto, Deltetto, La Corte, Malvirà, Negro, Pezzuto-Malot, Rabezzano.

Gavi Dry and rather neutral, its oily texture is cut by a steely acidity. Bergaglia, Carnevale, Castello di Tassarolo, Duca d'Asti, Deltetto, La Battistina, La Chiara, La Giustiniana, La Raia, La Scolca, Pio Cesare, Valmosè, Villa Banfi (Principessa), Villa Broglia.

Chardonnay Not yet DOC in the north-west, this trendy grape is making inroads into various corners of the zone. Styles range from fresh and creamy to full and oaky.
Piemonte: Coluè, Fontanafredda, Franco Fiorina, Gaja, Gomba, Pio Cesare.
Lombardy: Ca'del Bosco, Castello di Grumello.
Valle d'Aosta: Institut Agricole Régional.

Up to 45 per cent of Pinot Grigio is found in the blend, along with Pinot Bianco, used for Valcalepio Bianco. Produced east of Bergamo, on the western flank of Lake Iseo, it is a light, fresh and creamy dry white that never seems to have quite the charm of its red counterpart.

Pinot Bianco, Pinot Grigio and Chardonnay all figure on the eastern shores of Lake Iseo in the Franciacorta production zone, that extends as far east as Brescia. Franciacorta Bianco, made largely from Pinot Bianco, though the DOC discipline permits Chardonnay, is, like Valcalepio Bianco, seldom as enjoyable as the red. At best, it slakes the Italian thirst for fairly light and neutral dry white wines.

These grapes combine, along with the Pinot Grigio and Pinot Nero, in Franciacorta *spumante*. Some of Italy's most attractive sparklers are to be found in this zone, either non-vintage (made by the tank or Charmat method) or *méthode champenoise* vintage. From certain producers, these *méthode champenoise* wines can rival a good Champagne for quality, while still retaining their own individual character.

When it comes to *spumante*, Franciacorta is rivalled by the Oltrepò Pavese as the source of the north-west's best dry sparklers. The same four grape varieties are used to make the base wine, but whereas in Franciacorta most is sold under the DOC banner, in the Oltrepò only a small proportion cites the region of origin on the label, the rest being shipped to Piemonte where large producers use it as the base for the production of their proprietary brands.

The sparklers from both areas can be of excellent quality. In Italy, they represent good value, or at least have done until recently. In the early seventies, the Italian government imposed a punitive tax on imported sparkling wines in an attempt to wean people away from Champagne (for which Italy was the biggest export market) onto the native product. This gave a great boost to the *spumante* industry, but in 1988, the European Commission eventually got around to ruling that the tax was unfair. Now, the Italians are starting to realise what the export markets have been telling them for years: that their *spumante* is good, but it does not represent particularly good value alongside fine Champagne and certain other sparklers. Perhaps this renewed

Right: *Sediment working its way to the neck of this* spumante, *produced by the* Méthode Champenoise, *in Fontanafredda's cellars in Serralunga d'Alba.*

Below: *Chardonnay fermenting in stainless steel tanks in Angelo Gaja's cellars in Barbaresco. The wine is then given a spell of polishing in* barrique *before bottling.*

competition will spur on the *spumante* industry to endeavour to produce better wines at cheaper prices.

Certain of the wines can already match good Champagne for both quality and price. The Franciacorta *spumante* from Ca'del Bosco, especially his Dosage Zero, is outstanding, but it can come as something of a shock to a palate raised on Champagne. It is bone dry, without the extra *"dosage"* (a sweetener used to balance the high acidity of Champagne) found in Champagne. Without this, it can initially seem lean and austere, but the quality and purity of its fruit shine through so clearly that it soon becomes irresistible. It is just a pity that more producers are not making wines of this quality, but then that would be like wishing that all Champagne was on a par with Krug.

The Oltrepò specialises in another style of *spumante*, one that, though not unique, the Italians are beginning to make their own. The Pinot Nero *spumante* has the body and scent of the black grape combined with a remarkable delicacy that makes it quite distinct from a similarly produced Champagne. Indeed, these wines are not even attempting to emulate Champagne and will perhaps, as a result, show the *spumante* industry the route to survival.

The growing craze for Chardonnay could also help in this matter. Producers may find that they can add another line to the portfolio and sell their wine with greater ease if they separate the Chardonnay from their blend and produce a still varietal. Though it has yet to be granted a DOC in the north-west, some excellent *Vini da Tavola* are being produced. Foremost among these in Lombardy is Ca'del Bosco, with a stylish oaked version that promises the world on the nose but delivers slightly less on the palate. With time, though, as the vines get older, this flaw should be remedied.

The Piemontese seem more willing to embrace Chardonnay than they were Cabernet, a reflection, no doubt, of the strength of their red grapes as against that of their whites. Once again, Gaja has led the way with his oak-aged Gaia & Rey, but the wine has been less successful than Darmagi. It is fat, full and toasted on the palate, but lacks definition and nuance at the moment. I have little doubt, though, that with experience the wine will improve markedly.

Increasing experimentation has led to a growing number of Piemontese Chardonnays being released on the market. Styles range from the full and oaky (Pio Cesare's Piodilei is particularly good) to the light, creamy and non-oaked versions (Franco Fiorina's is very attractive). It is a trend that is bound to intensify, and as the producers gain more experience with Chardonnay, the overall level of quality is bound to rise. I doubt whether it will ever match that of the Moscato, let alone the great red grapes, but monitoring its progress will be one of the many things that will continue to make Italian wines so fascinating over the next few years.

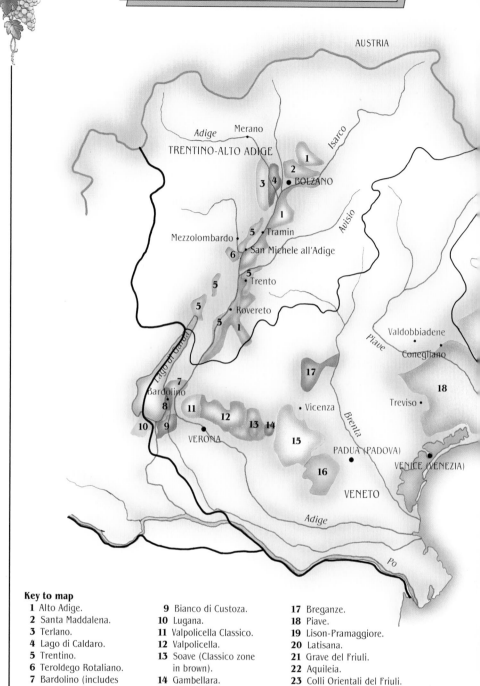

AUSTRIA

TRENTINO-ALTO ADIGE

Adige Merano

Isarco

1

2

3 **4** • BOLZANO

Avisio

1

Mezzolombardo •

5 •Tramin

6 • San Michele all'Adige

5 •Trento

5

5 •Rovereto

5 **1**

Lago di Garda

Bardolino

Piave

Valdobbiadene

Conegliano

17

18

7

8 **11**

10 **9** **12**

13 **14**

VERONA

• Vicenza

Brenta

Treviso •

15

PADUA (PADOVA) •

16

VENICE (VENEZIA)

VENETO

Adige

Po

Key to map

1 Alto Adige.	**9** Bianco di Custoza.	**17** Breganze.
2 Santa Maddalena.	**10** Lugana.	**18** Piave.
3 Terlano.	**11** Valpolicella Classico.	**19** Lison-Pramaggiore.
4 Lago di Caldaro.	**12** Valpolicella.	**20** Latisana.
5 Trentino.	**13** Soave (Classico zone	**21** Grave del Friuli.
6 Teroldego Rotaliano.	in brown).	**22** Aquileia.
7 Bardolino (includes	**14** Gambellara.	**23** Colli Orientali del Friuli.
area **9** also).	**15** Colli Berici.	**24** Collio.
8 Bardolino Classico.	**16** Colli Euganei.	**25** Isonzo.

The north-eastern zone is made up of Trentino-Alto Adige, the Veneto and Friuli-Venezia Giulia. The mountains dominate, whether they be the Dolomites of the Alto Adige or the Julian pre-Alps of Friuli. Despite the presence of these mountains, looming as they do over the northern rim of the zone, the North-East is characterised by two distinctly foreign influences.

Entering Italy from Austria, after coming through the Brenner Pass, there is little sense of anything having changed. The snow-capped Dolomites tower over the valley road, and the architecture remains alpine and Tyrolean. This is the Alto Adige, or, as a large part of the population would have it, Südtirol (South Tyrol). Part of Austria until the Austro-Hungarian empire was broken up and it was ceded to Italy in 1919, the dress, architecture, food and language remain very Teutonic in character.

The first language of much of the population is German, and many people, inclining their heads to the south, refer to Italy as "that country down there". They follow the Teutonic inclination to order, and this is reflected in their wines and wine laws. Over half the production is DOC, and the standard of

FRIULI-VENEZIA GIULIA

Tagliamento

21   Udine •
            23

• Pordenone

                    24 • Gorizia

20   22 25

19

                    • TRIESTE

eties grown on steep, hillside sites in the crisp mountain air, begin to find a market to the south.

As we move south into Trentino, the valley becomes broader, the vineyards are to be found on the valley floor as well as the gentler slopes and, as the Germanic influence recedes, a certain Italian flair (others might call it disorder) begins to make itself evident. Following the Adige river, we enter the Veneto, and are soon flanked by Lake Garda and Bardolino on one side and the hills of the Valpolicella Classico zone on the other. Swinging to the east with the Adige river, we skirt the southern tip of Valpolicella and pass through Verona, one of Italy's most beautiful and romantic cities, on the way to Soave.

The great Veronese trio is just a part of the varied Veneto wine scene. The gentle hills to the north, around Breganze, Vicenza and Conegliano, and the fertile plains of the Piave Valley, are home to a vast array of vines, making the Veneto the leading Italian region in terms of DOC production. Presided over by Venice, Vicenza and Verona, this region often seems to be the embodiment of all that is cultured and elegant in Italian life.

Moving to the north and east, the Italian influence fades as we approach the Yugoslavian border. Gorizia, in the heart of the Collio zone, is bisected by the border, and 80 per cent of Collio is to be found in Yugoslavia. Some producers, their names, features and heavily accented Italian betraying their Slavic origins, still have vineyards in Yugoslavia, and travel back and forth unhindered by frontier formalities.

Though in Friuli, as in the Veneto, a great number of vines are planted on the plains, the best sites are to be found on the hills. The two zones of Collio and Colli Orientali, in the provinces of Gorizia and Udine respectively, are the cradle of the Italian white wine revolution. Here, as in the rest of Italy, the white wines were dull and alcoholic until about 20 years ago, and were sold largely in bulk. Mario Schiopetto is widely credited with instigating the revolution. Earlier picking, a gentler pressing of the grapes and controlled fermentation temperatures, as well as the ability to protect the wines from oxygen, were all instruments of the revolution, enabling winemakers to retain the flavour and delicacy of the grape in their wines.

In the early seventies, the schools of oenology, especially Conegliano, turned out students who took up Schiopetto's call to arms, thus sweeping the revolutionaries to power. Today, Friuli, often at the crossroads of history, when her vineyards were trampled and turned to battlefields, is the undoubted capital of the Italian white wine scene. But there is a feeling that if the South Tyrol could harness its potential by reducing yields, then we would have an almighty tussle for vinous supremacy on our hands.

Above: *These Schiava vines, planted on the shores of Lago di Caldaro in the Alto Adige, produce a light and fresh red wine that is, at its best, drinkable if unexciting. It may also be called Kalterersee due to the German influence.*

quality is high. Much of the production, particularly the light reds from the Schiava grape, has historically been exported to the German-speaking markets to the north, but a recent reversal of this pattern has seen their whites, from German and French vari-

*O*f the native red grapes in the north-east, three are of great importance: Corvina, Rondinella and Molinara. Though they are only grown in a fairly small area, stretching from the eastern shores of Lake Garda, east to Verona and beyond, they are the major grapes of Valpolicella and Bardolino, two of Italy's best known wines.

Other grapes, local rarities like Negrara and national favourites like Sangiovese and Barbera, are also found in the blend, especially in Valpolicella, but these three varieties provide the vital ingredients that contribute to the character of these wines. Corvina is widely regarded as the finest grape, lending structure, perfume and finesse to the blend, while Rondinella imparts colour, acidity and a certain part of the bouquet, and Molinara gives a soft, easy drinking type of fruit.

Bardolino is the lighter of the two wines. Its Classico zone starts on the south-eastern shores of Lake Garda, where the campsites that flank the tiny lakeshore village of Bardolino give way to the gentle hills that run all the way to the Adige river. The Bardolino zone stretches north virtually to the border with Trentino, and curls around the southern tip of Lake Garda, where it meets the border with Lombardy. In Bardolino, unlike in Valpolicella, Classico does not necessarily mean better, as the excellent, non-Classico wines of producers like Fraterna Portalupi amply illustrate.

Above: *A ripe bunch of Corvina grapes. They lend their scent, structure and complexity to the best wines of Valpolicella and Bardolino, but their importance lessens on leaving Verona.*

There are two styles of Bardolino. The *rosso* is a light cherry colour and has a fragrant and delicate fruit, while the *chiaretto* is a delicious dry *rosato*, with a lively fruit and a bitter cherry aroma. The red can be "*superiore*" if it has an extra degree of alcohol (a minimum of 11.5°) and if it has been aged for a year. But given that Bardolino is almost invariably most attractive while young and fresh, this would only seem to indicate that the *superiore* is best avoided. This is not always the case, as producers like Masi, with their La Vegrona, and Guerrieri-Rizzardi, show, but they are the exception rather than the rule. The Castello Guerrieri from the latter producer is, though a *Vino da Tavola*, a fine, oak-aged blend of Sangiovese and the classic varieties that shows the depth and finesse that these wines, at their best, are capable of achieving.

Across the autostrada and the Adige river, north of Verona, lies the small and hilly Classico zone of Valpolicella. The mainly limestone soil has been home to these vines for centuries, and perhaps millennia, as the name would seem to indicate. It is thought to be derived from a mixture of Greek (poly) and Latin (cella) roots, meaning valley of many cellars.

The vines tumble down the hills that rise up out of the valleys of Fumane, Negrar and Marano in the heart of the Classico zone. They gently extend onto the plains beyond the Classico zone and back up into the valley of Valpantena, which produces wines that are sufficiently distinctive to merit an individual denomination, and then gather numbers as they once more roll down into the plain that stretches further east past Verona as far as Soave.

This sea of vines that floods the plain outside the Classico region is the source of the dilute, rather insipid liquid that finds its way onto supermarket shelves in the large, screw-cap bottles that sell at ridiculously cheap prices. That they manage to acquire the name Valpolicella along the way is a scandalous situation, one that arose in the fifties and sixties. It was a time when quantity was more highly prized than quality, so the production zone was expanded beyond the hills of Classico to take in the high yielding vines of the plains, which were greatly preferred to the niggardly bearers on the slopes. The resulting wine was, somewhat unjustly considering its low quality, permitted to call itself Valpolicella.

The large merchants urged farmers to plant on the plains, and to push yields to un-

acceptably high levels. But because they employed proficient technicians, the wines were at least acceptable. Good and great wines became very much the exception, yet quite often merchant's Valpolicella was, for many people, their first introduction to Italian wine. It is little wonder, then, that to this day many people remain unconvinced that Italian wine in general, and Valpolicella in particular, can seriously be classified in the ranks of fine wine.

Yet all the while the better producers have persevered in the production of small quantities of fine wine from specific vineyard sites in the Classico zone. The name of the producer and the vineyard is often highlighted, and that of Valpolicella, out of necessity, reduced to such a size that a close scrutiny of the label is required to find it at all. These people are now calling for new laws that will distinguish, not only between the true Valpolicella from the Classico zone and that

Below: Vines in the lakeside village of Bardolino tumble down gentle hills, stopping just before they reach the waters of Lake Garda. The wine is lighter than neighbouring Valpolicella.

from the plains, but also between the youthful and *riserva* quality wines.

There are, essentially, three types of Valpolicella. The first, and most recent, is the light, fresh and youthful style. It has slightly more depth than Bardolino, and, at its best, has a striking and cherryish purple colour and a fresh scent of black cherries, with a light but lively fruit on the palate. It is delightful, but several factors dictate that it should be so only on the rarest of occasions. Besides the obvious problems of elastic production zones and high yields that we have already encountered, there is also the fact that here, as in Bardolino, a wine called "*superiore*" must have both an extra degree of alcohol and an extra year's ageing. Except with wines like Allegrini's La Grola, where a superb site, a high proportion of Corvina grapes and low yields combine to produce a wine that can actually benefit from a certain amount of ageing, this stipulation often conspires to rob the wines of their freshness.

Nino Franceschetti, the superb winemaker at the fine firm of Masi, also feels that the grape mix is not suitable for the production of this lighter style. More Molinara is what is required for a young quaffing wine, he feels, and he has upped the proportion to 30 per cent for his newly developed "Fresco" style. Masi's Valpolicella Fresco epitomises the best of the basic style of Valpolicella.

Above: *Only those grapes from the steep slopes of the Classico zone are capable of imparting their inimitable finesse to the best wines of Valpolicella.*·

Franceschetti maintains that the grape mix to be found in the vineyards, and consequently enshrined in the DOC regulations of Valpolicella, is best suited for the production of the greatest of Veronese wines: Reciota della Valpolicella. The derivation of the name Recioto is uncertain. Some people maintain that it stems from the dialect word for ears, "*recie*", indicating that only the ripest grapes from the top and outside (hence the ears) of the bunches, are used in its production. Another version has it that it derives from the Latin "*recemus*", meaning "bunch of grapes".

Either way, the production of Recioto involves the use of carefully selected grapes, the best 10-15 per cent picked by a team of expert workers a week to 10 days before the rest are harvested. This early selection ensures that the grapes retain a good level of acidity, and that their skins are slightly harder than normal in order to endure the "*appassimento*". This is the period of drying for the grapes. They are, in the case of the top few producers, sorted by hand, and the best and healthiest bunches of grapes are

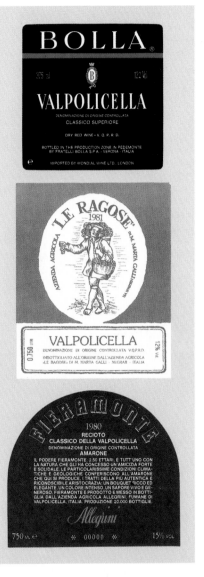

Below: *Grapes destined for use in Recioto are laid out on straw mats to dry, a process known as "appassimento". In two months, they will be shrivelled and rich.*

laid out on straw mats in dry, well-ventilated rooms. The conditions during the *appassimento* are as important as those encountered during the actual vintage. In 1982, humid conditions following an outstanding summer meant that little top quality Recioto was produced. The conditions required are cool, dry days and good ventilation.

The *appassimento* lasts until the end of January. During this time, the grapes lose about 30-40 per cent of their weight through evaporation. A small amount of *botrytis cinerea* (noble rot) occurs, but most producers try to avoid it, as it reduces acidity and colour and can lead to problems with oxidation and the formation of volatile acidity at a later stage.

At the end of January, the shrivelled grapes are crushed and a slow fermentation ensues. Some barrels stop fermenting and are racked off their lees once they reach about 13° alcohol, while they still retain a certain amount of residual sugar. Others bubble away and ferment to full dryness, reaching 15.5-16.5° alcohol. The former, often just called Recioto, or sometimes Recioto Amabile, are rich and sweet, with a wonderful scent of concentrated cherries and a herbal, bitter twist on the finish that prevents them from being cloying. If the wine drinkers of the world ever catch on to the fact that they are infinitely preferable to Vintage Port, being cleaner and in no way spirity, then the small amount produced will be in great demand. Top versions include Allegrini's, Quintarelli's Monte Ca'Paletta, Masi's Mezzanella, Tedeschi's Monte Fontana, and Serègo Alighieri's Casal dei Ronchi.

The latter, drier and stronger styles are called Amarone, from the Italian "*amaro*", meaning bitter. Though dry, their great concentration gives an impression of bitter sweet fruit, while their high level of alcohol is masked by a great range of flavours, from "musty" to "chestnutty" to "mossy". The styles range from the blockbusters of Quintarelli through the power and elegance of Masi's superb Mazzano to the elegant and restrained versions from Allegrini (Fieramonte) and Le Ragose.

These are magnificent creations, unique in the world of wine, and are known to the Veronese as "*Vini da Meditazione*". They are meditation wines in the sense that they are

Right: *The long tradition of winemaking in "the valley of many cellars" is threatened by industrial production.*

Below: *Sandro Boscaini, the dynamic head of Masi, standing next to a "botte" after a tour of the vineyard.*

Pick of Bardolino and Valpolicella

────────────────Bardolino────────────────

Top producers: Aldegheri, Bertani, Bolla, Boscaini, Cavalchina, Fraterna Portalupi, Girasole, Guerrieri-Rizzardi, Il Colle, Le Vigne de San Pietro, Masi, Montecorno, Santa Sofia, Tedeschi, Zenato.

────────────────Valpolicella────────────────

Top producers – *Rosso:* Allegrini (La Grola), Alighieri, Bertani, Bolla, Boscaini, Ca'del Monte-Zanconte, Campagnola, Girasole, Guerrieri-Rizzardi, Masi, Speri, Tedeschi, Tadiello, Zenato.

Top producers – *Ripasso:* Serègo Alighieri, Allegrini, Bolla (Jago), Boscaini (Le Cane), Le Ragose (Le Sassine), Masi (Campo Fiorin), Quintarelli, Santi (Castello d'Illasi), Speri, Tedeschi (Capitel San Rocco).

Top producers – *Recioto della Valpolicella and Amarone:* Serègo Alighieri, Allegrini, Masi, Quintarelli, Le Ragose, Tedeschi, Venturini.

────────────────Vintages────────────────

(The *rosso* style is best drunk within a year or two of the vintage, while the Ripasso and Recioto will age superbly.)

Great: 1986, 1985, 1983, 1981, 1977, 1974, 1971, 1967, 1964.
Average: 1980, 1979, 1978.
Below average: 1987, 1984, 1982.

---

best sipped and savoured, on their own, at the end of a long meal, when both the mind and palate are ready to accept them. The best versions are from a handful of producers, and can never be cheap, but they are worth every penny of what is paid for them.

The third style, produced in much larger quantities than Recioto, combines elements of both the lighter and more powerful versions, and is traditional to the area. It was, according to Nino Franceschetti, originally used to boost the strength of the lighter Valpolicella, thereby increasing its powers of preservation in the days before bottles and stainless steel. It involves pumping the just fermented Valpolicella into the fermenting vessels recently vacated by the Recioto and Amarone. The wine-soaked skins and lees that remain in these vessels initiate a slight re-fermentation, subsequently increasing both the alcohol and the body of the wine. This style, known as "Ripasso" although the term is not usually found on the label, gives the young wines an extra dimension and is, according to some producers, the only way to make real Valpolicella. Quintarelli, for instance, probably the greatest producer, uses only this method to produce his superb Valpolicella Classico Superiore from his Monte Ca'Paletta vineyard. It is more approachable and, in many ways, more subtle and impressive than his stupendous Amarone. Good examples of this style include Campo Fiorin from Masi, Le Sassine from Le Ragose, Serègo Alighieri and Bolla's Jago.

All the best wines, the perceptive reader will have noted, come from single vineyards, and there is, even among the larger producers, a move to making "cru" wines. This bodes well for the future of Valpolicella, but there remains the problem of nomenclature. If Valpolicella is to be judged on the wines produced by the likes of Quintarelli, Masi or Allegrini, rather than on the bulk wines from the industrial producers, then some distinction is going to have to be made between the three styles. The lighter style, for instance, could be called Rosso di Verona, with Recioto and Amarone being used only in conjunction with a vineyard or "cru" and the name Valpolicella being reserved solely for those wines that are made by the Ripasso method. Valpolicella, after all, is a great name greatly humbled; something must be done to restore it to the pre-eminent position it deserves in the vinous hierarchy.

---

*I*n the forefront of the drive to make Valpolicella great once again stand a handful of producers. All are to be found in the Classico zone, and they view with varying degrees of disbelief and contempt the wines from the plains that also carry the Valpolicella name.

The largest of these producers is undoubtedly Masi. Winemaker Nino Franceschetti produces a wide range of wines, from a youthful Valpolicella Fresco through an excellent Ripasso, Campo Fiorin, to some outstanding Recioto and Amarone. Their *cru* Mazzano is one of the greatest of Amarones, while the wines they make for the estate of Serègo Alighieri are outstanding. At the top end of the scale, their wines are superb.

Another fine producer is Renzo Tedeschi. A modest, delightful man, he and his wines have a great ability to revive both a jaded traveller and a tired palate. His Ripasso Capitel San Rocco is rich and concentrated, while his Amarone, Capitel Monte Olmi, is spicy and complex. His greatest wine, though, is his *cru* Recioto, Monte Fontana. It has a lively, rich and complex bitter sweet fruit that makes it one of the finest, after-dinner sipping wines that I know.

Few people in Valpolicella would deny that Giuseppe Quintarelli is the most outstanding

Above: *Conte Pieralvise Serègo Alighieri, a descendant of the poet Dante, samples a barrel of his great 1983 Amarone prior to bottling.*

Below: *The high-trained Corvina vines of Valpolicella save the strain on the pickers' backs. Careful selection and low yields are the keys to quality.*

producer. His wines are strikingly traditional, from his marvellous Valpolicella Classico Superiore, made by the *ripasso* style, to his array of stupendous (in terms of both quality and size) Amarone and Recioto. He also makes a Recioto from Nebbiolo which is magnificent, and an outstanding Cabernet called Alzero. It is not an exaggeration to say that he is one of the most outstandingly creative producers in the world of wine, and each glimpse of his distinctive green or tan labels, with their handwritten black script, is enough to make me forget my bank manager and reach for my cheque book.

If Quintarelli is the king of Valpolicella, his heir apparent is surely Franco Allegrini. Young and dynamic, he has been making the wines at the family estate since the death of his father in 1983. His style of wine, though, is distinctly different from Quintarelli. Where the latter gets power and complexity, Allegrini's wines are striking by their elegant perfume, vibrant fruit and silky texture. Franco, along with his sister Marilisa and brother Walter now look after the estate. It comprises about 35 hectares of vines. Marilisa looks after the sales and marketing side, while Walter, the oldest, manages the vineyards. Franco, the maestro of the cellar, freely admits that he can only make good wine if he

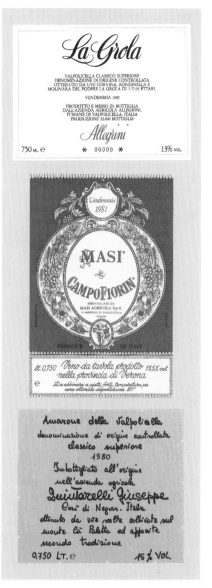

is working with the best grapes. Low yields (they use no chemicals in the vineyard) and excellent sites provide him with this.

Of their vineyards, Fieramonte produces some outstanding Amarone, tightly knit and supremely elegant, that will age for years. At Palazzo della Torre, a seven hectare site bought in 1979, they leave the grapes on the old vines until the end of November, getting rich, partially dried fruit. This produces a ripe, concentrated and spicy wine of immense character.

The greatest site, though, is La Grola, a 7.7ha vineyard that they bought in 1979. It had been abandoned at the turn of the century, so they invested 550 million lire to replant it and bring it back into production. Though the vines are still young, the wines are already setting new standards for Valpolicella. Their finesse and complexity are astounding, and the day is eagerly awaited when the vines reach maturity and are used for the production of Amarone. That, in all likelihood, will be the day when Valpolicella becomes the first zone to be presided over by two kings: Quintarelli and Allegrini.

D espite the renown of Valpolicella, and the reputation of the north-east's white wines, there are a number of other high quality native grapes that, along with some long-established French imports, make this a zone in which red wine production far outstrips that of white. Most of the native grapes, though, unlike the imports, generally thrive in confined areas, and seldom, if ever, achieve success beyond their own neighbourhood.

Friuli has two native reds of significance. The most popular is the Refosco del Peduncolo Rosso (the name, surely, is a marketing man's nightmare, and may indicate why it has failed to achieve international fame), which is DOC in all but two of the seven zones. It is a kind of north-eastern Dolcetto, a source of reliable, sound wines with a deep colour and a soft, direct and robust fruit. While it never really acquires great finesse, producers like Giovanni Dri make versions that are richly satisfying and capable of ageing quite well.

A sub-variety of Refosco, Terrano, is the main constituent of Carso Rosso and, naturally enough, Terrano del Carso, where it produces deep coloured wines with an even greater directness of character than elsewhere. In a rare foray outside its native Friuli, Refosco is also to be found in the eastern Veneto, where it is DOC in Lison-Pramaggiore.

Schioppettino, often talked about but seldom seen, is making something of a comeback in Friulian viticulture. Also known as the Ribolla Nera, it is found almost exclusively in the Colli Orientali, where it produces wines light in colour with a great perfume and an alluring texture that develops, once its acidity has settled down, after three to four years in bottle. Ronchi di Cialla's *barrique*-aged version is outstanding, but Vigne dal Leon and Ronco del Gnemiz also produce good versions which, though expensive, are worth seeking out.

Moving into the Veneto, the most important and exciting of the native grapes, apart from the Veronese trio, is Raboso. It thrives in the flatlands of the Piave valley north of Venice, where it produces full, characterful wines with a ripe depth of fruit and a tough, tannic bite. Little seems to find its way to foreign shores, being consumed instead in the myriad bars and restaurants to be found in Treviso and Venice.

Little else of great importance is made from indigenous varieties in the Veneto, though the Tocai Rosso (the DOC is the Colli Berici, the hills south of Vicenza) produces deep coloured wines that are enjoyable while youthful and robust. An even greater rarity is the Pelara, which is made, as far as I know, by only one producer. It was historically used in Valpolicella before phylloxera, but, because of its low yields, was not re-planted afterwards. Allegrini make a wine from it that can, in certain vintages, be astonishing, while in others it is no better than ordinary. It has an onion skin colour and, at best, a delicate yet

penetrating depth of fruit with a whole spectrum of flavours. Great care needs to be taken while making it, though, as it ages rapidly.

In the South Tyrol, home of crisp and perfumed dry whites, well over half the production is red, and much of this comes from the Schiava (or Vernatsch) grape. It is DOC in Alto Adige (Südtirol), and is the principal grape in Lago di Caldaro (Kalterersee) and Santa Maddalena (St. Magdalener). Most wines from the Schiava grape are light in colour, with a fresh cherryish perfume and a soft, easy fruit that is all the more quaffable when lightly chilled. Lago di Caldaro is the most popular, especially locally and in the markets to the north. If you are in Bolzano, the regional capital, and come across a bottle labelled Kalterersee Auslese, it means, not that the wine is sweet, but that it has achieved 11°, instead of 10.5°, of alcohol.

The best Schiava-based wine is probably Santa Maddalena, especially that from the steep and stunningly beautiful hills of the Classico zone. Despite its local popularity, its claim to fame these days rests more on the oft-repeated story of Mussolini's politically motivated attempt to place it, alongside Barolo and Barbaresco, in the Pantheon of great Italian wines. From producers like Schloss Rametz, Lageder, and Rottensteiner, it can be delicious, but the best wines today tend to be those where the Schiava element has been beefed up with a small proportion of Lagrein.

Lagrein is a local curiosity, a native of Bolzano, that is slowly acquiring a reputation for itself, both as a *rosato* (Kretzer) and as a *scuro* (Dunkel). The former, dry and deep flavoured with a muscular yet elegant character, is one of Italy's best rosés, while the latter, deep coloured with a brambley, bitter fruit, has, from producers like Tiefenbrunner, Niedermayer and, most outstanding of all, Conti Martini, a distinctive and appealing personality. At its best in the Trentino and Alto Adige DOCs, it deserves wider recognition.

Another local variety that has great appeal is the Teroldego. Grown only on the Campo Rotaliano, a plain north of Trento and south of Mezzolombardo, it produces wines that are deeply coloured and elegantly perfumed

---

Native Red Grapes: DOC Zones and Best Producers

Refosco
─────────────**Friuli-Venezia Giulia DOC Zones**─────────────

Aquileia Full, robust and soft, but with good grip and an attractive bitter twist on the finish. Ca'Bolani, Giacomelli, Valle.

Carso The grape, Terrano del Carso, is a different clone here, giving deep coloured, direct and full flavoured wines. Castelvecchio.

Colli Orientali The best zone for Refosco, producing wines of great depth with a touch of finesse. Abbazia di Rosazzo, Angoris, Arzenton, Bandut, Buiatti, Butussi, Ca'Ronesca, Dorigo, Dri, Livon, Nascig, Ronchi di Cialla, Ronchi di Fornaz, Rubini, Villa Belvedere, Volpe Pasini, Zambotto.

Grave del Friuli A large production of good and sometimes outstanding wines. Antonutti, Cantoni, Castello di Porcia, Fantinel, Pighin, Pistoni, Pradio, Villa Ronche, Vinicola Udinese.

Latisana Limited production, but quality can be good. Isola Augusta.

──────────────────────**Veneto DOC Zones**──────────────────────

Lison-Pramaggiore A recent DOC over the border in the Veneto. Initial results are promising.

Schiava
Also known as Vernatsch. There are three clones: Grossa, Gentile and Grigia. The former is the highest yielder, while the latter two give the best quality wines.

──────────────**Trentino-Alto Adige DOC Zones**──────────────

Alto Adige Light, cherry coloured wines with a fresh, quaffable fruit that can be very attractive when chilled. K. St. Michael-Eppan, Lageder, Niedermayer, Schloss Rametz, Tiefenbrunner, Walch.

Lago di Caldaro A light, fresh red, best drunk young and chilled, while its appealing cherryish perfume is still to the fore. Bellendorf, Gaierhof, Hofstätter, K. Kattern, Klosterkellerei Muri-Gries, Kuenberg, Lageder, Laimburg, H. Rottensteiner, Schloss Schwanburg, Tiefenbrunner.

Santa Maddalena Slightly fuller, especially when a dollop of Lagrein is added. Probably the best of the Schiava based wines. Bellendorf, Brigl, Hofstätter, K. St. Magdalener, Lageder, Hans Rottensteiner, Heinrich Rottensteiner, Walch.

Lagrein
Made as a *rosato* (known as ``kretzer'') and as a deep coloured red (known as *scuro* or ``dunkel'').

──────────────**Trentino-Alto Adige DOC Zones**──────────────

Alto Adige Styles range from fresh and approachable to deep-coloured, full flavoured with a brambley type of fruit and rich, bitter chocolate twist on the finish. Ages moderately well, but is usually best drunk within three to five years. Bellendorf, Hirschprunn, Lageder, Laimburg, Niedermayer, Sorni, Tiefenbrunner.

Trentino Similar in style, if perhaps broader and less well-defined. Barone de Cles, Conti Martini, Dolzan, Donati, Foradori, Gaierhof, C.P. Mezzacorona, C.S. Mezzolombardo.

Teroldego
──────────────**Trentino-Alto Adige DOC Zones**──────────────

Rotaliano Deep-coloured with a gripping, berried fruit that is as distinctive as, though distinct from, Lagrein. Barone de Cles, Conti Martini, Dolzan, Donati, Foradori, Gaierhof, Lechthaler, C.P. Mezzacorona, C.S. Mezzolombardo, Moser, San Michele all'Adige, Simoncelli, Zeni.

---

with a firm, full fruit that ages moderately well. From producers like Foradori, Conti Martini and Zeni, the wines are both delicious and memorable. Equally distinctive, if less memorable, is the Marzemino grape, more popular here than in the north-west. DOC in Trentino, it has a refreshing and juicy type of fruit with a tangy acidic bite on the finish. Though its fame in Mozart's day saw it reach Don Giovanni's table, it is now largely confined to Trentino, where people like Simoncelli excel.

By far the most popular of the north-east's red grapes, though, is Merlot. It is long-established here, having taken root in the wake of the Napoleonic invasion, and produces vast quantities of quaffable table wine,

as well as being DOC in, at last count, 15 zones. Some producers, like Russiz Superiore in Collio, produce splendidly fat, ripe and plummy wines that put one in mind of a good Pomerol, but the prevailing fashion in Italy for light, fresh reds means that some producers feel that they have to serve up a more anaemic version if they are to have a chance of selling. They macerate on the skins for only a couple of days, extracting a modicum of colour and a skeletal varietal character, and produce gaunt, ill-balanced wines that cry out for a little more flesh.

The same problem exists, especially in Friuli, for Cabernet. Traditionally, Cabernet Franc has been the most widely planted, but little distinction has been drawn between the two. Up until recently, only Collio stipulated Cabernet Franc in the discipline, with the others leaving the choice to the producer. Now though, zones like Aquilea, Lison-Pramaggiore and Trentino have made room for both Cabernet Franc and Sauvignon within the DOC regulations.

The preferred style of Cabernet has generally been the fragrant, grassy and lively, similar to, say, a Chinon from the Loire Valley, but with greater depth. This continued to be the case, especially in the South Tyrol, Friuli and the eastern Veneto. Some producers, though, are now choosing to emphasise the blackcurrant character of the Cabernet Sauvignon. Supreme among these is Fausto Maculan's Frata, made from late harvested, partially dried grapes that are aged in *barrique*, resulting in a wine that is the essence of Cabernet Sauvignon.

A trend fast gathering steam here is the use of Merlot and Cabernet to produce a Bordeaux blend. These now abound, and vary both in the proportion of each grape in the blend and the amount and type of oak ageing the wine receives. Some, like Borgo Conventi's Braida Nuova, spend a year in used *barrique*, and appear very much to be wearing a Bordeaux mask on a Collio face. Others in Friuli, like Borgo del Tiglio's Rosso della Centa or Russiz Superiore's Cuvee Rosso, let the mask slip a bit, while Castel San Michele and Foianeghe, both from Trentino, are, despite the French garb, distinctly native. Venegazzù della Casa, one of the first to use this blend, seems less successful than it once appeared to be.

Attempts are also being made to blend the best of the French and the indigenous vines. Vigne dal Leon, Volpe Pasini's Le Marne (Cabernet, Merlot, Pinot and Refosco) and Tiefenbrunner's Linticlarus (Lagrein, Merlot and Pinot) are just three of this new breed, which should produce more interesting results than the numerous Bordeaux blends that, though good, always suffer by comparison with the grandeur of the Médoc.

Another Bordeaux native, the Malbec, is also found here, making distinctive varietals in western Friuli and eastern Veneto, as well as playing a minor rôle in some of the Bordeaux blends. Another component of some

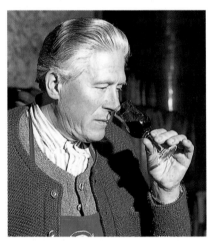

Above: *Herbert Tiefenbrunner, a South Tyrolean "Kellermeister", produces some of the region's most aromatic wines.*

French Red Grapes: DOC Zones and Best Producers

Merlot
————————Friuli-Venezia Giulia DOC Zones————————
Aquileia Large production of light, quaffable wines, but little of lasting interest.
Colli Orientali Capable of producing fuller, richer wines of great class. Butussi, Dorigo, I Moros, Pascolini, Ronchi di Fornaz, Valle, Villa Belvedere, Volpe Pasini.
Collio Some light wines, lacking depth, others full, plump and startlingly good. Borgo Conventi, Borgo del Tiglio, Caccese, Marco Felluga, Gradnik, Roncada, Russiz Superiore, Schiopetto, Radikon, Villa Russiz.
Grave del Friuli Huge production of soft, sound wines. Pighin, Conti di Maniago.
Isonzo Better than average, while never reaching the heights of Collio or Colli Orientali. Eddi, Gallo Stelio, Prandi d'Ulmhort, Zampar.
Latisana Fresh and supple, best drunk young. Isola Augusta, Zaglia.

————————Veneto DOC Zones————————
Colli Berici Round and plump, with good depth and capable of taking several years' ageing. Castello di Belvedere, Dal Ferro-Lazzarini.
Colli Euganei Soft and easy drinking. C.S. Colli Euganei.
Lison-Pramaggiore With its ripe, fleshy fruit, this is, from the better producers, the best of the Veneto's Merlots. La Fattoria, Sant'Anna, Sant'Osvaldo, Villa Frattina.
Montello e Colli Asolani Round and plummy, the best can age for a couple of years. C.S. di Valdobbiadene.
Piave Large production of soft, sound wines that are consistently good. Abbazia di Busco, Bertoja, Del Majno, Maccari, Rechsteiner, Verga.

————————Trentino-Alto Adige DOC Zones————————
Alto Adige Chunky and herbaceous, and, though better than Trentino, seldom aspiring to the same heights as Cabernet. Hofstätter, K. Muri-Gries.
Trentino Only a few producers manage to instil a certain class into Merlot, but when they do, it can be very classy. Bossi Fedrigotti, Barone de Cles, Letrari, De Tarczal.

French Red Grapes: DOC Zones and Best Producers

Cabernet

Friuli-Venezia Giulia DOC Zones

Aquileia Either Franc, Sauvignon or just plain Cabernet. Fairly light and undistinguished. Ca'Bolani, Valle.

Colli Orientali Either Franc and/or Sauvignon, some of the north-east's best Cabernets come from this zone. Arzenton, Budini, Brova, Buiatti, Butussi, Dorigo, Pascolini, Ronchi di Fornaz, Ronchi di Manzano, Rubini, Villa Belvedere, Zambotto.

Collio Lively, fresh and herbaceous Cabernet Franc. Burdin, Ca'Ronesca, Marco Felluga, Gradnik, Jermann, Pintar, Russiz Superiore.

Grave del Friuli Cabernet, Cabernet Franc or Cabernet Sauvignon, as the producer prefers. Largely the lighter, grassier style of Cabernet Franc. Collavini, Conti di Maniago, Pistoni.

Isonzo Either Franc or Sauvignon, among the best wines of this zone. Eddi, Gallo Silvano, Gallo Stelio, F. Pecorari, Prandi d'Ulmhort.

Latisana Franc or Sauvignon produce fresh, light wines. Volderie, Zaglia.

Veneto DOC Zones

Breganze Usually very fine Cabernet Franc, though Maculan makes excellent Cabernet Sauvignon.

Colli Berici Sound Cabernet Franc, with a small amount of Cabernet Sauvignon, Costozza, Dal Ferro-Lazzarini, Da Schio.

Colli Euganei Light, from either or both of the Cabernets. Villa Sceriman is the best producer in the zone.

Lison-Pramaggiore Revised DOC has made room for all three types. Can be excellent. La Fattoria, La Frassinella, Sant'Anna.

Montello e Colli Asolani Fuller in style, needing a few years ageing. Asolani and Tomasella are two producers of note, though the Venegazzù (non-DOC) of Loredan Gasparini is the most famous.

Piave Most often the herbaceous style of Cabernet Franc, though Sauvignon is making inroads. Bortoluzzi e Pajer, Del Majno, Mercante, Castello di Roncade.

Trentino-Alto Adige DOC Zones

Alto Adige Blended but labelled Cabernet. Made in a number of styles, though generally herbaceous with good ageing capacity. Bellendorf, Hirschprunn, Lageder.

Trentino A blend of the two produces consistently full, fleshy wines with a grassy, dusty aroma. Bossi Fedrigotti, Endrizzi, Guerrieri in Gonzaga, Letrari, Longariva, Mandelli, San Leonardo, San Michele all'Adige, Rossi, De Tarczal.

Pinot Nero

Friuli-Venezia Giulia DOC Zones

Colli Orientali Consistently disappointing when measured against the potential of this great grape. The wines are, at best, light, fragrant and sound. Butussi, Dorigo, Ronchi di Manzoni, Volpe Pasini.

Collio Usually fresh with a raspberryish perfume, and sound if unexciting. Marco Felluga, Gradnik, Jermann (Englewhite), Komjanc, Schiopetto, Villa Russiz.

Grave del Friuli Recently elevated to DOC status. Should produce light, fragrant wines of some charm. Antonutti, Collavini and Giacomelli are among the better producers.

Veneto DOC Zones

Breganze Light and lively, best drunk young. The grape's name on the label is seldom sufficient to convince people that there is even a tenuous link with red burgundy. Bartolomeo da Breganze, Maculan.

Piave The plains are more suited to Merlot and Cabernet than to this fragile vine. Liasora, Verga.

Trentino-Alto Adige DOC Zones

Alto Adige Also known as Blauburgunder, it is usually meagre and inconsequential, but some producers in certain years can produce wines that rival good red burgundy for varietal character and ageing capacity. Bellendorf, Brigl, C.S. Colterenzio (Cornell), Hofstätter, Tiefenbrunner.

Trentino Light, fragrant and finely balanced. Much of what is produced goes into sparkling wine production. Foradori, Pojer e Sandri, San Michele all'Adige.

of these blends is the Pinot Nero, but it is more often seen on its own. Seldom, though, is it wholly successful. Often vinified to produce the younger, fresher style, this usually results in wines that lack both stuffing and character. An exception is Pojer e Sandri's light, almost rosé-like version.

Producer after producer, though, expresses frustration at not being able to get the best from this grape. Some of the best versions are produced in the South Tyrol (Hofstätter and Brigl both make long-lived wines), while in Friuli, Marco Felluga has had some success after abandoning the youthful style. It has probably been least successful in the Veneto, where a great deal is used for *spumante*, though Maculan's *rosato*, Costa d'Olio, is pleasant and fragrant.

The white wines of the north-east are dominated by French and German grape varieties. This is not due, as is the case in Tuscany, to a recent influx, but rather to the fact that much of this zone was under Hapsburg rule until just after the First World War. As a result, grapes like Riesling Renano, Pinot Grigio (or Ruländer, as it is called in the South Tyrol) and Pinot Bianco (Weissburgunder) have, like Merlot and Cabernet, been planted here for nigh on two centuries.

Traditionally, they have been blended together to produce a simple *vino bianco*. But, as we have seen, this is the home of the modern Italian white wine. When new technology became available to the growers, they used it to produce clean, crisp and well-defined wines. And the easiest way to produce these wines was to use a single grape variety, so that the clever winemaker could capture its particular character in a bottle.

This led to an abandonment of the traditional style. The varietal became, and remains, the preferred style. These fresh, perfumed wines, with their distinctive varietal character, are now great favourites on the home market. Friuli is the source of many of the bottles that adorn the tables in Milan's smarter restaurants, while winemakers in the rest of Italy are craning their necks northward to glean some advice from the producers of the South Tyrol's crisp and racy whites.

The most popular variety, at present, is the Pinot Grigio. Although occasionally still found in the traditional ``ramato'' style (copper coloured, from macerating the grapes on their reddish-tinged skins), most is now vinified ``*in bianco*''. At its best, it has a broad, nutty character, different in style to, but at a similar level of quality with, the Tokay d'Alsace. It boasts many DOCs, not only in Friuli and the South Tyrol, but also in Trentino and the Veneto. It can, from some producers, be one of Italy's great dry white wines, but, as it is also a favourite of the industrialists, its name can also be found on bottles whose contents, insipid and meagre, are of questionable provenance.

As elsewhere in the world, Chardonnay's star is on the rise, and it is already rivalling the Pinot Grigio in the north-east in terms of quality and popularity. Although DOC in relatively few zones, the best producers are experimenting with it, turning out some highly

priced *Vini da Tavola* that vary greatly in style. These range from the non-oaked versions, which combine the crispness of a Chablis with the breadth of a Mâcon, that are particularly prevalent in the South Tyrol and Trentino (Tiefenbrunner, Lageder and Pojer e Sandri all make good versions) to the oakier wines, either full and fat (Gallo Stelio in Friuli stands out) or refined and smokey (Gravner and Borgo Conventi are just two of the many fine producers).

The increase in the volume of Chardonnay produced is due not only to its increased popularity and to its growing number of DOCs, but also to the fact that much of what was previously grown and sold as Pinot Bianco was, in reality, Chardonnay. The insouciance with which these grapes were previously mixed together has been replaced by a concerted effort to separate and correctly identify the two varieties in the vineyard. The

result has been a large decrease in the amount of Pinot Bianco produced, but it remains DOC in six of Friuli's seven zones, and is widely planted in Trentino and the South Tyrol. It produces fresh, crisp and creamy wines that bear more than a passing resemblance to Chardonnay; indeed, in many instances, it surpasses the latter variety for quality.

Both Pinots are used, along with Chardonnay and a small amount of Pinot Nero, in the production of sparkling wine. A great deal of *spumante* is produced by the Charmat method, much of it sound but unexciting, but a small and growing amount of it is made by the *Méthode Champenoise* (``Metodo Classico'' they call it on the labels). Trentino, in particular, is home to some producers who, like Ferrari, are capable of matching a good Champagne, both for quality and price.

Sauvignon, unlike its French counterparts, has only had limited success here. Despite being DOC under a number of zones in the north-east, producers seem to have as much difficulty expressing its varietal character as they do with Pinot Nero. It seldom has the nettley, herbaceous fruit of a

Below: *Mountains flank the narrow strip of vineyards in northern Trentino. The church steeple reminds us that Austrian rulers once presided over this region.*

good Loire or New Zealand Sauvignon, being instead broad and slightly earthy, more akin to a Bordeaux Sauvignon. Some producers, though, like Ca'Ronesca in Friuli, are showing that they may finally have got the measure of this grape, while others, like Gravner, are actively seeking the restraint and complexity of the Bordeaux style and eschewing the direct varietal character of the Loire.

Of the Germanic varieties, Rhine Riesling, or Riesling Renano, as distinct from Riesling Italico, a lesser, native variety, stands supreme. It is DOC in the South Tyrol, where Tiefenbrunner makes a delicately aromatic and steely version, and in four of Friuli's zones, but the best versions come from producers like Jermann and Schiopetto. Though both are *Vini da Tavola* (the grape is not DOC in Collio), they are fuller and more concentrated than the South Tyrolean versions (probably because of lower yields) and are exquisitely perfumed and very fine.

Müller-Thurgau, the Riesling-Sylvaner cross that is responsible for a great deal of innocuous and vapid German wine, is found in pockets here. Recent experimentation has produced good results in Friuli, but nothing has yet matched the perfumed delicacy of Pojer e Sandri's Müller-Thurgau di Faedo, nor the steely grandeur of Tiefenbrunner's Feldmarschall. The latter, from a vineyard at 1,000 metres, is taut and dumb in its youth but opens out with age to express a subtle and diverse range of flavours.

Two Germanic varieties of minor importance are worth trying if you come across them. Sylvaner, DOC in the South Tyrol, has a

pleasantly earthy grapiness (the best is probably from Tiefenbrunner) while the Veltliner, DOC in the Valle Isarco, produces nicely scented wines that are, at best, quaffable.

After the roll-call of famous French and German varieties that are in production in the north-east, the cast of native varieties can, on first appearance, seem prosaic by comparison. There are no real stars of international renown, just some solid, workaday varieties. But in the right hands, these varieties can produce wines that equal and, in some cases surpass, those made from their more famous foreign kin.

Garganega, for instance, is hardly a name that springs to mind when we consider great white grapes. Its importance is confined to certain areas of the Veneto, where it is DOC in the Colli Berici hills south of Vicenza, and is the most important variety in Soave, Gambellara and Bianco di Custoza.

Soave has come a long way from being the local wine of Verona to its present position as Italy's best selling dry white DOC. This is quite a remarkable feat if you consider the size of Soave, a small town nestling beneath vine clad hills topped by a handsome and well-preserved castle. But here, as in Valpolicella, the authorities bowed to pressure from the larger producers and stretched the production zones onto the plain that runs as far west as Verona. A massive volume of insipid wine was churned out, and Soave, often seen beside Valpolicella on supermarket shelves in over-sized bottles, became synonymous with cheap, neutral plonk.

Soave Classico is a fairly small, hilly zone, 90 per cent of which is to be found in the

Above: *Low yields are the key to quality in Soave. Each July, Leonildo Pieropan* *goes through his vineyards and reduces quantity to increase quality.*

plains were used for growing maize and other cereal crops, but the mentality of the fifties, when quantity was more important than quality, has become so deeply ingrained here that it seems unlikely that the vines will now be uprooted. There are now moves afoot actually to increase the permitted yields, a situation that leaves good producers like Anselmi and Pieropan, who reduce their production by 20-30 per cent by summer pruning, shaking their heads in dismay.

At its best, Soave has a fresh, herbal and slightly nutty aroma, is bone dry on the palate with a medium depth of flavour and an almondy fragrance on the finish. Drunk on its own, it can be refreshing without being memorable, but with a seafood risotto in a trattoria in Venice or Verona, it can appear every bit – well, almost – as magical as white burgundy.

There is also a small amount of Recioto di Soave produced, but it lacks the stature of Recioto della Valpolicella. Pieropan, though, produces a subtly honeyed example using only Garganega grapes, while Anselmi's Recioto Capitelli, aged for a year in *barrique*, is rich, smokey and luscious, and is similar in style to good Sauternes, though lacking the distinctive *botrytis* character of the latter.

Unlike Valpolicella, Soave never boasted half a dozen or so small producers who kept ahoist the flag of quality. Until the early seventies, there was only Leonildo Pieropan. A quiet, unassuming man, he was only, as he sees it, carrying on a tradition that stretches as far back as his great-grandfather, who was the first man to bottle Soave. He believes passionately in Soave. His first concern is the vineyard, for this, he maintains, is where great wine is made. Low yields and a careful selection of Garganega clones (he expounds passionately on the character and importance of each clone) planted on carefully selected sites give him the right raw materials to produce not only an outstanding Soave Classico and a fine Recioto, but also two "crus" from the Calvarinho and La Rocca vineyards. The latter, from 40 year old vines, tends to be fuller and more expressive than the former, and is probably the finest Soave produced.

In Pieropan's hands, Soave is a wine of great interest. His example, more than any-

commues of Soave and Monteforte. Here, the Garganega is blended with up to 30 per cent of Trebbiano di Soave, which, according to some growers, has a similar biochemical make-up to the Verdicchio and Riesling Italico grapes. It is lower yielding than the Trebbiano Toscano, which some people mistakenly planted a few years back, and is valued for the perfume it adds to the wine.

The permitted yields for Classico are, ridiculously, the same as for the plains, where growers produce double the grapes yet receive more than half the price than those from the hills fetch. Before the war, the

---

Pick of Native Veronese White Wines

Soave Aldegheri, Anselmi, Bertani, Bolla, Boscaini, Campagnola, C.S. di Soave, Guerrieri Rizzardi, Masi, Marcato, Pegaso, Pieropan, Pra, Santa Sofia, Santi, Scamperle, Suavia, Tadiello, Tedeschi, Tommasi, Villa Girardi, Zenato, Zonin.

Lugana Ambrosi, Ca'Furia, Co' de Fer, Dal Cero, Fraccaroli, Pasini, Pellizzari, Prandell, San Grato, Venturelli, Villa Flora (Zenato), Visconti.

Bianco di Custoza Arvedi d'Emilei, C.S. di Custoza, Cavalchina, Fraterna Portalupi, Le Tende, Le Vigne di San Pietro, Menegotti, Pezzini, Gianin Piccoli, San Leone, Tedeschi, Zenato.

Gambellara C.S. di Gambellara, Zonin.

Foreign White Grapes: DOC Zones and Best Producers

Pinot Grigio

Friuli-Venezia Giulia DOC Zones

Aquileia Ca'Bolani, Ca'Vescovo, Giacomelli, Valle.

Colli Orientali One of the top zones for the production of Pinot Grigio. Concentrated and nutty, either white or *ramato* (coppery). Buiatti, d'Attimis-Maniago, Livio Felluga, Volpe Pasini, Zambotto.

Collio Similar in style and quality to the Colli Orientali, but with a little less breadth and better definition. Buzzinelli, Gradnik, Gravner, Jermann, Komjanc, Puiatti, Radikon, Schiopetto, Villa Russiz.

Grave del Friuli Large production, but from certain producers it combines the breadth of Colli Orientali with the crispness of Collio. Castello di Porcia, Collavini, Giacomelli, Pradio.

Isonzo Light, fresh and sound, for everyday drinking. Angoris, Burdin, Cantina Cormons, Gallo Stelio, F. Pecorari.

Latisana Small production of light, fresh wines at reasonable prices. Isola Augusta is generally regarded as the best producer here.

Veneto-DOC Zones

Breganze Soft, round and slightly coppery, though never matching the Tocai for quality locally. Little is produced.

Lison-Pramaggiore New addition to the DOC discipline; the *ramato* Pinot Grigio of La Fattoria promises high quality here.

Piave Brisk, refreshing varietals lacking substance and complexity. Rechsteiner, Santa Margherita.

Trentino-Alto Adige DOC Zones

Alto Adige Also known as Ruländer, the grape here has good depth and breadth, but is less perfumed than it is in Friuli. There are many fine producers, with Bellendorf, Hirschprunn, Hofstätter, Lageder, Tiefenbrunner and Walch leading the way.

Trentino Either white or *ramato*, the vine is less well-established here, but promises plenty. Cavit, Barone de Cles, Lechthaler, Pojer e Sandri.

Valle Isarco Lighter and more delicate here than either the Alto Adige or Trentino. K. Eisacktaler, Stiftskellerei Neustift.

Chardonnay

This trendy grape is DOC in a growing number of zones, including Grave del Friuli, Collio, Isonzo, Alto Adige, Trentino and Lison Pramaggiore, but it is also widely produced as a *Vino da Tavola* where official recognition has yet to be granted. At present, styles seem to vary more according to producer than to zone of origin.

Friuli Best producers include Abbazia di Rosazzo, Borgo Conventi, Ca'Ronesca, Gallo Stelio, Gradnik, Gravner, Jermann, Puiatti and Villa Ronche, with many others joining this elite each year.

Veneto This region has been slower to latch onto the Chardonnay craze, but they are now seeking to make up for lost time. Maculan makes a stylish, oaked version.

Alto Adige and Trentino Among the best producers are Lageder, Pojer e Sandri and Tiefenbrunner, though many others are rising to their level at a rapid rate.

Pinot Bianco

Friuli-Venezia Giulia DOC Zones

Aquileia Crisp, creamy and aromatic. Good overall quality but little that is outstanding. Giacomelli, Valle, Villa Chiozza.

---

thing, has spurred other producers to aim for quality, and now, each vintage seems to bring another name of repute. Thankfully for Soave, Pieropan no longer stands alone, but he still leads the way.

Though it never reaches the heights that it does with Pieropan, the Garganega continues to flourish in Gambellara, a small town east of Soave on the road to Vicenza, where it produces dry whites similar in style to Soave, as well as Recioto and a small amount of Vin Santo. It also thrives in the hills of Valpolicella, where it is mixed with Trebbiano di Soave and, in the case of Masi's fine Masianco, with Sauvignon, to produce some excellent dry white *Vini da Tavola*, or is made into a Recioto, the most exciting of which are Allegrini's stunning Fiorgardane, Masi's Bianco Campociesa, Tedeschi's Vin de la Fabriseria and, as we might expect of him, Quintarelli's Il Bandito.

West of Soave, on the southernmost shores of Lake Garda, another local clone of the ubiquitous Trebbiano, the Trebbiano di Lugana, produces a dry white wine of considerable distinction. Though largely in Lombardy, and therefore geographically in the north-west, Lugana belongs stylistically to the Veronese wines, and thus in the north-east. It has more concentration and a finer scent than all but the very best Soave, and really comes into its own, like the rest of the Veronese whites, as an excellent accompaniment to a plate of seafood.

Foreign White Grapes: DOC Zones and Best Producers

Colli Orientali Biscuity and fragrant with a tightly drawn varietal character. Fine without being showy. Abbazia di Rosazzo, Arzenton, Budini, Buiatti, Butussi, I Moros, Pascolini, Rubini, Villa Belvedere, Zambotto.

Collio Perfumed and delicate, though quite often lacking complexity. Borgo Conventi, Gradnik, Marco Felluga, Jermann, Pintar, Princic, Puiatti, Schiopetto.

Grave del Friuli Fair breadth but lacking the definition of those wines from the hills. Morassutti, Pistoni, Pradio, Russolo.

Isonzo The low lying land of this zone lends itself more to the broader, biscuity style of Pinot Bianco. Attems, Gallo Silvano, P. Pecorari, Prandi d'Ulmhort, Zampar.

Latisana Pleasantly varietal without being exceptional. Isola Augusta, Volderie.

────────────**Veneto DOC Zones**────────────

Breganze Crisp and fresh, performs better here than elsewhere in the Veneto. Maculan and Bartolomeo da Breganze (the local co-operative).

Colli Berici Lean, steely and fresh, best drunk young. Little stands out, except for the fine wines from dal Ferro-Lazzarini.

Colli Euganei Can be either dry or *abboccato*.

Lison-Pramaggiore A new addition to this recently expanded DOC. I have yet to come across an example, but quality should be good once production gets under way.

Piave Pinot Bianco is not one of Piave's great success stories, though Rechsteiner makes a good example.

────────────**Trentino-Alto Adige DOC Zones**────────────

Alto Adige Also known by its German name, Weissburgunder. Consistently good if currently unfashionable, the wines are perfumed, crisp and biscuity. K. St. Pauls, Bellendorf, Lageder, Tiefenbrunner.

Terlano Fresh, dry and lively, with a high overall level of quality. Brigl, K. St. Michael-Eppan, Lindner, K. Terlan.

Trentino Broader and fuller than the racier wines from the South Tyrol, these wines are still impressive. Conti Martini, Longariva, Zeni.

Riesling Renano

────────────**Friuli-Venezia Giulia DOC Zones**────────────

Aquileia Lacks perfume and delicacy here.

Colli Orientali Dry, perfumed and delicate, quality is on the rise here. Buiatti, Livio Felluga, Ronchi di Fornaz, La Viarte, Volpe Pasini.

Collio Though not DOC here, some of the zone's better producers turn out some of Italy's finest examples of this great grape. Jermann, Schiopetto.

Grave del Friuli Small production, but can be good. Light and fragrant.

Isonzo Delicate and flowery, creditable rather than awe-inspiring. Angoris, Gallo Stelio.

────────────**Trentino-Alto Adige DOC Zones**────────────

Alto Adige The cool, hillside sites yield crisp, dry and nervy wines that develop well with age. Rivals Collio as the source of Italy's best real Riesling. Bellendorf, Elzenbaum, Hofstätter, Tiefenbrunner.

Terlano Light and delicate, without the grandeur of the Alto Adige. Brigl, K. St. Michael-Eppan, Schloss Schwanburg.

Trentino Good crisp wines, though lacking the tantalising brilliance of this grape at its best.

────────────**Veneto**────────────

No DOCs as yet, but Fattoria di Ogliano, near Conegliano, makes a fine version.

From Lake Garda, as we curve around the southern shore and move up towards Bardolino, we enter the Bianco di Custoza zone. Once again, the Veronese mix comes into play in the production of this light and lively dry white, but here a small amount of Tocai adds an extra dimension to the wine, making it, to some people, the most elegant and characterful of the wines of this region.

This distinction can be attributed to Tocai, probably the most important (in terms of quality) of the north-east's native white grapes. Both its provenance and the origin of its name remain matters for debate. Some people claim that it was originally brought to the north-east, through Friuli, from Central Europe several centuries ago, while others maintain that it is related to the Sauvignon, and acquired its name because the sweet, "passito" style wines that used to be made from it were adjudged to be similar in style to Hungarian Tokay. Many people in the Anglo-Saxon world, more familiar with the wines of Alsace than with those of Friuli, often make the mistake of associating it with the Pinot Gris (Tokay d'Alsace), but there is no relation between the two.

Though it adds a certain lustre to Bianco di Custoza, Tocai really shines on its own. In the Eastern Veneto, it excels in Lison-Pramaggiore and Piave, while further east it is to be found in the Colli Berici. It is also the mainstay of Breganze Bianco and Maculan's excellent Prato di Canzio. In Friuli, it is DOC in six of the seven zones, but reaches its greatest heights in the hills of Collio and the Colli Orientali. Broad and concentrated with an intriguing nutty perfume, it has a round, slightly oily texture that is cut, in the best years, by a good level of acidity. It produces some of Italy's finest dry white wines, and is usually worth a try.

Tocai's rise to prominence is directly attributable to the ability of the winemaker to capture its elusive varietal character. The sensible application of modern winemaking techniques has given us wines like Schiopetto's Tocai Friulano, a masterful combination of richness and nuance. Modern winemakers have done a great deal to rescue Tocai, and a number of the north-east's other native white varieties, from the anonymity of the blends by giving them sufficient character to stand on their own.

One such variety is the Malvasia, which will become more prominent as we move further south. It is a delicate variety that is easily oxidised, so great care is needed when handling it. A small amount is made in Friuli from a local clone, the Malvasia Istriana, which is DOC in Carso and Isonzo, and in Collio, where the best versions are to be found. In the hands of a producer like Borgo del Tiglio, it has a dry, appley and honeyed fruit that is intense yet delicately scented on the finish.

Until recently, the producers in the hills of Friuli blended the Malvasia with the Tocai and Ribolla Gialla grapes. The latter would give a firm acidity to the fatness of the Tocai and

Above: *The Collio Goriziano zone produces some of Friuli's finest wine. This vineyard, in the commune of Oslavia, abuts the Yugoslavian border.*

Left: *Silvio Jermann is one of Friuli's finest young producers. He consistently achieves a rich varietal character in each of his wines, through low yields and great skill in the cellar.*

the delicacy of the Malvasia. But while its erstwhile partners went on to better things, the Ribolla languished, a victim of its high acidity which, it was generally felt, did little for its commercial appeal. With low yields and careful handling, though, it has shown that it is quite capable of standing on its own. The best examples are to be found in Collio, especially in the commune of Oslavia, which straddles the border with Yugoslavia, where Gravner and Radikon in particular produce waxy, appley wines that are subtle and restrained in character.

With this ability to isolate the components of their traditional blends, the Friulian producers have come to understand and appreciate the characteristics of their native varieties. This understanding has led to an increased willingness to reconstitute the blends, often with different mixtures from

those traditionally used. A number of people are now producing these blends, which are more and more being viewed as a vehicle for expressing individuality. A Tocai is a Tocai is a Tocai, say some people (though Schiopetto's Tocai and Tocai from Aquileia are obviously not the same wine), but an individual blend of say, Tocai, Malvasia, Pinot Bianco and Ribolla, aged briefly in *barrique*, is unique to a particular producer.

Some of the most successful of these blends include Schiopetto's Blanc Di Rosis (Tocai, Sauvignon, Pinot Bianco and Malvasia) and Jermann's outstanding Vintage Tunina (Pinot Bianco, Chardonnay, Sauvignon and Picolit), but probably the most characterful is the Vino Gradbreg of Francesco Gravner. It is a blend of Malvasia, Ribolla, Pagadebit and Glera (the local name for Prosecco) from a small vineyard of old vines. Gravner, a tall Slavic figure with a broad frame and a crew cut that makes him look like a farmer in the American mid-west, produces it to keep a tradition alive. It is not a great wine, he says, but those are the varieties traditional to Oslavia, the district in which his vineyards are to be found.

Above: *A view of Combai, near Valdobbiadene in the northern Veneto. The Prosecco vine rules here, producing soft, scented sparklers of great charm.*

This wine seems to sum up Gravner's philosophy. He is a strong believer in tradition, but one who is also constantly innovating. He is a staunch individualist, seemingly unconcerned with what other producers are worrying about. While they are concerned with picking early to retain acidity, Gravner picks later, risking rot and natural calamity, to get a fuller ripeness and, he feels, better results. And while others fret if the fermentation temperature nudges over 20°C, he quite happily allows it to run as high as 25°C, believing that this allows the wine to express fully the grape's character and flavour. "To ferment a wine at low temperatures is like expecting an athlete to run the 100 metres with a gag around his mouth," he says with a shrug and a smile.

He is individual, but in no way loud or brash. Any claims he makes are in his wines, and they are superb. His Chardonnay is probably Italy's best, simply because, like the rest of his wines, it is not only technically correct, but is also infused with tremendous character and interest. In a region where one cannot help marvelling at the technical wizardry of the winemakers while bemoaning the lack of passion in their wines, it is gratifying that the two unite so well in Gravner's wines.

Above: *Francesco Gravner samples his Chardonnay. Later, he will blend it with a batch in tank to strike the balance that makes his wines so fine.*

While the wines and winemakers of Friuli continue to grab the headlines, a number of lesser known white vine varieties are quietly flourishing throughout the north-east. One of these is the Verduzzo, which produces lean and acidic dry whites in the eastern Veneto and Friuli and sweet wines in the Colli Orientali. Giovanni Dri's Verduzzo di Ramandolo (a distinct and superior sub-denomination in the Colli Orientali) has a restrained and subtle sweetness that is cut by a tangy, lemony acidity, and is one of Italy's great sweet wines. At Marco Felluga's Russiz Superiore winery, Californian in look and layout with its vaulted wooden ceilings and glass partitions but set against a dramatic backdrop of the Julian pre-Alps, they produce a Verduzzo that has been refined further by a short spell in barrique. One taste of either of these versions and you will wonder why Picolit, and not Verduzzo, was ever hailed as Italy's answer to Château Yquem. This ridiculous assertion only serves to give Picolit a vaunted reputation and an inflated price that the wine can never match. A shy-bearing variety, it produces attractively honeyed wines (Volpe Pasini's is especially recommended) that never quite match the breed of a good Verduzzo.

Another grape that, because of its high natural acidity is more suited to the production of sweet wines, is the Vespaiola. Though DOC for dry wines under Breganze, it is at its best, along with Tocai, in Maculan's outstanding Torcolato, a rich, luscious and honeyed wine made from partially dried grapes, aged in *barrique* and acquiring, with age, great finesse.

Riesling Italico, distinct from, and usually inferior to, the Riesling Renano, is sprinkled around the north-east. Though DOC in Trentino and the South Tyrol, it seldom produces anything out of the ordinary. The same could be said of the Veneto, with the exception of Pieropan's herby, tangy version, and of Friuli, where only Gravner and several others contrive to make wines of real style.

Visitors to Venice seeking a diversion from the crowds of San Marco or the Lido should go off in search of a small bar and order a bottle of Prosecco di Conegliano. The Prosecco grape is widely planted in the hills north of Treviso, especially around the towns of Conegliano and Valdobbiadene, and produces still light wines, softly foaming *frizzante* wines and fully fledged sparklers. The best sparklers, made by the *"Cuve Close"* method, are from the DOC of Prosecco di Conegliano, some of which can, when from a small area around Valdobbiadene noted for its superior wines, be labelled Cartizze.

At their best, these wines have a fresh, fragrant character and a soft, appealing fruit, and are just the thing to revitalise the tired and thirsty tourist. Producers like Carpene Malvolti and Antica Quercia have boosted the level of quality to such a point that, should the thirsty Venetians ever allow us to have a little, it could have great success as a good value, refreshing sparkler.

Of the other white grapes of the northeast, the Nosiola, found only in Trentino, must certainly be the most obscure. It makes distinctive dry whites and a sweet and nutty Vin Santo. Of substantially greater renown is the Gewürztraminer, famous in Alsace but named after the South Tyrolean village of Tramin. Until recently, little care was taken to distinguish it from its less spicy relative, the Traminer, but both make soft and attractively perfumed wines in Friuli and the South Tyrol. You will not find the full-blown spiciness that is so typical of Alsatian Gewürztraminer, though, as the Italian taste tends to the less aromatic style.

The Moscato, though nowhere near as prominent here as it is in the north-west, is to be found both in some fine sweet versions in Trentino and the South Tyrol (where it is known as the Goldmuskateller) and several excellent dry versions (Conti Martini and Tiefenbrunner excel). In addition to the Moscato Giallo, there is the Rosenmuskateller, or Moscato Rosa, which has a pale pink colour and an astonishing perfume of dried rose petals. Tiefenbrunner makes a fine dry version, but *the* outstanding Rosenmuskateller, sweet and scented and complex, is made by Graf Kuenberg.

EMILIA-ROMAGNA

milia-Romagna is a unique region. It virtually bisects Italy, stretching from the Ligurian/Piemonte border in the west to the Adriatic coast in the east. The Po River separates it from Lombardy and the rest of Northern Italy, while the Apennines to the south define the border with Tuscany and the rest of the Central zone. Though it shares certain grape varieties with both Tuscany and the regions to the north, it has managed to establish enough of an individual identity to be considered as a separate zone.

This may come as something of a surprise to those who have driven along the old Roman road from Piacenza to Rimini, the Via Emilia. It runs unswerving, from Emilia in the west to Romagna in the east, over the flat, monotonous terrain of the Po Valley. The monotony is only broken by cities like Parma and Bologna, both of which are worth a visit. Bologna has some splendid towers and *campanili*, is home to the oldest University in Europe (founded in the 11th century) and is celebrated for the excellence of its cuisine, as is Parma.

The native foods of the region have achieved greater fame than its wines. Parma ham, thinly sliced, is a great delicacy, while Parmesan cheese, bought hard and crumbling from a freshly cut block, is one of the world's great cheeses. Its pastas, from *cappelletti* to *lasagna*, are renowned, as is Bolognese sauce, for the wonderful textures and richness they offer. Even lowly vinegar can achieve greatness in Emilia, where the oak-aged Aceto Balsamico di Modena, produced in minute quantities, is a marvel of concentration and exploding flavours.

With such a fabled cuisine, it is little wonder that the wines have been content to play a supporting role. The style of the wines, generally *frizzante* in Emilia, still in Romagna, is admirably suited to the local dishes. This is recognised in the DOC disciplines, guardians of tradition that they are, but things are changing here as they are in the rest of Italy.

The flatness of the Po Valley is ideal for the cereal crops that are grown here in abundance, and for the Lambrusco grapes, but most of the DOC wines, and the best of the *Vini da Tavola*, are to be found in the Apennine foothills. South of Piacenza, the hills play host to a number of the same vines that are to be found in the neighbouring region of Oltrepò Pavese. These hills, the Colli Piacentini, were granted a DOC in 1984. This incorporated the previous DOCs such as Gutturnio (a delicious Barbera/Bonarda blend) as well as defining disciplines for other, largely varietal based wines. Like the Oltrepò Pavese, its potential has yet to be realised fully.

Further east, the hills of Parma and Bologna are home to the Colli di Parma and Colli Bolognesi DOCs respectively. In the case of the latter, the DOC is further split into

Key to map
1 Colli Piacentini.
2 Colli di Parma.
3 Lambrusco Reggiano.
4 Lambrusco Salamino di Santa Croce.
5 Lambrusco di Sorbara.
6 Lambrusco Grasparossa di Castelvetro.

Right: *Best known for Lambrusco, Emilia-Romagna also turns out fine white wines from grapes like Malvasia.*

Emilia-Romagna DOC Zones

Albana di Romagna DOCG

Bianco di Scandiano

Colli Bolognesi, Monte San Pietro or Castelli Medioevali Eight categories (Barbera, Bianco, Cabernet Sauvignon, Merlot, Pignoletto, Pinot Bianco, Riesling Italico, Sauvignon)

Colli di Parma Three categories (Malvasia, Rosso, Sauvignon)

Colli Piacentini 11 categories (Barbera, Bonarda, Gutturnio, Malvasia, Monterosso Val d'Arda, Ortrugo, Pinot Grigio, Pinot Nero, Sauvignon, Val Nure, Trebbianino Val Trebbia)

Lambrusco Grasparossa di Castelvetro, Reggiano, Salamino di Santa Croce, di Sorbara

Sangiovese di Romagna

Trebbiano di Romagna

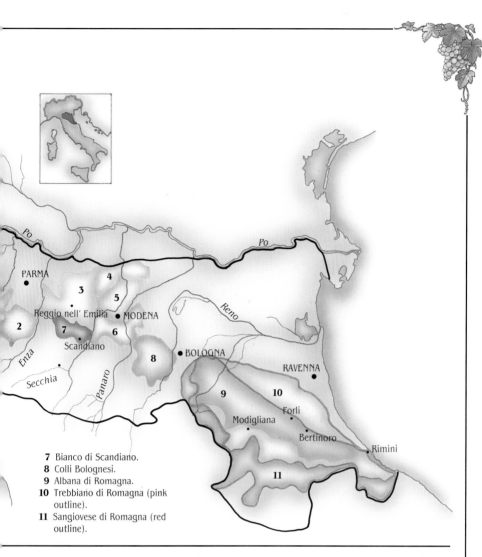

7 Bianco di Scandiano.
8 Colli Bolognesi.
9 Albana di Romagna.
10 Trebbiano di Romagna (pink outline).
11 Sangiovese di Romagna (red outline).

two sub-zones, Monte San Pietro and Castelli Medioevali, either of which may be seen on the label. The last great Emilian wine is Lambrusco, the wine of the plains between Parma and Bologna. Traditionally dry and frothing, it is said to be the ideal partner to many of the local dishes.

The spread of DOCs has been matched by a growing awareness of the need for quality among many of the producers. This is shown by a reduction in quantity of wine produced, with the 1985 crop down to one-third of the level it reached in the record 1980 vintage. Lambrusco is probably immune to this trend, but it is very much in evidence in the two Romagna DOCs, Trebbiano and Sangiovese, and its recent DOCG, Albana di Romagna. Stretching from Bologna to the Adriatic, the Romagnolan hills have traditionally produced light, quaffing wines, but producers like Mario Pezzi of Fattoria Paradiso and Gian Matteo Baldi of Castelluccio are showing just how much potential there is here if quality is the sole aim.

In this respect, Emilia-Romagna differs little from the rest of Italy. New grape varieties are being imported, and experimentation is taking place in the production and ageing of wines. But the style remains unique to the zone. Whether the grape variety is grown throughout Italy (like Barbera, Sangiovese or Malvasia), is French in origin (as with Sauvignon and Cabernet Sauvignon), or is strikingly native (like Lambrusco), it will be handled in such a fashion that the resulting wine will complement one or other of the local specialities. And the originality of the cuisine, which certainly rates among Europe's finest, has given birth to an interesting array of wines, some of which are capable of standing with Italy's greatest.

*T*hree native varieties predominate in Emilia-Romagna when it comes to red grapes. Indeed the region could be carved up into three fiefdoms: Barbera holding sway in the Colli Piacentini to the west and in a thin strip of the Apennine foothills, running as far as Bologna; Lambrusco holding the plains between Parma and Bologna by sheer force of numbers; and Sangiovese, firmly entrenched in the Romagnolan hills. There are a few pockets of foreign resistance, and several eccentric natives who conform to few rules, but the supremacy of the three remains unchallenged.

Barbera is the most important grape in the Colli Piacentini, where it represents part of the large swathe of the vine that cuts across Piemonte and Lombardy before sweeping down into Emilia. It does not reach the heights of quality here that it does in Alba or Asti, but produces a rustic, sometimes fizzy style that lacks pretension and can be quite attractive.

Another vine that thrives here, as in the Oltrepò Pavese, is the Bonarda. Its deep coloured wines, round and plummy, often have a hint of sweetness enhanced by a slight sparkle, and are best drunk young, ideally with a rich pasta dish. But its major rôle here is to complement the Barbera in a blend, the most prominent being Gutturnio. This now comes under the Colli Piacentini umbrella of DOCs, and is made from about 60 per cent Barbera and 40 per cent Bonarda, with the former giving acidity and structure to the blend and the latter providing soft, fleshy fruit. Its name is derived from a large drinking cup *(gutturnium)* from which the wines of the hills of Piacenza were quaffed by the Romans. Just as in Roman times, the wines are still best when drunk young, though some producers in good vintages create wines that can age well for up to five years.

Above: *Vineyards silhouetted against the town of Ziano Piacentini. The Colli Piacentini is found on the western tip of Emilia-Romagna, where the borders with Piemonte and Lombardy converge.*

Below: *The wines of the Colli Piacentini have more in common with those of nearby Oltrepò Pavese than with the rest of Emilia-Romagna.*

A similar mixture forms the base for Colli di Parma *rosso,* a DOC zone centred on the hills south of Parma; the wines resemble Gutturnio in style, though they have yet to match them for quality. Barbera emerges from the anonymity of a blend further east to form the most popular category in the Colli Bolognesi DOC zone. The style is robust and workmanlike, and, though the Barbera can be tempered with up to 15 per cent Sangiovese, the producers often contrive to leave a hint of sweetness in the wine to tone down its naturally assertive acidity.

Once we move past Bologna into the Romagnolan hills, we enter the stronghold of the Sangiovese grape. This variety dominates the plantings of Central Italy, where it is the principal constituent of Chianti. Here, however, they have their own clone, a higher yielding vine that produces larger berries than its Tuscan cousin, and these two factors account for the wines being noticeably different. Much of what is produced (about 10-15 million litres annually) is consumed locally; at best, it is light and gulpable, at worst thin and austere.

The best producers attribute this fairly low level of quality to the use of the Sangiovese di Romagna clone. They use the Tuscan clone instead, and the lower yields and smaller berries give more concentrated wines with a better varietal character and a sturdy, tannic structure. As a result, they age well, showing a style that matches some of the best that Tuscany can offer.

Mario Pezzi, for instance, at Fattoria Paradiso, combines the use of low yielding Tuscan clones and a perfectionist approach to winemaking to produce one of Italy's outstanding Sangiovese-based wines. His single vineyard *riserva,* Vigna delle Lepri, is aged for two years in large and small casks before being bottled, and develops great finesse and character in bottle. Capable of ageing for at least seven to ten years, it is one of the finest wines of these hills.

Another producer who is leading the way in this area is Gian Matteo Baldi of Castelluccio. His three 100 per cent Sangiovese wines, Ronco dei Ciliegi, Ronco Casone and Ronco delle Ginestre, all named after the hill (Ronco) on which they are grown, are aged in new *barriques* (oak casks of 225-litre capacity). Their class is enhanced by the spicy vanilla scent of the oak, and they could easily be mistaken for a new-style Tuscan in a blind tasting. Indeed, one look at the label, with its fashionable Vino da Tavola di Modigliana denomination, and a glance at the price (expensive), and you could easily be convinced that it was Tuscan. But it is just the Tuscan ethos of quality, embodied by consultant oenologist Vittorio Fiore, that imbues these wines and sets them apart. With time, they would seem capable of setting new standards for the level of quality that Sangiovese can reach when grown in the Romagnolan hills.

Though Sangiovese accounts for much of the red wine in Romagna, there are a few curiosities planted here and there that are worth looking at. One is Cagnina (a grape that is, according to Mario Pezzi, the Terrano (or Refosco) of Friuli), which is made into a dessert wine of the same name. Its striking colour and round grapey fruit, sometimes slightly frothing, is just the thing to refresh a jaded palate at the end of a long meal. Drunk young and slightly chilled, it is delicious with nuts and fruit, filling a similar rôle to port but without the alcoholic punch. Fattoria Paradiso make a very good one, as do Ravaioli and the Cantina Sociale Forli.

An even rarer vine is the Barbarossa, grown only by Mario Pezzi at Fattoria Paradiso. Pezzi discovered these vines growing on his estate and saved them from extinction by nurturing a small vineyard to maturity. The resulting wine is remarkable, needing about five years to shed the deep, tannic style of its youth and show its true complexity. It is worth searching out, and is not, when you consider the quality, all that expensive.

Of the French grapes that are grown in this zone, Cabernet Sauvignon has been historically the most important, and it is once again becoming increasingly prominent. This is especially true in Emilia, where it has been granted DOC in the Colli Bolognesi. Some producers in the Apennines are using it in Bordeaux type blends, though the best, a varietal, is undoubtedly made by the Vallania family on their Terre Rosse estate at Zola Predosa, located in the hills south-west of Bologna. Established in 1961, the reputation of this fine estate was originally built by Enrico Vallania, a physician who turned to winemaking. He developed a particular style of wine, unusual in Italy at the time, in which he saw the expression of the grape's varietal character as one of the most important elements. After his death in 1985, control passed into the capable hands of his children, Giovanni and Elisabetta, and they are carrying on the tradition of quality instituted by their father.

Other than a tiny proportion of Merlot, Cabernet Sauvignon is their only red grape variety. At 38 hl/ha, their yields are about half those of most other producers in the region. This, combined with a careful selection of grapes (they do two or three pickings at vintage time in order to ensure that they select only the ripest and healthiest fruit), guarantee that they have excellent raw materials. The method of vinification aims to maximise the fruit character that they have worked so hard to achieve in the vineyard: gentle pressing, a fairly brief maceration (five to twelve days, depending on the nature of the vintage) followed by fermentation at the relatively low temperature of 20-22° Celsius. The wine is then aged for three years, but only in stainless steel. It was Enrico Vallania's belief, and that of his children as well, that wood ageing impaired the full expression of Cabernet character that he sought.

As a result, the wine has a tremendously youthful character, moderate tannin and a ripe, concentrated and blackcurrant character. Because its production methods favour a forward style of wine, it can be drunk from four to five years after the vintage, but will age well for up to ten years. Though most Cabernet-based wines in Italy have set out to emulate Bordeaux, few have succeeded as well as Vallania, whose wines manage to retain a distinctively Italian style, despite the use of French grapes.

Of the other Bordeaux grapes, Cabernet Franc is increasing in importance, but at the

Below: *The Cabernet Sauvignon produced at Terre Rosse is, thanks to low yields, one of Italy's finest.*

moment its greatest rôle is in support of the Sangiovese and Pinot Nero in Vallunga's Rosso Armentano, one of Romagna's few Franco-Italian reds. Merlot, on the other hand, is quite widely planted, especially in the Po delta, where the vine thrives in conditions similar to those of the neighbouring Veneto. Here, as in the Veneto, it is largely valued for its ability to yield high amounts of soft and fairly gulpable wine that is sold as *Vino da Tavola*. Further west, in the Colli Bolognesi, it performs with enough distinction to be granted a DOC. The yields, though high, are lower than those to the east, and the hillside sites give soft, supple wines that are attractive when youthful.

Another French variety that is finding favour in Emilia is the Pinot Nero (Pinot Noir). It has long been planted in the Colli Piacentini, as in the Oltrepò, for use in sparkling wine production, and was granted DOC in 1984. It is also used to make a light and fairly youthful red wine that, thankfully, makes no attempt to ape red Burgundy.

Below: *The Vallania family at Terre Rosse. On the right are Giovanni (seated) and Elisabetta; on the left, their mother, Adrianna, with a friend.*

*L*ambrusco is fast replacing Chianti as the most widely known of all Italian wines, though there are those who would dispute its claim to be called a wine at all. It is seen by many as being nothing more than a soft drink with alcohol, cola with clout, rather than as a wine. Yet viewed within a certain context, it can be delicious, and from certain producers it can reach quite remarkable heights of quality – even if quality Lambrusco is not quite on a par with the best Chianti.

It is churned out in astonishing volumes on the plains between Parma and Bologna. This is the flat, dreary country of the Po Valley, where the rich, fertile soil supports bountiful crops, one of which is the Lambrusco grape. Flatlands and fertile soil are not usually associated with wine production, but then Lambrusco is not your usual wine.

The Lambrusco vines (there are numerous sub-varieties) are trained high on trellises, and sometimes trees, forming in August and September wonderful arbours, hanging from which are ripe, plump bunches of grapes. It is an ancient Etruscan manner of training the vines, and viewing such a scene you would half expect to see some corpulent Roman voluptuary reclining in the shade, gorging himself on grapes popped into his mouth by a coterie of nymphs. But your reverie is likely to be shattered by the sound of a tractor, moving up and down the rows harvesting the grapes.

From there, the grapes will most likely be taken to one of the large co-operatives like Riunite, or one of the large private firms like Giacobazzi, for transformation into that semi-sparkling, semi-sweet phenomenon called Lambrusco. Its sales abroad are massive, accounting for a large proportion of the total amount of Italian wine exported to the United States and Great Britain. This sweet, frothing beverage has, for many people, removed the element of mystery (and pretension) that surrounds wine, and has given them the confidence to drink it on a fairly regular basis. They do not need to worry about committing any heinous social "*faux pas*" while serving it, but only need to enjoy its uncomplicated and lively sweet fruit.

Sweet Lambrusco, though, is a fairly recent development. It was traditionally produced as a dry, *frizzante* wine of fairly low alcohol and high acidity. This vibrant, light bodied character made it an excellent partner for the rich meals that are a staple part of Emilian life. A great deal of wine is needed to wash down a meal consisting of a plate of succulent Parma ham, followed by *cappelletti* or *tortellini* in a rich *bolognese* sauce – and those are only the starters. You will then get a plate of *zampone* (pig's feet sausage), or something equally rich, that has been cooked in Aceto Balsamico di Modena vinegar that will set your senses reeling and stretch your stomach to bursting point. The richness of the cooking is exceeded only by its fineness, for this is the epicurean heart of Italy, the equivalent of Lyons in France.

Above: *Ripe and plump when harvested, these Lambrusco grapes are transformed into semi-sweet, semi-sparkling wines that have gained popularity abroad.*

Below: *Harvesting Lambrusco is not so much a back-breaking as arm-stretching task. The high-trained vines produce grapes high in acidity, so a touch of sweetness is needed for balance.*

To complement this cooking, rather than to compete with it, something simple is required, something of which you can drink copious amounts without suffering adverse effects. Something, in fact, like a dry, frothing Lambrusco. Its froth is derived from a slight sparkle, about one-third as strong as that of a Champagne. And it was by using the Champagne method of making a wine sparkling (second fermentation in bottle) that Lambrusco was traditionally given its sparkle. After the wine had finished its second fermentation though, it was not aged on its lees, as the aim was to drink it as young as possible, and nor did it undergo *dégorgement,* so it retained a slight sediment. The locals did not mind this sediment, they just took care in pouring when they reached the bottom of the bottle.

This was all very well as long as the wine was not exported. Once the American market was taken into consideration, however, there was a growing realisation that the sensibilities of people being weaned from high-tech drinks like cola or beer had to be respected. Fortunately, the urge to export was preceded by the development of the ``autoclave'', a large, hermetically sealed, stainless steel tank in which the wine could undergo a second fermentation and be decanted from its lees prior to bottling. In addition, these ``autoclavi'' made it easier for the producer to stop the fermentation when required in order to leave the wine with a predetermined degree of sweetness.

Thus the scene was set for the launch of Lambrusco on the export markets. It was an inexpensive wine, and price became a more and more important consideration in the battle for sales. So naturally, human ingenuity being what it is, ways of cutting corners during production were devised. Put simply, the second fermentation was dispensed with, wholly or partially, and carbon dioxide was pumped into the wine to give it its sparkle. This is (or could be) known as the "bicycle pump" method, and is strictly illegal. Some producers use it, others do not, but like politicians, those who do contrive to deny in public that they use it, but tacitly admit to it in private.

A great deal of Lambrusco is *Vino da Tavola*, though there are four DOCs which are based on particular zones and sub-varieties of the grape. The classic zone is generally considered to be Lambrusco di Sorbara, located north-east of Modena. South of Modena is Lambrusco Grasparosso di Castelvetro, the former term being the grape while the latter is the village at the centre of the zone. The top producer here is Barbieri, and he gets a 3 star rating for his Cru Magazzino from Luigi Veronelli in his "*Catalogo dei Vini d'Italia*". The last two zones are Reggiano, situated around Reggio Emilia, home of the best Parmesan, and Salamino di Santa Croce, located about 25km north of Modena.

To qualify for DOC, the wine must be sealed by a cork, not by a plastic or metal cap. These latter options are a cheaper and, in many cases, a more reliable, means of sealing wine, so many producers prefer to use these and label their wine simply as a *Vino da Tavola*.

There is not, as yet, a DOC for Lambrusco Bianco, a style that has become increasingly popular. Nor are there any white Lambrusco grapes, this style being made as a "*blanc de noirs*". The black grapes are crushed, the

Above: *The bottling line at Riunite. The bottles of Lambrusco are just about to enter the pasteurisation tunnel, a process that ensures stability.*

Above right: *Prior to bottling, Riunite, and all the large commercial producers, filter the wine to a fine degree to remove any harmful organisms.*

Below: *These "autoclavi" are full of Lambrusco undergoing a secondary fermentation, thus gaining its sparkle.*

juice is immediately separated from the skins to prevent it from taking on any colour, and then vinified in an autoclave. Much of what is available is very poor indeed, but Cantina Cavicchioli's has a dry, grapey character that easily distinguishes it from the rest.

Despite the volume that is produced, and the relative ease with which it can be sold, there are still a few producers who are preserving the tradition of quality Lambrusco. They continue, for instance, to practise the traditional second fermentation in bottle, producing vibrant, characterful wines that

are as far removed from the common Lambrusco as they can be. Good examples of this style are Cavicchioli's Tradizione and Lambrusco dal Picol Rosso from Moro. The *autoclave* is also used to good effect by these producers, whose wines are consistently more interesting than those produced by the larger concerns. They are, as a result, also more expensive, and cynics have often wondered how long they will be able to survive in a market where price is of prime importance. But they sell all they can produce, and may just have the last laugh, as the effect of the diethylene glycol and methanol scandals on Lambrusco sales in the important United States market has been devastating.

Riunite, the large communist-controlled co-operative who made it big in the United States by joining forces with American-owned giant Villa Banfi, have seen their sales drop from 14 million cases a year to 8 million. They have countered by launching fruit-flavoured Lambrusco, and have been successful in a market that has gone wild on "coolers" — the fruit juice and wine mixers. But what will happen once this fad begins to dwindle, as signs already indicate it has? Let us hope that they will continue to produce the same old reliable product that has enabled them to fulfil the prime function of a co-operative: to benefit its members.

This reliability has been the key to Lambrusco's success. At best, it is a fun wine, and is, as Luigi Veronelli has called it, "human". True, it has shown to the world another, less serious side of Italian wines, and some people have criticised it as having damaged the reputation of Italy's great wines. But surely such wines have done a good enough job of this themselves, as evidenced by all the dreadful examples of Barolo, Valpolicella and Chianti that can still be found today. Lambrusco was never meant to be great, but, when dry, bubbling and slightly chilled, it *was* meant to be enjoyed.

Among the white wines of Emilia-Romagna, there is nothing as popular as Barbera and Sangiovese are for the reds. True, Malvasia is prominent in Emilia and Trebbiano vies with Albana for supremacy in Romagna, but there are a host of other varieties that are of far more than local interest.

Malvasia is beloved by the Emilians, no doubt because of its versatility. It can be made dry or sweet, still or *frizzante*, or used to enhance a blend of other grape varieties. Because of the local preference for *frizzante* wines, the DOCs for Malvasia in Colli di Parma and Colli Piacentini are usually off-dry and semi-sparkling. They may seem slightly unusual on first encounter, but they become more attractive each time the acquaintance is renewed. Perhaps the most attractive of the zone's Malvasia is the *Vino da Tavola* made by Terre Rosse. Its medium sweet fruit is enlivened by a slight effervescence, and it has a remarkably fresh perfume of apricots. Like most Malvasia, it is best drunk young, as these wines have an unfortunate tendency to oxidise easily.

Under the Colli Piacentini DOC, Malvasia is also to be found in several blends. It constitutes up to 50 per cent of Monterosso Val d'Arda, along with Moscato and Trebbiano, and makes up the same amount of Val Nure, with the local variety Ortrugo replacing the Moscato element. Ortrugo, which also has a DOC of its own, is blended with Malvasia and Trebbiano to produce Trebbianino Val Trebbia, a fresh, sometimes *frizzante* wine of little distinction. This DOC is located in the valley of the River Trebbia, which claims to be the original homeland of the Trebbiano.

If this is true, the Romagnolans can be thankful, for their local clone, Trebbiano di Romagna, is DOC in a large area that stretches from Bologna to the Adriatic coast. The annual production of around eight million litres is usually fairly neutral, dry and fresh but seldom distinguished. In the hands of Mario Pezzi at Fattoria Paradiso it has a certain character, but even he cannot overcome its intrinsic neutrality.

Trebbiano is also grown in the hills south of Bologna, where it is mixed with Albana to make Colli Bolognesi Bianco. Albana, a fairly ancient variety native to the Romagnolan hills, is less prodigious than the Trebbiano but usually surpasses it for quality. Its annual production of about three million litres covers several styles, from dry to *amabile* and still to *spumante*.

Quality is variable, and even at best, from the likes of Fattoria Paradiso (whose Vigna dell'Olivo is excellent), Trerè and Vallunga, it seldom climbs above mediocrity. It was surprising, then, when on 1 November 1987 it became the first white wine to be granted DOCG. Many other white wines achieve greater consistency at a higher overall level of quality, so many feel that the DOCG had more to do with political considerations than any such fanciful notion as "quality wine production".

It is best drunk young, when it has a creamy, nutty character, and chilled. The *amabile* is more light and honeyed than rich and cloying, and is enjoyable as an aperitif. I have drunk many good bottles of Albana di Romagna, and think of it in similar terms as I do of a good Bordeaux Blanc: a fresh and pleasing aperitif wine, but not in the same

Above: *Albana grapes at vintage. Albana, grown in the Romagnolan hills, was given a DOCG in 1987.*

Right: *Harvesting Riesling Italico at Terre Rosse. Their version, perfumed and elegant, is the best in the zone.*

league as the *Grands Crus Classés* of the Médoc. This, however, is the sort of recognition the authorities have granted it by elevating it to DOCG status.

Another Romagnan variety that some consider superior to Albana is the delightfully named Pagadebit, which means "Pay a Debt". Though not widely seen, it is grown in pockets around Bertinoro, and produces lightly sweet "amabile" wines that some consider to be among Italy's finest dessert wines. But this seems to be a slightly exaggerated claim, for the wine, delicate with a hint of walnuts in its richly flavoured fruit, is attractive without being great. Once again, Mario Pezzi probably turns out the best version, a complex and refined wine that would be overwhelmed if matched with sweet food. It is probably best drunk young and moderately chilled on its own, a wine to be sipped rather than quaffed.

More widely seen than Pagadebit is Riesling, more often the lesser Italico than the noble Renano. It usually makes soft fresh wines with a vaguely herbal fragrance and, occasionally, a *frizzante* character. DOC in the Colli Bolognesi, it seldom distinguishes itself, although Vallania at Terre Rosse makes a version of notable quality, perfumed and elegant, that could easily be mistaken for a Rhine Riesling.

Until fairly recently, Riesling Italico was often confused with Pignoletto, a native vine of obscure origin. The latter, distinct from, though similar to, the former, has now been given a separate DOC, and tends to produce wines that are fresh, vaguely aromatic and dry, though the law permits them to be *amabile* and *frizzante*.

G iven the amount of wine churned out by Albana and Trebbiano in Romagna alone, there would seem to be little room for outsiders to find a hillside to cling to. Yet foreign white grapes have been more successful in this zone than the reds, and only in the North-East of Italy can they be said to have had more success with the likes of Sauvignon.

The green, grassy style of Sauvignon at its best has eluded producers all over Italy. The Loire Valley and parts of New Zealand produce marvellously assertive Sauvignons, but in Emilia-Romagna the grape bows to local tastes and is made in a variety of styles. It makes up at least 85 per cent of Bianco di Scandiano, a DOC zone situated south-west of Reggio Emilia. The wine can be dry or medium dry, still, *frizzante* or *spumante,* so should be suited to a number of tastes. Sauvignon is also DOC in Colli di Parma and the Colli Piacentini, for still and *frizzante* dry wines. These wines, along with Bianco di Scandiano, are pleasant and quaffable, ideal with fish soups or light pasta dishes. They do not seek to emulate the best Sancerres, so it is important not to approach them expecting a grassy, gooseberryish fruit. They are appealing, but often the only clue to their grape variety is the attractive bite of acidity on the finish.

The most attractive Sauvignon wines, under DOC, are produced in the Colli Bolognesi. Here, a number of good producers aim to make wines with a fuller and better defined varietal character. The best wines, from people like Montebudello al Pazz, Bruno Negroni and his Tenuta Bissera and, of course, Terre Rosse, are excellent. They have a nicely restrained varietal character that, while not up to the standard set by Sancerre, can usually match the best of what the North-East has to offer.

While the producers in the Colli Bolognesi look to the Loire Valley for inspiration with their Sauvignon, Gian Matteo Baldi at Castelluccio turns to California. As with his three Sangiovese *crus,* he ages his Sauvignon, Ronco del Re, in 350-litre Limousin oak casks for between six months and a year. First produced in 1981, it has been greeted with rave reviews. It has great concentration and depth of flavour, and shows considerable finesse on a long finish. This vintage alone established it as one of Italy's best and most exciting new-style white wines, and the ones that have followed have only served to confirm this position.

Sauvignon's popularity, and level of quality, is on the increase throughout the zone. This seems slightly surprising, given the predilection for Chardonnay in other areas, until we discover that the EEC has not given the go-ahead for Burgundy's noble grape to be officially planted in Emilia-

---

Pick of Emilia-Romagna

Best Producers

Colli Bolognesi Conti, Montebudello al Pazz, Negroni, Terre Rosse

Colli Piacentini Cascina di Fornello, Castello di Luzzano, Clementoni, Crosignani, Molinelli, Mossi, Pusterla, Romito, Solitario, Stoppa

Lambrusco Barbieri, Cavicchioli, Chiarle, Contessa Matilde, Giacobazzi, Masetti, Ca'de Medici, Moro, Oreste Lini, Riunite, Severi Vini

Romagna Baldrati, Le Calbane, Camerone, Castelluccio, Conti, Fattoria Paradiso, Ferrucci, Guarini Matteucci, Monsignore, Pasolini dall'Onada, Picchi, Plauto, Ravaioli, Ronchi, Spalletti (Sangiovese *cru* Rocca di Ribano), Tenuta Amalia, Trere, Zanetti Protonotari (Sangiovese *cru* Villa I Raggi), Zerbina

Vintages

Most red and white wines of Emilia-Romagna are drunk young, the exceptions being Ronco del Re (white) and Cabernet, the better Sangiovese and Barbarossa.
The best recent vintages are:
Red 1987, 1986, 1985, 1983, 1982
White 1987, 1986, 1985, 1983
(1984 produced some good wines, but was generally variable.)

Above: *The sparse yields contribute greatly to the high quality of Terre Rosse's Chardonnay. From the 1988 vintage, they will be allowed to use the name of the grape on the label.*

Romagna. The positive side of this is that it permits producers to experiment with other native and foreign varieties. It is doubtful, for instance, if Sauvignon would have reached a similar level of pre-eminence if Chardonnay was a permitted variety.

However, one of the best Sauvignons is made at Terre Rosse, and they are among the few people who admit to planting Chardonnay. The wine cannot be labelled Chardonnay, so is only called Giovanni Vallania Vino da Tavola. It is initially very confusing, and I remember, upon first encountering this wine, thinking that somebody was greatly mistaken. I had ordered their Chardonnay, yet I had only been given their Vino da Tavola, which was quite obviously (or so I thought – why else should they not put Chardonnay on the label) a Trebbiano-based blend. But this was before I knew their wines very well, and the first taste was a great education. It erased all doubt from my mind. The pronounced melony character on the nose gave way to an intense biscuity fruit on the palate that finished long and nuanced. It was un-

mistakably Chardonnay, and a very good one at that.

In common with their Cabernet Sauvignon, and the other varietals that they produce, Terre Rosse do not age their Chardonnay in oak. Instead it spends six months in stainless steel before being bottled. The concentration and finesse that is so evident in the wine is derived from low yields (32-39hl/ha), careful selection in the vineyard and a controlled fermentation. Very few Chardonnays in Italy (or anywhere else, for that matter), oaked or non-oaked, can match it for quality and character.

Despite this quality, Vallania's Chardonnay is an isolated example. Pinot Bianco and Pinot Grigio are permitted grape varieties, and are therefore more widely seen. The former is DOC in the Colli Bolognesi, where Bissera and Montebudello al Pazz both produce good versions, while the latter makes both a still and *frizzante* wine in the Colli Piacentini. Once again, though, the best Pinot Grigio in the region is made at Terre Rosse. If tasted blind, it could easily be mistaken for one from Friuli.

One fairly recent import to the Colli Piacentini is the Müller-Thurgau. Though not covered by a DOC, there have been some successful wines produced from this German grape around Ziano by producers like Mossi and Molinelli.

THE CENTRE

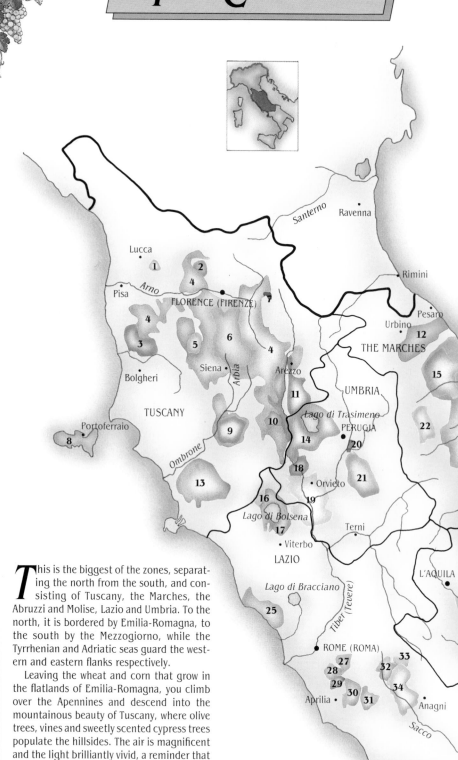

This is the biggest of the zones, separating the north from the south, and consisting of Tuscany, the Marches, the Abruzzi and Molise, Lazio and Umbria. To the north, it is bordered by Emilia-Romagna, to the south by the Mezzogiorno, while the Tyrrhenian and Adriatic seas guard the western and eastern flanks respectively.

Leaving the wheat and corn that grow in the flatlands of Emilia-Romagna, you climb over the Apennines and descend into the mountainous beauty of Tuscany, where olive trees, vines and sweetly scented cypress trees populate the hillsides. The air is magnificent and the light brilliantly vivid, a reminder that these hills were once home to the likes of Michaelangelo and Leonardo.

The solid, workaday Romagnolans, with their rich cuisine, yield place to the proud Tuscans, whose rich heritage is balanced by a simple cooking based on the bounty of the forests and the hills. Little can match a plate of *funghi porcini* (wild mushrooms) garnished with the best of Tuscan olive oil (there is no better in the world), followed by a Florentine steak and a bottle of Chianti. Florence, and its historical rival, Siena, are the twin jewels of Tuscany.

Landlocked Umbria, gently hilly and forested, is seen by some, particularly those who cannot afford the price that a crumbling, grey stone farmhouse fetches in Tuscany, as little more than an extension of its northern neighbour, but those willing to explore a little will find beautiful lakes and splendid medieval cities and idyllic hillside villages.

Key to map

1 Montecarlo.
2 Carmignano, Vinruspo.
3 Montescudaio.
4 Chianti.
5 Vernaccia di San Gimignano.
6 Chianti Classico.
7 Pomino.
8 Elba.
9 Brunello di Montalcino, Rosso di Montalcino.
10 Vino Nobile di Montepulciano, Rosso di Montepulciano.
11 Bianco Vergine della Valdichiana.
12 Bianchello del Metauro.
13 Morellino di Scansano.
14 Colli del Trasimeno.
15 Verdicchio dei Castelli di Jesi.
16 Aleatico di Gradoli.
17 Est! Est!! Est!!! di Montefiascone.
18 Orvieto.
19 Orvieto Classico.
20 Torgiano.
21 Montefalco.
22 Verdicchio di Matelica.
23 Rosso Conero.
24 Rosso Piceno.
25 Cerveteri.
26 Montepulciano d'Abruzzo, Trebbiano d'Abruzzo.
27 Frascati.
28 Marino.
29 Colli Albani.
30 Velletri.
31 Cori.
32 Cesanese di Olevano Romano.
33 Cesanese di Affile.
34 Cesanese del Piglio.
35 Pentro.
36 Biferno.

ANCONA

23

24

Ascoli Piceno

Pescara

26

Pescara

ABRUZZI

35   **36**

MOLISE

35 CAMPOBASSO

To the south of both Tuscany and Umbria lies the border with Lazio, at the centre of which is Rome. The sandy Tyrrhenian coast gives way to the volcanic hills in the north, the Roman Campagna and, of course, the spine of Italy, the Apennines in the west, which rise to their highest point in the adjacent Abruzzi and its equally mountainous neighbour to the south, Molise. The Abruzzi area, always one of Italy's wildest and most rugged and isolated regions, has been opened up since the sixties by a motorway that links it with Rome, but it remains a splendid place to visit for those in search of solitude and tranquillity.

To the north of the Abruzzi lies the Marches, whose Adriatic coastline attracts tourists in the summer, while further inland, hilltop towns, especially the magnificent Urbino, take on something of a Tuscan or Umbrian air.

Vinously, there are several threads that draw together this apparently disparate zone. The most important of these is the Sangiovese grape. Though it has already put in a brief appearance in the Romagnolan hills, it is in the Central zone, and especially in Tuscany, that this grape comes to dominate the stage. The wines that are based on it in Tuscany range from the great and renowned like Chianti and Brunello di Montalcino, through those of increasing importance, notably Morellino di Scansano, to newer style, highly priced *"Vini da Tavola"* that, while still seeking a firmly established rôle, have shown just how great the wines of this grape can be. Also of note are the *"rosati"* made from the Sangiovese, some of which rank with the world's finest dry rosés.

Following the thread of Theseus laid down by the Sangiovese through the hilly labyrinths of the Central zone, we come to such wines as Torgiano in Umbria, Velletri in Lazio and Rosso Piceno in the Marches. In this latter wine, the Sangiovese is blended with Montepulciano, the other great grape of the Central zone. This plays an important rôle in the Marches and a lesser one in Lazio, but is the only red grape of any significance in the Abruzzi and Molise.

The same connecting strands that exist for red grapes can be traced for the white grapes, particularly Trebbiano and Malvasia, that populate this zone. But just as this thread of cohesion is being drawn tighter as the full potential of the Sangiovese is being realised, so is it loosening for the whites as better varieties are being brought in to replace the Trebbiano Toscano. These imports, led by the Chardonnay (especially in Tuscany), are beginning to transform the quality of the white wines of this zone, traditionally dull and nondescript. But at the same time as several Tuscan Chardonnays are pointing to the great and unfulfilled potential of this region for white wines, other producers throughout the zone are showing signs of reaching previously unthought of levels of quality with lesser known white grapes. This, combined with the exciting results that have been produced by the experimentation with red grapes, makes the Central zone, with Tuscany firmly at the helm, the most dynamic and commercially important of all Italy's wine zones.

The most important grape variety, red or white, of Central Italy is the Sangiovese. From the flatlands of Lazio to the coastal valleys of the Marches, only the Montepulciano grape can approach it for importance. In Tuscany, however, it remains unrivalled. In the 1970s, the French interloper, Cabernet Sauvignon, seemed set to unseat the Sangiovese from its exalted position, but it has proved to be merely a pretender to the Tuscan throne.

Tuscan by origin, its name is thought to be derived from "*sanguis Jovis*", blood of Jupiter. Until quite recently, the colour of many Sangiovese-based wines might have indicated that Jupiter was an anaemic deity. Generally, they tend to have a moderately ruby colour rather than a dark blood purple, with a marked acidity and a fairly high level of tannin. The numerous variations on this theme are due to differing soils, altitudes and micro-climates, but perhaps the most important influence on the style of wine is the particular clone of the Sangiovese that is cultivated by individual producers.

At the last count, there were fourteen different clones. For the sake of convenience, it is easiest to categorise these under two headings: the Sangiovese Grosso and Piccolo. Paradoxically, the "Grosso" is, in fact, small but important (in terms of quality), while the "Piccolo" is large but minor. Under the heading of Sangiovese Grosso, we find all the best Chianti clones, the Prugnolo used in Vino Nobile di Montepulciano and the Brunello di Montalcino. These particular clones are all low yielding, and give smaller berries than the larger Sangiovese Piccolo, which is widely planted in Lazio, the Marches and, as we have already seen, Romagna.

The importance of these small berries cannot be overstated. In their thick skins reside the aromatic substances that give the wine its distinctive perfume, and the tannins which provide the capacity for ageing. Once crushed and placed in the fermenting vat, the berries yield a must (the unfermented grape juice) with a higher proportion of skins to juice, and this invariably means that the resulting wine will have more of the grape aroma, and better tannin for ageing, than a wine made with larger berries.

This partly explains the legendary ageing capacity of a wine like Brunello di Montalcino, and its assertive character. In Montalcino, the Sangiovese is used on its own, but in most other areas it is blended with other grapes. In Chianti, Carmignano and Torgiano, other varieties are used to temper the natural austerity of the Sangiovese, to give it a balance and harmony that it might otherwise lack. The grapes used to perform this softening rôle include Canaiolo and Cabernet

---

Sangiovese Based Wines

Barco Reale; Bolgheri (Rosato); Brunello di Montalcino; Carmignano; Cerveteri; Chianti (7 sub-zones); Colli Altotiberini; Colli del Trasimeno; Colli Perugini; Colline Lucchesi; Elba Rosso; Maremma Rosso; Monte Antico; Montecarlo Rosso; Montefalco Rosso; Montescudaio; Morellino di Scansano; Parrina Rosso; Pomino Rosso; Predicato di Cardisco; Rosso di Montalcino; Rosso di Montepulciano; Rosso Piceno; Sangiovese dei Colli Pesaresi; Sangiovese di Aprilia; Torgiano; Vinruspo.

Sauvignon. In Carmignano, Cabernet has been permitted in the blend since 1976, and in small amounts it does for the Sangiovese what the Merlot does for Cabernet in Bordeaux: it gives it a fullness on the mid-palate and a roundness at the edges that it badly needs.

Unlike the Cabernet, however, the Sangiovese character, restrained and nuanced, is easily overshadowed by a more assertive personality, so needs to be blended with something less dominant if it is fully to express its sleek, delicate character. In Chianti, the Canaiolo has selflessly played this supporting

Right: Harvesting the Sangiovese at Fattoria dei Barbi in Montalcino. Down here, the grape is known as the Brunello because of the brownish hue it displays when ripe.

Above: *The Canaiolo grape, though scorned by some producers, can serve to soften the austerity of the Sangiovese.*

Right: *Ripe Sangiovese grapes, prior to harvest, at Fattoria Selvapiana.*

part for years, enabling the Sangiovese to display its true elegance with time. Recently though, many producers have been experimenting with 100 per cent Sangiovese wines, often aged in *barrique.* The soft wood tannins replace the harsh grape tannins, thus obviating the need for another grape variety. Some of these wines have been notable successes, and are clear indications that the Sangiovese grape, while already dominant in terms of quantity, is set to enhance its position in terms of quality.

*T*he name Chianti summons up many images. For those who have been to Tuscany, it evokes a scene of unparalelled beauty, of pink-roofed, grey stone farmhouses firmly anchored in an undulating sea of vines, olive trees and cypresses. For others, who have come to know it at the local trattoria, it is a youthful and usually quaffable wine that comes in a straw covered bottle called (not inappropriately, some would say) a *"fiasco"*, while the odd few, fortunate enough to have been introduced to the finer estate wines, will know it as one of the world's great red wines.

Great or not, it is certainly one of the most famous names in the world of wine. Like the Italian language, it sprung out of the Tuscan hills, and remains today perhaps the most quintessential Italian wine. Nobody really knows the derivation of the name, but it is extant in documents that date back to the thirteenth century. By 1716, it was well enough known for Cosimo Medici III, the Grand Duke of Tuscany, to issue a decree defining the area from which Chianti could come. This move, making Chianti the first delimited wine zone in the world, was an attempt to prevent other wines unscrupulously capitalising on the fame of Chianti.

This delimited area stretched from south of Florence to north of Siena, is what is today the Classico zone. This did nothing, though, to prevent the name being used by the other wines of the central Tuscan hills, and this eventually led to the development of the other six sub-zones that we now know in Chianti (Rufina, Colli Fiorentini, Colli Senesi, Montalbano, Colli Aretini, Colline Pisane).

The wines of these central Tuscan hills historically served to quench the thirst of the artists, poets and politicians of Florence and Siena. A little found its way to London in the seventeenth century, but even its distinctive flask made little impression on the claret-besotted English.

The *fiasco* became synonymous with Chianti, but recently the high-shouldered Bordeaux bottle has eclipsed it in importance. Each represents one of the two basic styles of Chianti. The flask, unsuited for laying down, was used as a receptacle for the fresh and fruity *"normale"* wines that were meant to be drunk young, while the Bordeaux bottle, an ideal shape for binning, contained the *"riserva"* wines that were deemed suitable for ageing.

Several other factors influence the style. Each has its particular *"uvaggio"* (or grape-mix), and this varies from producer to producer, as well as from zone to zone. The *riserva* wines have a higher proportion of Sangiovese and, historically, would have con-

Right: *Vineyards near Panzano in Chianti Classico. This large zone has many sub-zones, each of which produces quite distinctive styles of wine. Those from the south-facing slopes of Panzano are noted for their finesse.*

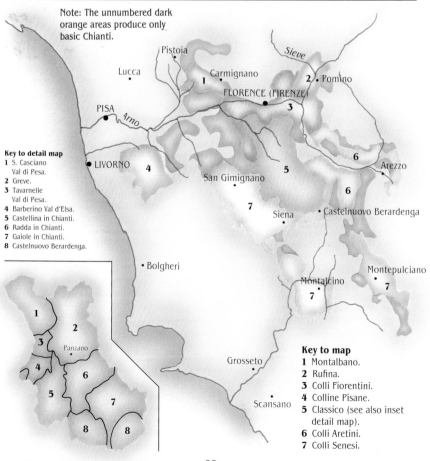

Note: The unnumbered dark orange areas produce only basic Chianti.

Key to detail map
1 S. Casciano Val di Pesa.
2 Greve.
3 Tavarnelle Val di Pesa.
4 Barberino Val d'Elsa.
5 Castellina in Chianti.
6 Radda in Chianti.
7 Gaiole in Chianti.
8 Castelnuovo Berardenga.

Key to map
1 Montalbano.
2 Rufina.
3 Colli Fiorentini.
4 Colline Pisane.
5 Classico (see also inset detail map).
6 Colli Aretini.
7 Colli Senesi.

Chianti Zones

Classico A hilly zone between Florence and Siena. The wines are amongst the finest and longest lived of Chianti.

Colli Aretini Most easterly zone, from the hills around Arezzo. The wines tend to be medium bodied and are best drunk young.

Colli Fiorentini Borders the Classico zone to the north, and extends to the southern border of the Rufina zone. Produces good quaffing Chianti as well as some of the finest *riservas*.

Colli Senesi The largest Chianti zone in the hills around Montepulciano, and south of the Classico zone from San Gimignano to Castelnuovo Berardenga. Wines can be excellent for early consumption or ageing, or can be of the worst quality available. The name of the producer is all important.

Colline Pisane Most westerly zone, from the hills south-east of Pisa. Light and fresh, they are best drunk young.

Montalbano In the hills west of Florence and south of Pistoia, at the centre of which is the Carmignano zone. Usually soft and scented and best consumed within several years of the vintage.

Rufina The smallest and coolest zone, in the Sieve valley, north-east of Florence. The wines are usually fuller, with a higher acidity, than other Chiantis. Some of the best and longest lived wines are produced here.

tained a certain percentage of white grapes, while the *normale* wines would have included less Sangiovese and a higher proportion of Canaiolo and white grapes. The use of Malvasia and Trebbiano, essential ingredients in Barone Ricasoli's classic formula (Ricasoli was the man who established the basic Chianti blend in the 1860s), probably started as a way of softening a wine from a poor year in order to make it drinkable sooner.

Another practice that was used to improve the wines from poor years was the use of "*mosto meridionale*". Said to have originated in the cool Rufina zone, where the wines tend to have a higher acidity, this involved the blending of a small proportion of deep coloured, high strength wine from Puglia to the thinner, more acid Chianti, thus

making it rounder and suppler. This was also achieved by the "*governo toscano*", where the addition of dried grapes to the young wine induces a secondary fermentation, with a consequent increase in alcohol and body and a decrease in acidity. However, the drying of grapes is an expensive process, so when concentrated grape must became available, it was seen as a feasible and cheaper alternative. That it was not as good as dried grapes was not the point; it was cheaper, and therefore to be preferred.

As these practices emerged and became firmly established in the winemaker's repertoire, they were resorted to with increasing frequency. All favour the production of a young wine, so the *normale* came to be the most common style of Chianti, and the *fiasco* became synonymous with the wine. Several quality-conscious houses like Antinori, Frescobaldi and Ruffino, and the rare estate like Badia a Coltibuono, continued to produce small quantities of *riservas*, but these were difficult to sell while the world clamoured for Chianti in the straw flask.

Young Chianti can be delicious. Its youthful ruby tint and cherry-scented fruit is imbued with a rustic charm, and it is capable of imparting enjoyment far above the level that its lowly price would suggest. But to suppose that each Chianti zone is as adept at producing this style as the next is as ridiculous as presuming that all of the Gironde can produce good Bordeaux rouge. Some parts of the Gironde, like the Haut-Médoc, are particularly well suited to the production of wines that are capable of ageing for years, while others, like the Côtes de Bourg, excel at producing suppler wines that are best drunk while still young.

The same regional differences exist in Chianti. The wines of Classico and Rufina, for instance, are generally reputed to be the finest and longest lived of all, something that can be attributed to the well-drained soils and the slightly cooler micro-climates. The wines are fairly tannic in their youth, with a higher natural acidity. Those from the Colline Pisane or the Colli Aretini, on the other hand, are generally drunk younger, as they have a lighter, more pliant fruit, and *riservas* from these zones are generally regarded as the exception rather than the rule.

Another factor that favoured the *fiasco* over the Bordeaux bottle was the social situation that existed in Chianti until the 1950s. It was, in reality, a feudal zone, where even medium sized estates were inhabited by as many as 100 people. A share cropping system was in operation, the workers being paid with part of the oil, wheat and wine that was produced. The estates were self-sufficient, and few people had the desire, and even fewer the means, to travel as far as the next village.

The estate owners had neither the time nor the inclination to bottle their own wines. They were not worth much anyway, so most people were quite happy to sell them to the merchant houses like Antinori, Ruffino and Melini. They in turn were content to put them into *fiaschi* if it would provide a certain identity for the wines and help with sales.

In the first couple of decades of this century, there was concern that, despite the best efforts of Cosimo Medici III, of all the wine being sold in *fiasco* as Chianti, very little of it was actually from the Tuscan hills. This prompted a group of merchants to band together to protect the name of Chianti. In 1924, the Chianti Classico Consorzio was born, taking as its symbol the Gallo Nero (or black cockerel), while in 1927, the producers of the other zones organised themselves into the Chianti Putto Consorzio, and decided to adorn their bottles with a Cherub (Putto) as a seal of authenticity.

The Consorzio worked hard to improve quality. They defined zones, stipulated cer-

Right: *Signor Torello with his Chianti in Pontassieve. It is still bottled in the traditional rounded flask and is meant to be drunk while still young.*

tain grape varieties and prescribed specific practices, all to make the wine "typical" of the Chianti zone. Despite their efforts, the image of Chianti continued to plummet, and while France was enacting *Appellation Contrôlée* laws in the mid-1930s, Italy was struggling with fascism. It was a fascist Italy in which the trains ran on time, but also one in which the wine industry was in a seemingly irreversible decline.

The post-war period saw Italian wines generally, and Chianti specifically, reach their nadir. At the same time, Italian society was being dramatically transformed, with many people leaving the farms to find work in the cities. As this exodus coincided with a sharp decline in the sales of Chianti in the mid-fifties, many owners were faced with a crisis. They had to adapt to survive, and if they failed to do so, had to sell their estates.

The buyers were often people who had made their money in Rome or Milan. They were more attuned to the needs of the modern world, and it did not take them long to appreciate the natural attributes that had come with their weekend retreats.

This brought a little light into the darkness of Chianti. By the time DOC was introduced in 1967, Chianti was already on its way back. But DOC provided the impetus for a viticultural revolution. The vineyards, in the late sixties, were planted as they had been for centuries, in a system of promiscuous culture. Less

Above: *Signs informing you that you are in the Gallo Nero zone are scattered along roadsides. The Black Cockerel is the emblem of the Chianti Classico Consorzio.*

titillating than it actually sounds, this merely described the manner in which the vines were planted with olive trees and other crops in a system of mixed, rather than specialised, culture. The first step towards revitalising Chianti was to re-plant the vineyards in a system that was better suited to modern agricultural practices. Olive trees and cereal crops were given their own plots, while the vines were planted in rows and trained along wires rather than up trees.

Unfortunately, something went wrong. The prevailing contemporary theory was that good winemaking could overcome any deficiencies that Nature exposed in the vineyard, so little attention was paid to the type of Sangiovese that was planted. Indeed, little was known about its various clones at the time, and the general view was that high yields were an economic necessity, given the depressed price of Chianti. As a result, the vines recommended for planting by the authorities were the high yielding Sangiovese Piccolo clones. The scale of this folly was not fully appreciated until the early eighties, so today the beautifully contoured hills of Chianti are planted largely with an inferior clone.

With the establishment of a DOC in 1967 came regulations covering production. These were largely based upon the controls implemented over the years by the Consorzio. This resulted in regulations that stipulated a minimum percentage of white grapes in the blend, and permitted the blending of up to 15 per cent of *mosto meridionale* with Chianti, as well as the use of *governo*. As we have seen, these were developed to help produce softer, rounder wines suitable for earlier drinking.

Once the vineyards were re-planted, attention then focused on the cellars. The lead was taken by many of the new estate owners, and the best oenologists that money could hire were drafted in to modernise the cellars and winemaking practices of Chianti. People like Giacomo Tachis of Antinori, Vittorio Fiore, Maurizio Castelli and, latterly, Franco Bernabei, brought a new and dynamic approach to winemaking, the aim of which was to change the face of Chianti.

Like plastic surgeons, they set about altering and removing various features of the

familiar face. Their first act was the excision of white grapes from the blend. The thought that they could ever do anything for a red wine other than dilute it was anathema to these modern winemakers. Their aim was to produce a *normale* with the emphasis on fruit, and *riservas* with the structure necessary for longevity. As white grapes would only dilute the former and weaken the latter, the law, which stipulated a minimum of 10 per cent and a maximum of 30 per cent, was ignored. The proportion of Sangiovese in most Chiantis was increased, a situation tacitly recognised by the authorities when, in 1984, the newly formulated DOCG laws reduced – but did not remove! – the minimum percentage of white grapes.

The next victim was the *governo*. This ancient Tuscan practice was deemed to give Chianti a dullness, when what was required was vibrancy. Recently, however, some estates have re-introduced it, notably those where Franco Bernabei is the consultant oenologist. He feels that by using dried grapes (rather than concentrated grape must, a cheaper but inferior method) to initiate the re-fermentation, he gets more richness in his wines and a decrease in acidity, but does not in any way reduce their capacity for ageing. This latter point is a criticism often levelled at *governo*, yet estates like Felsina Berardenga and Fontodi, where Bernabei uses it, are among the finest and longest lived of Chiantis.

Governo may be finding favour again, but gone for good is the use of *mosto meridionale* – at least from the better Chiantis. Its use remains permitted in the regulations for Chianti DOCG, though this is a somewhat absurd provision in a law that is supposed to "guarantee" quality. A dollop may have been a useful antidote to high yields and diluted wines, but these days it just serves to mask the subtler nuances of the Sangiovese. Of course, if a producer were to push his yields well beyond the permitted maximum (70hl/ha for Chianti, still far too high for a quality wine), then the result would be thin, acidic wines that would certainly then benefit from the addition of a soft, fat and deep-coloured wine.

Above: *The bottling line at Isole e Olena. The wines of many estates have improved in recent years due to greater care being exercised at bottling.*

While not wanting to see their delicate Chianti overwhelmed by coarse blending wine, the modern winemakers were also keen to ensure that it did not lose too much of its fruit flavours through protracted cask ageing. Traditionally, Chianti was aged and stored in large casks of chestnut or Slovenian oak, and the wines would be sold either in bulk, to the merchants, or in demi-johns. In the sixties, though, the estates began to bottle their own wines. But because there was insufficient space to store bottles, only

enough wine to fulfil a specific order would be bottled. This meant that there could be, on an average sized estate, four or five different bottlings of a particular vintage, with perhaps four years separating the first from the last bottling. Because more oxygen comes into contact with a wine the longer it spends in cask, thus accelerating its development, the result was a marked variation in style between the different bottlings.

With an eye focused clearly on Bordeaux, there has been a move in recent years to bottling the vintage all at once, and to reducing the amount of time the wine spends in cask. Instead of spending, say, three to five years in oak, today's Chiantis may be bottled a year or two after the vintage. The exact time depends very much on the estate and the nature of the vintage, but there is generally a greater awareness of the need to protect the wine during this ageing in order to preserve its youthful aroma and fruit, and to ensure that the end result is a sound, healthy wine, capable of ageing in bottle. A Bordeaux bottle, more likely than not.

Many of the large casks of chestnut or Slovenian oak are now being complemented by small, new oak *barriques* (225-litre casks used in Bordeaux) in order to give the wine a little more complexity. *Barriques* are now a common sight in many of the cellars of Chianti, especially in Classico, but they only came to be widely used at the beginning of the seventies, at the same time as another Bordelais native, the Cabernet Sauvignon, was making its presence felt.

Chianti Vintages

1988 Early indications are that this will top even 1985 for quality, possibly because quantity was down by almost 30 per cent. A wet Spring gave way to a long, hot Summer, and the grapes were in perfect condition when harvesting began. By the time all but the last of the Sangiovese was in, rain fell and diluted this part of the crop. Few producers minded, as the rest of the vats are showing tremendous colour, fruit and alcoholic degree. Time will tell just how good the wines are.

1987 The Cabernet and the early ripening grapes were harvested in perfect conditions, but the heavens opened just as the Sangiovese was being brought in. Some communes were hit worse than others, so it is even more difficult than usual to generalise. Selection will be the key. The best wines look like having good colour, medium weight and a well-defined and attractive perfume, and a moderate capacity for ageing.

1986 A patchy summer was followed by perfect autumn weather. The wines lack depth, especially when set against the magnificent 1985s, but make up for this with a forward, accessible fruit. They are distinctively perfumed and are for drinking in the medium term.

1985 A magnificent vintage. The sun took up its post high in the sky in early summer and refused to budge until the autumn, though drought caused problems in some areas. High temperatures at harvest created trouble for those who lack refrigeration facilities, so some wines, despite having good depth, have an unattractive baked character and an unacceptably high level of volatile acidity. The best wines, though, are stunning. They have great concentration of fruit and have sufficient grip to enable them to age for years. Volpaia, Isole e Olena, Felsina and Selvapiana were especially successful.

1984 The gods made evident their displeasure with the muddle of DOCG by dumping buckets of rain over the central Tuscan hills in 1984. The vintage was generally a washout, though some estates, either by rigidly selecting only the best vats or by judiciously blending the meagre 1984 with a small amount of sturdier 1983 or 1985, have produced attractive, drinkable wines. Badia is particularly delicious.

1983 A hot summer produced ripe, thick-skinned grapes that gave wines which were, in their early stages, austere and tannic. As they age, though, they are shedding their tannic shell to display a tremendously elegant fruit. Classic, long-lived wines.

1982 Though initially lauded because of their ripe, delicious fruit, the 1982s, like a child prodigy, are having trouble coping with adolescence. What maturity will bring is difficult to say, but their low acidity does not augur well. While 1982 was better in Brunello, 1983 seems to have the edge in Chianti. The Sangioveto of Badia, though, is outstanding.

1981 Rain in early summer was followed by a long, dry and warm spell of weather that brought the grapes to full ripeness. The wines are generally well-defined and forward, though lacking the charm of the 1982s and the structure of the 1983s. Rufina fared better in this vintage, with Vetrice and Selvapiana producing particularly outstanding wines; Selvapiana's Vigna Bucerchiale is one of the greatest Chiantis ever produced.

1980 Late flowering and patchy weather during the summer led to a late harvest. The wines have fair depth, medium tannin and good acidity that has enabled them to develop well in bottle. At its peak now and over the next couple of years.

1979 A fine summer and a lack of vigilance in the vineyard led to a large crop. The wines were attractive early, but few have had sufficient depth to age well.

1978 Not as abundant as its successor, and perhaps consequently more tannic. Some good, long-lived wines were produced, but generally they lack balance and finesse. Most are at their peak now, though Frescobaldi's Montesodi, has a good few years ahead of it yet.

1977 A small quantity of ripe, sturdy wine was produced. As in 1981, Rufina was better than Classico, with Selvapiana producing an outstanding *riserva* that still has some way to go.

Good earlier vintages 1975, 1971, 1970, 1967, 1964, 1961.

Cabernet Sauvignon is not a newcomer to Tuscany. Thanks to a particularly Francophilic ancestor, Frescobaldi have had it planted on their Nipozzano estate for well over a century. But it is really only in the last twenty years that this grape variety has started to become an important factor in Tuscan viniculture.

The search for direction in the sixties sent Conte Ugo Contini Bonacossi to Bordeaux, where he obtained some cuttings of Cabernet Sauvignon from a friend who also happened to be the owner of Château Lafite-Rothschild. He brought them back to his Villa di Capezzana estate, nestled in the Montalbano hills northwest of Florence, and, once they came into production, he started to blend them with his own wines.

At the same time, Piero Antinori had recently taken over the family business and was keen to make an impact. This was next to impossible with Chianti, given the low esteem in which it was held, but with a little help from Bordeaux, in the shape of Emile Peynaud, the legendary oenologist, and his own winemaker, Giacomo Tachis, he set about developing a wine that was to prove to the world that Tuscany was indeed capable of producing great wines.

Out went the white grapes (except for a small amount of Malvasia) and up went the percentage of Sangiovese, carefully selected from a special vineyard on their estate at San Casciano, in the north of the Classico zone. The wine was then aged in new *barriques* for about two years to soften the austerity of this novel Sangiovese/Canaiolo blend. The first vintage was 1971, but by 1975, the Malvasia and Canaiolo elements had been eliminated and 10 per cent of Cabernet Sauvignon had been injected into the blend in their stead. The result was international success on a Byronic scale. People who would not previously have drunk Chianti, let alone bought

Carmignano

Carmignano was one of the four zones demarcated by Cosimo Medici III in 1716. This was not only because of the fame of the wine, but also because of the interest that the Medici family had in this small village. They had built summer residencies in the hills, and had planted vines, some of which, due to their links with France, were French varieties. Ugo Contini Bonacossi of Villa di Capezzana believes that one of the French varieties was Cabernet Sauvignon. After the devastation caused by phylloxera, the Cabernet disappeared, but it was replanted at Capezzana in the sixties, and it was on this basis that Carmignano was granted its DOC. Because of its well-drained, rocky soil, and its proximity to the Apennines, Carmignano produces a distinctly different style of Sangiovese, one which, according to Contini Bonacossi, benefits greatly from the addition of a small amount of Cabernet.

The DOC also covers a rosé, Vinruspo, which is one of Tuscany's most attractive, and a Vin Santo.

Top producers Ambra, Artimino, Bacchereto, Capezzana, Il Poggiolo, Trefiano.

Best Vintages 1988, 1985, 1983, 1979, 1975.

Super Tuscans: Sangiovese and Cabernet Blends

This is a selection of the better known wines, with approximate percentages of each grape indicated. However, this often changes from vintage to vintage.

Wine	Producer
Alte d'Altesi (70 per cent Sangiovese, 30 per cent Cabernet)	Altesino
Balifico (70 per cent Sangiovese, 30 per cent Cabernet)	Castello di Volpaia
Bruno di Rocca (70 per cent Sangiovese, 30 per cent Cabernet)	Vecchie Terre di Montefili
Ca' del Pazzo (50 per cent Sangiovese, 50 per cent Cabernet)	Caparzo
Concerto (80 per cent Sangiovese, 20 per cent Cabernet)	Castello di Fonterutoli
Grifi (85 per cent Sangiovese, 15 per cent Cabernet Franc)	Avignonesi
Sammarco (25 per cent Sangiovese, 75 per cent Cabernet)	Castello dei Rampolla
San Giorgio (80 per cent Sangiovese, 20 per cent Cabernet)	Lungarotti
Tignanello (80 per cent Sangiovese, 20 per cent Cabernet)	Antinori
Vigorello (85 per cent Sangiovese, 15 per cent Cabernet)	San Felice

Left: *Three generations of the Antinori family. Albiera flanked by father Piero and grandfather Nicolo. Piero Antinori, a brilliant marketing man, has done much to raise Tuscan wines to their present level of international esteem.*

it, were gladly forking out the same amount of money as they would for a good claret to enjoy the new Antinori blend, Tignanello. Throughout the seventies, the proportion of Cabernet continued to rise until it reached 20 per cent, which, with the 80 per cent of Sangiovese, is now aged for about 18 months in new *barrique*. Its success has meant that it has outgrown the original Tignanello vineyard at San Casciano, so other, carefully selected, Sangiovese is bought in to give Antinori the quantity they need.

Tignanello's success gave impetus to other growers who were experimenting with Cabernet. Conte Ugo's efforts resulted in Carmignano being the first DOC, in 1976, to allow Cabernet in the blend, and this was joined, in 1983, by Pomino, where Frescobaldi is the top producer. Today, Barco Reale, based on the same grape mix and from the same zone as Carmignano, though lighter in style, continues to prove the benefits that can be derived from a dollop of Cabernet. All, by separate paths, had reached the point where white grapes were replaced by Cabernet, which tempered the Sangiovese's natural austerity and gave it a richness and complexity that some felt it lacked.

It was not long before other producers noted the extra refinement of these wines and started to plant Cabernet in their own vineyards. Some of this was used to bolster their Chianti, so much so that when the DOCG regulations were formulated in 1984, there was a provision made for up to 10 per cent of "other grapes" (ie Cabernet) in the blend.

Most, however, was destined for use in the "fantasy" wines that the producers set out to create. Antinori's Cabernet-based Tignanello may have been the prototype, but it is more in the Italian character to create rather than to imitate, so each producer developed a wine that suited the style of his estate. These wines have earned themselves the dubious sobriquet of Super Tuscans, possibly because they have soared to price levels that others have only ever dreamed of reaching. And this despite the fact that they bear the lowly *Vino da Tavola* denomination. They are considered on the subsequent four pages.

s the concept of the Super *Vino da Tavola* spread, producers set out to create a wine that reflected their own character, and that of their estate. Some, taking their lead from Tignanello, favoured a judicious amount of Cabernet Sauvignon to fill in what often seemed to be the slightly hollow mid-palate of many Chiantis.

This was, in a sense, the substitution of Cabernet for the traditional *mosto meridionale.* A great deal of this blending wine used to come from Squinzano, in Puglia, where the Malvasia Nera grape was grown. Winemaker and consultant Maurizio Castelli, impressed by the way in which some of the better Chiantis, bolstered by a small amount of Squinzano, had aged, decided to bring the Malvasia Nera grape to Chianti, where he planted it at Castellare. He used it in a blend with 70 per cent Sangiovese, which was then aged in *barrique,* to create the stylishly perfumed and distinctive I Sodi di San Niccolo. Since 1985, though, he has reduced the proportion of Malvasia Nera to 10 per cent of the blend, largely because of its pronounced and dominant perfume.

Other producers sought out other grapes to blend with their Sangiovese. Recently, a great deal of Pinot Noir has been planted, but this will more likely be used to make a varietal wine rather than for blending with Sangiovese. There is a feeling among some producers that the Pinot Noir, a difficult

Super Tuscans: Cabernets

Wine	Producer
Cabernet di Miralduolo	Lungarotti
Ghiaie della Furba (Equal proportions of Cabernet Sauvignon, Cabernet Franc and Merlot)	Villa di Capezzana
Sassicaia	Marchese Incisa della Rochetta
Solaia	Antinori
Tavernelle	Villa Banfi

grape to grow at the best of times, will perform well in Chianti's cool climate, especially in those vineyards at about 400-600 metres.

Others, though, have wholeheartedly embraced the Cabernet Sauvignon. Foremost among these is the Marchese Incisa della Rochetta, whose Sassicaia was catapulted to international fame when, in 1978, it topped a tasting held by *Decanter* magazine in London of Cabernet Sauvignons from around the world. Included in the tasting were some of the top properties from Bordeaux, so Sassicaia became, virtually overnight, something more than just another Tuscan Cabernet.

Below: *Piero Masi, the estate manager at Isole e Olena, inspects their new plantings. Replanting with clones or new varieties is a constant process.*

Made at Tenuta San Guido, due west of Siena, inland a bit from the Tyrrhenian coast at Bolgheri, Sassicaia often thrives in vintages that are indifferent in the rest of Tuscany. Low yields (30-32hl/ha), fermentation in stainless steel, maceration on the skins for about 12-14 days and ageing in French and Slovenian oak *barriques* (three-quarters of which are new) for anything from 18-22 months, depending on the nature of the vintage, are the particular production techniques that lend character to Sassicaia.

Sassicaia is, without doubt, a fine wine, especially from vintages like 1968, 1972 and 1982, but part of its success can probably be attributed to the mania for Cabernet that has swept the world of wine in the last decade or so. Unlike Tignanello, or some of the other Super Tuscans where Cabernet forms a small percentage of the blend, Sassicaia's Tuscan provenance is difficult to discern in a blind tasting. Its appeal lies on an international level, as indeed does that of the other Tuscan wines where Cabernet is the predominant feature in the blend.

The swelling sea of Cabernet prompted some producers to experiment with different grape varieties. At Isole e Olena, Paolo de Marchi felt that the naturally spicy character of his wines would be better suited for blending with Syrah, the peppery grape of the Northern Rhône, than with Cabernet. He planted a small amount of each variety in the early eighties, but, while waiting for them to come into production, found that, by reducing the yields from his Sangiovese vines to 40-45hl/ha, he was able to achieve sufficient concentration in his wines to obviate the need for blending with either Cabernet or Syrah.

This simple factor has only really become economically viable following the improvements that have been wrought in the cellar. The subsequent improvement in quality has meant that the better estate wines, especially those in Chianti Classico, are now able to fetch a higher price for their wines. But the level of investment required is still such that, in 1987, Piero Stucchi-Prinetti of Badia a Coltibuono could say that the only way to make a small fortune in Chianti was to have started with a large one.

In any case, the use of carefully selected Sangiovese grapes, from low yielding vines grown in particularly favoured vineyards, was found to produce wines of great concentration. Many of these wines came from older parts of the vineyard, from vines that had survived the ravages of the sixties. They tend to be austere in their youth, but this characteristic is moderated by a short spell in *barrique.* The results have been impressive. The first of this style, Le Pergole Torte, was produced at Monte Vertine by Sergio Manetti in 1977. Others, like Flaccianello della Pieve from Fontodi and Sangioveto from Badia a Coltibuono, have followed. Today, the best of these 100 per cent Sangioveses are, in my opinion, the most exciting of the Super Tuscans on the market.

They gave producers a renewed faith in the ability of Sangiovese to produce world-class wines. Still, though, they carry the *Vino da Tavola* denomination, simply because there is no room, in Chianti, for a wine that is made solely from Sangiovese, but also because, sadly, the producer could not charge the high prices necessary to cover production costs (and, it must be said, to satisfy their egos) if the wine was simply labelled Chianti.

But there are signs that this may be changing. Some producers, notably Silvano Formigli at Castello di Ama, are producing single vineyard wines that are labelled as Chianti Classico and sold at Super Tuscan prices. This belief in Chianti, allied with the new-found confidence in Sangiovese, has led many producers to feel that while Cabernet may be alright in Tuscany, it has no place in the blend that goes to make up Chianti. It is an indication of the ineffectual nature of much of the DOCG discipline for Chianti that, just when the law had caught up with the prevailing situation, the producers had already begun to move off in a new direction.

DOCG was, to a large extent, a great muddle. Although undoubtedly a step in the right direction, it failed to proceed far enough along the road of quality. Compromises, like the retention of the provision for blending up to 15 per cent of wine from outside the zone (ie *mosto meridianale*) for Chianti DOCG, were blows against quality and victories for the industrialists.

Positive elements include the reduction in white grapes, an increase in the minimum percentage of Sangiovese and the provision for up to 10 per cent of other grape varieties in the blend, giving the producers at least a semblance of freedom to experiment. But most producers feel that the greatest benefit has been the reduction in yields, even though the best obtain much lower than the maximum that is permitted. The important thing here is that it has encouraged (or forced) those other than the best to decrease their yields and, one hopes, to make better wines.

DOCG may have been successful at raising the overall level of quality, but it has done nothing to draw back into the fold the black sheep of Chianti, the Super Tuscans. In the sense that they represent top quality, their existence should be cheered by every wine lover, but even the closest follower of the Tuscan scene will have trouble keeping tabs on the latest developments, and on which blend relates to which name – and from which estate?

Super Tuscans: Sangioveses

This is a selection of the better wines rather than a comprehensive list.

Wine	Producer
Brunesco di San Lorenzo	Montagliari
Capannelle Rosso	Capannelle
Cepparello	Isole e Olena
Cetinaia	Castello di San Polo in Rosso
Coltassala	Castello di Volpaia
Elegia	Poliziano
Flaccianello della Piave	Tenuta Fontodi
Fontalloro	Felsina Berardenga
Grosso Senese	Il Palazzino
Il Sodaccio (85 per cent Sangiovese, 15 per cent Canaiolo)	Monte Vertini
I Sodi di San Niccolo (90 per cent Sangiovese, 10 per cent Malvasia Nera)	Castellare
La Corte	Castello di Querceto
Le Pergole Torte	Monte Vertine
Palazzo Altesi	Altesino
Querciagrande	Podere Capaccia
Sangioveto	Badia a Coltibuono
Sangioveto Grosso	Monsanto
Solatio Basilica	Villa Cafaggio
Vinattieri Rosso	Maurizio Castelli, Burton Anderson, Carlo Mascheroni

Above: *Paolo de Marchi tasting from barrel in the cellars of his Isole e Olena estate. Thanks to his incessant pursuit of quality, his wines now rank with the very best in Classico.*

A group of larger producers, led by Antinori, Frescobaldi and Ruffino, as well as the Consorzio del Putto, have recently banded together and created a system which they hope will accommodate the Super Tuscans. The wines will be called "Vini con Predicato", and are subject to a number of stringent production regulations. The delimited area for these wines, the Colli della Toscana Centrale (Central Tuscan hills) is quite large, but specific stipulations include the altitude at which the vines must be planted (minimum of 150 metres), the number of plants per hectare (an important quality consideration), yields (60hl/ha maximum) and ageing requirements in wood.

There are four different sub-divisions, each being based on a particular grape variety. Predicato di Cardisco must have a minimum of 90 per cent Sangiovese, the remaining 10 per cent being any other red grape other than Merlot or Cabernet. The Predicato di Biturica must in theory be a blend of a minimum of 30 per cent Cabernet and Sangiovese, and up to 10 per cent of other red grapes. In practice though, as the name would suggest (Biturica is the Latin name for Cabernet, an indication, perhaps, that the recent influx is more a homecoming than a foreign invasion), the wines have a predominance of Cabernet. A fine example is Frescobaldi's Mormoreto, which has 85 per cent Cabernet Sauvignon, 5 per cent Cabernet Franc and 10 per cent Sangiovese. The other two Predicato categories are for white grapes, and will be looked at under that section later in the book.

Predicato is an interesting concept, but whether it can impose some order on the chaos that currently exists, or whether the numerous names involved will only add to the confusion, remains to be seen. But there is a feeling among smaller producers that they would do better to avoid it. As one of them said to me, when I asked him if his excellent 100 per cent Sangiovese, aged in *barrique* for a year, was a Predicato: "It could be," he said, and paused tantalisingly for a moment. "But I would really prefer it to be my Chianti Classico Riserva."

*T*oday, the producer in Chianti is at a crossroads. He could turn away from the whole DOCG discipline, like Raffaele Rossetti at Capannelle or Sergio Manetti at Monte Vertine, and sell his wines solely on the basis of the name he has acquired for quality. Alternatively, he could see that his future lies with Chianti, and move forward accordingly. It is a great name that has become tarnished through lack of care; a little bit of hard work could make it shine once again.

He could even throw his hands up in horror at the various options open to him and turn back in the direction from whence he came, and resume selling to the merchants. This, after all, was the method by which Chianti used to be marketed. The merchants would buy from various estates and bottle and sell the wine under their own name.

This situation, in many ways a legacy of lethargy, was what the new proprietors inherited. Historically, the farmers had little incentive to produce quality, as they were paid the going rate – and no more – by the merchants, who in turn were more concerned with promoting their own names than that of Chianti. The individual identities of the estates were submerged in the homogeneous blend of the merchants, a situation akin to Château Margaux and Château Lafite being blended together and sold as "Mr Jones' Médoc".

The new estate owners soon realised the absurdity of the situation and set about establishing an identity for their property. They engaged the services of people like Fiore, Castelli and Bernabei, peripatetic oenologists who, as we have seen, transformed the winemaking techniques and, ultimately, the wine, of Chianti. The result was a profusion of estates, each producing a wine called Chianti. But in each case, the wine varies according to a number of factors.

Chianti is a huge zone, with wide variations in soil, altitude and micro-climates. In this respect, it is quite similar to Bordeaux. And just as various Bordeaux Châteaux have different grape mixes, so the numerous estates in Chianti use varying proportions of Sangiovese, Canaiolo and other grapes.

All these factors contribute to the great diversity of styles that exist in Chianti today. Add to this the different yields, the rigour of selection (not all grapes will be fit for use, so the care that goes into sorting the good from the bad is vital) and, of course, the style of winemaking, and you come up with a situation where there are as many styles of Chianti as there are estates.

It also means that the most important item on the label is not the DOCG, nor the name "Chianti", nor the Gallo Nero emblem, but rather the name of the estate. As yet, though, there is no classification of estates in Chianti that could be compared with the one that exists in Bordeaux. What is required is more research into what actually makes a great Chianti, so that the producers can confidently move forward and establish the primacy of the estates.

Below: *Selvapiana's vineyards in Rufina produce some of the greatest and longest-lived of all Chianti.*

One of the most celebrated of Chianti estates, Castello di Nipozzano, is located in Rufina. Owned by the Frescobaldi family, who also run a large merchant firm, it has, unusually, been bottled separately since the 17th century. The oldest bottle remaining in their cellars dates back to 1864. Its distinctive style can be attributed to its altitude (250-380 metres), its *"uvaggio"* (80 per cent Sangiovese, 10 per cent Canaiolo and 10 per cent of other grapes, including Cabernet), the 18 months that just under half the wine spends in *barriques* and, naturally enough, the luck of the vintage.

This is in stark contrast to the Villa Antinori Riserva. Produced by Antinori, the large and venerable merchant firm based at San Casciano, the wine is a blend of grapes bought from other areas in the Classico area and those grown on their own estate. Fortunate in having at their disposal the services of

Giacomo Tachis as winemaker, the style owes more to his skill as a blender than to any of the intrinsically natural advantages that Nipozzano has. They have recently increased both the amount of Cabernet in the blend and the proportion of wine that goes into *barrique,* so the wine, while remaining at a very high level of quality, becomes less distinctively Tuscan in character with each succeeding vintage.

Antinori seem to have recognized that the future for Chianti lies with the estates, for they have recently bought the I Peppoli vineyard and are starting, with the 1985 vintage, to market it separately. It is a good wine, and underlines the fact that, with so many estates coming on to the market, now is the time to move away from the safe merchants' blends and experiment with, and get to know, the great diversity of styles that Chianti has to offer.

A Guide to Good Chianti

This is very much a personal guide, and makes no attempt to be comprehensive. It reflects my preferences and tasting experience; there are, I have no doubt, many other fine producers waiting to be discovered by the adventurous taster. The name in parentheses after the estate indicates the commune in which it is situated; this is followed by the DOCG zone.

The Best

Badia a Coltibuono (Gaiole) Classico: An ancient and beautiful Abbey, owned by Piero Stucchi-Prinetti and managed by his son, Roberto. Maurizio Castelli is the consultant oenologist. Old vines give the wines a certain toughness in their youth, but they age very well. Their Sangioveto di Coltibuono, pure Sangiovese aged for a year in *barrique* and another year in "*botte*", is magnificent. Made from vines planted just after the war, yields are as low as 15-20hl/ha. Concentrated and austere when young, it unfolds after a decade.

Castello di Ama (Gaiole) Classico: Silvano Formigli has brought this estate into the top flight over the past few years by concentrating his efforts on the production of single vineyard wines. His cru Bellavista and San Lorenzo, both *barrique* aged, are excellent. Located at an altitude of 400-480 metres, Ama's wines are characterised by a deep colour and concentration, attributable to low yields, and an elegance and distinctive perfume, derived from the *barrique* ageing (which can, at times, be overdone) and about 5 per cent of Malvasia Nera in the blend.

Castello di Volpaia (Radda) Classico: Giovanella Stianti owns this splendid estate which sits atop a hill at about 600 metres altitude in the heart of the Classico zone. Since Maurizio Castelli, the winemaker, grafted the vineyard from the Brunello that was mistakenly planted there to his preferred clone of Sangiovese, the wines have shown a marked improvement. They are amongst the finest of Chiantis, but the *riservas* and Coltassala, as well as the fairly recent Balifico (1985 was the first vintage), all show excellent ageing potential.

Fattoria Selvapiana (Pontassieve) Rufina: Francesco Giuntini is the latest, and, as he is a bachelor, probably the last, of his family to run this estate, which they have owned since 1827. With the help of oenologist Franco Bernabei, he produces one of the most distinguished of all Chiantis. The wines have a great concentration of fruit but are quite hard in their youth, opening out with age into magnificent bottles.

Felsina Berardenga (Castelnuovo Berardenga) Classico: Since Franco Bernabei became consultant oenologist here in 1983, the wines have begun to live up to the potential that they displayed all along. Owner Giuseppe Mazzocolin has also brought out a single vineyard *riserva*, Vigneto Rancia, which is outstanding. The wines combine a chunkiness that is typical of the commune with a certain elegance. They age well, and all signs are that they will continue to improve. Their *Vino da Tavola*, Fontalloro, is one of the best.

Tenuta Fontodi (Panzano) Classico: This is another estate where owners Dino and Domiziano Manetti employ the services of Franco Bernabei. The wines are characterised by their finesse. The *normale* takes about two to three years to begin to show at its best, with the *riserva* and the *Vino da Tavola*, Flaccianello, needing a little longer. The latter, with its finely integrated oakiness, is one of the most harmonious and ultimately impressive of the new breed. Their white, Meriggio, a blend of Pinot Bianco, Sauvignon and Traminer, is also good, if lacking the class displayed by the reds.

Isole e Olena (Barberino Val d'Elsa) Classico: Paolo de Marchi arrived at Isole, the estate his father bought in 1954, from Piemonte in 1976. His tenure has seen the wines improve greatly, yet he is adamant that they still have a long way to go to fulfill their potential. His excellent *normale* has a brilliant colour, a distinctive spiciness on the nose and a vibrant yet concentrated fruit on the palate. He makes a small amount of *riserva* and his *Vino da Tavola*, Cepparello. Though using a small amount of *barrique* for all his reds, it never dominates. He is due to release soon a Cabernet and a Syrah, as well as an outstanding Chardonnay (non-oaked). His Vin Santo is one of the best.

Monsanto (Barberino Val d'Elsa) Classico: Despite being only several kilometres down the road from Isole e Olena, the wines of Monsanto are markedly different. When young, they are intense and closed, but as they unfurl, often over a couple of decades, they display an astonishing array of flavours. As a result, the *normale* often lacks charm, and the real stars are the *riserva* and Il Poggio, their single vineyard *riserva*. The estate has been owned by Fabrizio Bianchi since 1961.

Montesodi (Pelago) Rufina: Montesodi is a 12 hectare vineyard on the Frescobaldi estate of Castello di Nipozzano. This fine estate produces excellent wines in its own right, but Montesodi is something special. First produced in 1974, it is made from old and low yielding (30hl/ha) Sangiovese and Cabernet vines. It is aged for about 20 months in *barriques* (half of which are new), and needs about eight to ten years to start to show its true magic. It is deeply coloured, finely scented and has a velvety elegance on the palate.

A Guide to Good Chianti

─────**Very Good**─────

Capannelle* (Gaiole) Classico
Castellare (Castellina) Classico
Castell'in Villa (Castelnuovo Berardenga) Classico
Castello di Nipozzano (Pelago) Rufina
Castello di Querceto (Greve) Classico
Castello dei Rampolla (Panzano) Classico
Castello di San Polo in Rosso (Gaiole) Classico
Il Poggiolino+ (Tavarnelle) Classico
La Querce (Impruneta) Colli Fiorentini
Le Masse di San Leolino (Panzano) Classico
Lilliano (Castellina) Classico

Fattoria di Montagliari (Panzano) Classico
Monte Vertine* (Radda) Classico
Podere Capaccia (Greve) Classico
Podere Il Palazzino+ (Gaiole) Classico
Poggio Reale (Rufina) Rufina
Prima Vigna, Castello di Vicchiomaggio (Greve) Classico
Riecine+ (Gaiole) Classico
San Cosma (Castelnuovo Berardenga) Classico
Savignola Paolina (Greve) Classico
Vecchie Terre di Montefili+ (Greve) Classico
Villa Cafaggio+ (Panzano) Classico

*Both producers have now opted out of Chianti Classico DOCG. Both continue to produce wines of the highest quality.
+Wines which, on recent form, seem set to join the top rank before long.

─────**Above Average**─────

Aziano (Ruffino) Classico
Castello di Cacchiano (Gaiole) Classico
Castello di Fonterutoli (Castellina) Classico
Castello di Gabbiano (Mercatale) Classico
Castello di Uzzano (Greve) Classico
Castello Vicchiomaggio (Greve) Classico
Fattoria dell'Aiola (Radda) Classico
Fattoria dell'Ugo (Tavarnelle Val di Pesa) Colli Fiorentini
Fattoria di Artimino (Carmignano) Montalbano
Fattoria di Guicciardini-Strozzi (San Gimignano) Colli Senesi
Fattoria di Petroio (Castelnuovo Berardenga) Classico
Fattoria di Pietrafitta (San Gimignano) Colli Senesi
Fattoria di Vetrice (Rufina) Rufina
Fattoria di Vistarenni (Gaiole) Classico
Fattoria La Ripa (San Donato) Classico
Fattoria Lilliano (Antella) Colli Fiorentini
Fattoria Quercebella (Greve) Classico
Fossi (Florence) Classico

Il Poggiolo (Carmignano) Montalbano
Lamole (Panzano) Classico
La Querce (Panzano) Classico
Machiavelli Riserva (Serristori) Classico
Pagliarese (Castelnuovo Berardenga) Classico
Poggio Al Sole (Sambuca Val di Pesa) Classico
Poggio a Remole (Frescobaldi) Rufina
Poggio Rosso, San Felice (Castelnuovo Berardenga) Classico
Rocca della Macie (Castellina) Classico
Ruffino Riserva Ducale (Pontassieve) Classico
San Fabbiano (Castellina) Classico
San Felice "Il Grigio" (Castelnuovo Berardenga) Classico
Tenuta di Capezzana (Carmignano) Montalbano
Vignale (Radda) Classico
Vignamaggio (Greve) Classico
Villa Antinori, (Florence) Classico
Villa Cilnia (Pieve al Bagnoro) Colli Aretini
Villa La Selva, (Pietraviva di Bucine) Colli Aretini

Chianti was long established when, in the middle of the last century, Clemente Santi started to experiment with the vines that were growing on his family's farm near Montalcino, a small town south of Siena. The wine had traditionally been sold as Chianti, but he concentrated his attention on isolating and propagating a particular clone of the Sangiovese, known locally as the Brunello because of the brownish hue of its grapes.

His grandson, Ferruccio Biondi-Santi, carried on the experiments, and was probably the first person, in 1870, to make a wine solely from the Brunello grape, using neither white grapes nor *governo* in the process. His Brunello di Montalcino was obviously a success, for he was soon replanting his vineyards with this clone, being in the fortunate position of being able to take shoots from established vines rather than having to buy them from the local authorities.

The wine soon gained a reputation for longevity, and while his neighbours continued to use *fiaschi,* Biondi-Santi put his wines into Bordeaux bottles. Vintages such as the 1888 and 1891 soon acquired legendary stature. The wines derived this fabled longevity from a long maceration with the skins and stalks (thus extracting extra tannins), followed by a protracted ageing in cask. Long a feather in its cap while Chianti remained unable to achieve it, this capacity for ageing has become something of a problem in recent years. The wines are hard and unyielding in their youth, taking years to come around to a state where they are actually pleasant to drink. In these modern times. when interest rates are high and time is money, few can afford to wait this long.

Thus Brunello currently faces a dilemma. Its claim to greatness has been predicted largely upon its longevity (and an inflated price), but harmony, balance and finesse are all important components of any wine that makes such a claim. These are elements missing from many Brunello, largely because the makers have blindly followed the old ways. How easy is it to make a good wine in the small zone of about 700 hectares? "Very easy," says Maurizio Castelli, winemaker at Castiglion del Bosco, "because the grapes are always fully ripe and healthy, unlike in Chianti." This he attributes to its lower altitude and the hotter summers. But, according to Franco Bernabei, who makes the wine at Lisini, it is much more difficult. "They have good grapes in Montalcino, but very poor winemaking equipment," he says. They do not have the means to control the tempera-

Below: *These small bunches of Brunello grapes were found on Biondi-Santi's "Il Greppo" estate in Montalcino. The clone was first isolated here and the resulting wine gained a world-wide reputation for its quality and longevity.*

ture during fermentation, and he maintains that this results in wines that are unable to stand up to long ageing in cask.

Some producers, recognising this problem, have taken action. They have installed stainless steel in the cellars, thus enabling the fermentation temperature to be controlled, and have shortened the maceration. Unwilling to see this carefully extracted fruit become attenuated during a prolonged period in cask, they ignore the DOCG (granted in 1980) regulations, which call for three and a half years ageing in cask, and instead bottle their wines after 1-2 years, depending on the nature of the vintage. These new style wines, from producers like Altesino and Il Poggione, have finesse and balance, and do not seem to have sacrificed any of their ability to age. Indeed, they positively need to be aged before they start to show their true breed, and even then, after seven to ten years, will only do so after they have been allowed to "breathe" for a couple of hours.

As with Chianti, the biggest benefit of the introduction of DOCG has been a reduction in yield from 70 to 56 hectolitres per hectare, and the prohibition of the addition of wines from outside the zone. However, the permitted yield is still higher than that achieved by the best producers, who would never, in any case, countenance the use of a coarse southern wine just to boost the alcohol level of their treasured creation. The name of the producer on the label remains as important here as it is in Chianti.

The top producers will only bottle their very best wine as Brunello. Their lesser vats, made from younger vines, or those that do not have sufficient structure to age, will either be sold off in bulk or, if they are deemed attractively youthful, will be bottled and sold as Rosso di Montalcino. This DOC, instituted in 1983, replaced the previous Rosso dei Vigneti di Brunello. The wine, robust and chunky, can be excellent, and often provides better value and (dare I say it!) more enjoyment than most Brunello. It is a wine for drinking rather than ageing, and is a similar price to a decent Chianti Classico *normale.* Lacking the latter's finesse, its enjoyment is derived from its gutsy fruit and lack of pretension.

In the long term, it could be this pretension that robs Brunello of its greatness. Some producers have worn this cloak of pretension for nigh on a century as though it were a family heirloom, but all wines must justify their claims to greatness with each successive vintage. The Bordelais recognise this, as do the new Chiantigiani and the Piemontese, but today only producers like Lisini, Altesino and Il Poggione seem to be aware of it in Montalcino.

East of Montalcino, around the beautiful village of Montepulciano, the Sangiovese grape, because of its plummy colour, is called the Prugnolo. Here, it is used to make both Vino Nobile di Montepulciano, which was the first DOCG to be released on the market in 1983, and Rosso di Montepulciano.

There were more than a few raised eyebrows when the Noble Wine of Montepulciano was granted its DOCG, for it had long failed to live up to its name. True, it was said, the town is Noble, perched as it is on a hilltop surveying the Tuscan countryside with a benign and aristocratic gaze, but the wine is, at best, a good Chianti. The grape mix of 50-70 per cent Prugnolo, 10-20 per cent Canaiolo and up to 25 per cent white grapes made it quite similar to Chianti, and the wine from most producers was, frankly, poor. Only in the hands of a top producer like Boscarelli did it show why it merited special attention.

With the advent of DOCG, the white grapes were reduced by law but eliminated in practice, while the proportion of Prugnolo was increased. But the greatest improvement wrought by the introduction of DOCG seems to have been in the minds of the producers. Not only are they more aware that quality should be their aim, but they are also finding that they can obtain a higher price if they achieve it. The better producers are now making a much more careful selection, selling only their very best wines as Vino Nobile. The rest they previously sold as Chianti, but, eager to escape from the shadow that name casts, they were granted a new DOC in 1987, Rosso di Montepulciano.

Modelled as it is on Rosso di Montalcino, it is an indication that the best producers are keen to emulate the success of Brunello. The wines of Avignonesi, for instance, surpass many a Brunello for finesse, if not for longevity. By restricting their yields to 30hl/ha, and by reducing the time it spends in cask, they produce a wine which, though austere when young, unfolds after about five to seven years and displays an elegance that puts one in mind of fine Classed Growth claret. Their wine is probably the best in the zone, due to their unceasing pursuit of quality. Others, like Poliziano and Boscarelli, both of whom employ the services of Maurizio Castelli as winemaker, seem to have their sights set on the top position, so the future looks better for Vino Nobile today than it has at any time since the introduction of DOCG.

Further south of Montepulciano, across the Tiber from Perugia, is Torgiano, last outpost of quality Sangiovese. There is no competition here for title of top producer, for the

Pick of Vino Nobile di Montepulciano and Torgiano

Vino Nobile di Montepulciano

Best Producers Avignonesi, Boscarelli, Poliziano

Very Good Casalte, Casella, Carletti della Giovampaola (Poliziano), del Cerro, Baiocchi, Gracciano, Fognano, Montenero, Vecchia Cantina, Fassati, Valdipiatta

—Vintages—

Excellent 1985, 1983

Very Good 1987, 1986, 1982, 1979, 1978, 1977

Torgiano

—Vintages—

Excellent 1985, 1982, 1975, 1971

Very Good 1987, 1986, 1983, 1980, 1977

Above Average 1981, 1979, 1978

Cantina of father, Giorgio, and daughter, Teresa, Lungarotti is by far and away the best. They account for almost half the production of Torgiano, and so dominate the zone that their trademark Rubesco is almost better known than the DOC.

Two co-operatives account for the rest of the production of Torgiano, which is made from 50-70 per cent Sangiovese, 15-30 per cent Canaiolo, 10 per cent Trebbiano and 10 per cent Montepulciano and Ciliegiolo. Lungarotti age their Rubesco in oak for about 12 months, with the Riserva seeing some *barrique* in its 15 month tenure in wood. The latter, from a single vineyard, Vigna Monticchio, can be one of Italy's finest red wines, especially from vintages like 1985, 1982 and 1975. It has a velvety Burgundian richness, a svelte texture and great length – and a Burgundian price. But it does show that Sangiovese can be capable of greatness.

Perhaps the fairly high level of consistency achieved by Lungarotti's Rubesco *normale* over the years palls after a while, but it does seem less exciting these days than it once was. There is no question of the quality slipping, just that where it once stood out among Central Italian reds as a paragon of quality, many others have now caught up and surpassed it – in terms of quality, if not in price. Still, it remains a trusted friend, and a reliable one.

Below: *The beautiful village of Montepulciano, located south of Siena, is renowned for its "Noble Wine". It was one of the first DOCGs.*

S uch is the predominance of Sangiovese in the Central zone that you could be forgiven for thinking that few other native grapes are worth mentioning. This is emphatically not the case. Indeed, it could be convincingly argued that several native red grapes are of intrinsically higher quality than the Sangiovese.

Foremost among these is the Montepulciano. Widely planted in the Abruzzi and the Marches, its name, it is claimed, is derived from the Montepulciano of Vino Nobile fame. Tuscan traders are said to have transported the Sangiovese grape to the Abruzzi, where it was named after the wines it produced around the village of Montepulciano. Yet another version has it that these traders noted a similar level of quality between the native wines and those made from the Sangiovese grape around Montepulciano, and called the wine of the Abruzzi after the Tuscan village.

The latter seems a likelier explanation, as the Montepulciano produces wines that are distinctly different from those of the Sangiovese. They are deep coloured with a soft, ripe and supple fruit and a peppery character that puts one in mind of the wines of the Rhône Valley. The grape ripens later than the San-

giovese, and the wines have a lower acidity and lack the assertive tannins of, say, a Brunello di Montalcino. This combination of low acid and tannin and ripe fruit accounts for its growing popularity. At all levels, from the humblest table wine through its many DOCs, it produces a highly appealing and delicious wine of great generosity.

The finest Montepulciano comes from the Abruzzi, the ruggedly mountainous zone on Italy's Adriatic coast. The vast DOC zone covers the coastal part of the region and extends inland to the hills. Although it can include up to 15 per cent Sangiovese, the best versions are made solely with Montepulciano. They range from the soft and quaffable, like the one from Cantina Tollo, through a darker, more concentrated wine with a slightly chocolatey edge, as exemplified by Illuminati and Cornacchia, to the intensely peppery, velvety and complex version from Edoardo Valentini.

Below: *These vineyards belong to the esteemed producer of Montepulciano and Trebbiano d'Abruzzo, Dino Illuminati. His Montepulciano is one of the best examples of this fine grape.*

Above: *A sign points the way to the Cantina Sociale del Conero. The co-operatives play an important rôle in this part of Italy, the eastern coastal region of the Marches.*

Valentini sells off most of his production in bulk and concentrates his efforts on the finest grapes. He ages them for about 18 months in cask before bottling, but refuses to release the wine until he feels it is ready for drinking. The 1977, for instance, was only released in 1986, by which time it had acquired an astounding nuance of flavour and suppleness of texture. It is an outstanding wine, one of Italy's greats, acquiring with time the character that only the very best Hermitage otherwise does.

Though none can match Valentini, there are many other good producers, including Emidio Pepe, a staunch traditionalist whose highly individualistic production methods result in an alarming variability of quality. That his best bottles come close to matching Valentini makes his others, which are no better than ordinary, very disappointing.

Just south of the Abruzzi is the tiny region of Molise, where Montepulciano is DOC in Biferno and Pentro, and *Vino da Tavola* in a blend with Sangiovese that its producer, Masseria di Majo Norante, calls Ramitello. Here, as in the Abruzzi, it also makes an excellent *rosato*, the full flavour of the grape complementing the freshness of the style. Once again, Valentini's Cerasuolo, an unusually aged version, is pre-eminent.

To the north of the Abruzzi, in the Marches, Montepulciano vies with Sangiovese for supremacy. In the Rosso Piceno DOC, 60 per cent Sangiovese is blended with 40 per cent Montepulciano to produce a wine of fair depth and moderate elegance. With time, this zone would seem to be capable of great improvement, but for now Rosso Conero, from 100 per cent Montepulciano (though up to 15 per cent Sangiovese can be included), has more to offer. Its strapping, robust fruit can often match a good Abruzzese version in its youth, softening with age into a wine with good richness and a certain distinction.

Experimentation is not solely a Tuscan phenomenon, and Villa Pigna are proving that it can produce just as dramatic results in the Marches as it can anywhere. Their Tenuta di Pongelli, made from Montepulciano, Sangiovese and Cabernet, has great finesse, while their Vellutato, 100 per cent Montepulciano, has good depth and style.

From the east coast, Montepulciano spreads west and south, and its individuality becomes submerged in blends. In the Castelli Romani, the hills south of Rome, it adds a little roundness to the Sangiovese and Cesanese grapes in wines like Velletri DOC, and forms the largest portion of the Cori Rosso DOC, blended with Cesanese and Nero Buono di Cori, North-east of Rome, in the Cerveteri DOC zone, it produces a soft, moderately full wine in conjunction with Sangiovese, Cesanese, Barbera and Canaiolo. To the North, it is used in Umbria with Sangiovese to make Corbara, but is at its best with Sangiovese, Merlot and Barbera in Castello di Montoro, a wine that needs about 5 years to begin to show at its best.

As if to test the theory that Montepulciano originated in Tuscany, several producers have recently planted it there to gauge the results. Unfortunately, it tends to ripen too late for the cool Tuscan autumn, but in certain years, when full ripeness is achieved, the fatness of its fruit should add a nice fleshiness to Sangiovese's austere frame. Of the two producers that I know who are experimenting with Montepulciano, Fattoria Artimino, with their Rosso di Artimino, have had more success than Villa Cilnia's Le Vignacce. Both wines are made with Sangiovese, Cabernet Sauvignon and Montepulciano, but neither has yet achieved the refinement of other Tuscan blends.

In theory, the Montepulciano would seem to be a better bet than Cabernet for blending with Sangiovese, as it is less likely to submerge the latter's character; in practice, however, this has not proved to be the case. If it did originate in Tuscany, it has, like a long exiled person, lost any affinity it ever had for its native land.

Several other varieties native to the Central zone, though less widely diffused than Montepulciano, can produce wines of a similar quality. One is Umbria's Sagrantino, which fell into disfavour for a long time after the war, largely because of its low yields. Its

Above: *Vines near Velletri in the Colli Albani. Though not as well known as Frascati, the white Velletri can provide an agreeable alternative at a good price.*

name is thought to be derived from the Sacrament, and its religious pedigree is further enhanced by a vague association with St Francis of Assisi. It is a venerable variety, and the recent upturn in its fortunes is due largely to the DOC it was granted around Montefalco, south-east of Perugia.

Traditionally made from dried grapes, the "*passito*" style still makes the most exciting wines. Its rich and raisined fruit is sweet or "*abboccato*", but a bitterness on the back of the palate, similar to that which cuts the fruit on a Recioto della Valpolicella, gives it a dry finish, making it ideal with strong blue cheeses. The best producer of this style is Adanti. His dry version, though, tends to be tough and tannic, at least in its youth. Others produce a deep coloured, lively and generous wine, always with the characteristic bitter twist on the finish but usually lacking something of the personality of Adanti's wines.

Sagrantino is also blended with Sangiovese and Trebbiano to make the lighter Montefalco Rosso, though Adanti conspires to

Above: *A sign for "Il Casale" in the DOC of Colonna Montecompatri, a neighbour of Frascati in Lazio.*

turn out a wine that combines the fullness of Sagrantino with finesse of Sangiovese. But the future for Sagrantino lies with the varietal versions, and, on recent evidence, they should achieve fame well beyond the confines of Umbria's borders.

An even more ancient variety struggling to adapt to the modern world is the Aleatico, a grape that makes dark, alcoholic wines in Tuscany and Lazio. Aleatico di Gradoli, a DOC zone north of Rome, makes sweet, silky wines that can also be fortified. Perhaps the best versions, though, are made on Elba, around the villages of Portoferraio and Lacona. They are always sweet and rich, and usually finely perfumed and characterful, making them well worth searching out.

Cesanese, Lazio's native red grape, while seldom being worth a detour, can prove to be a reliable quaffing wine if you happen to be in the area. The three major zones for Cesanese, Piglio, Affile and Olevano Romano, are all located east of Rome, but as a grape, it seems destined to achieve fame by virtue of the company it keeps. With Sangiovese and Montepulciano, it makes Velletri, a good value wine from the Castelli Romani, and it is also to be found in the blends that make up Torre Ercolana and Colle Picchioni, Lazio's two best red wines.

Torre Ercolana, made around Anagni, south east of Rome, from equal portions of Cesanese, Cabernet and Merlot, was first made by Luigi Colacicchi in the early sixties, and is now perpetuated by his nephew, Bruno. Produced in minute quantities (about 150 cases a year), it has, over the years, acquired a great reputation. Because of the different ripening cycles of its three grapes, it varies markedly from year to year, but is usually of a very high quality.

Colle Picchioni is made by Paola Di Mauro in the Castelli Romani and carries, like Torre Ercolana, the humble *Vino da Tavola* denomination. Here, the Cesanese is blended with Merlot and a bit of Sangiovese and Mon-

tepulciano, and is as refined as Torre Ercolana, if not as ultimately impressive.

The torrent of Barbera from the north-west has been reduced to a trickle by the time it reaches the Central zone. Adanti uses it to great effect with Canaiolo and Merlot in his delicious Rosso d'Arquata, while Falerno, an ancient wine from southern Lazio, where the South and Central zones overlap, is made from Barbera and Aglianico. Its history as Falernum, the fabled wine of ancient Rome, is often more exciting than the wine itself.

Of the numerous other varieties that are sprinkled here and there throughout the zone, the Ciliegiolo, or "little cherry", produces a lightly coloured but finely scented wine that adds a certain character to Velletri and Torgiano, among others. Once widely planted in Chianti, it was replaced with Sangiovese during the sixties, and is now to be found only in small, scattered pockets. Maurizio Castelli holds it in high esteem, and includes a small proportion in the magnificent Sangioveto of Badia a Coltibuono.

Just as Chianti dominates the red wines of Central Italy, so do its white grapes, Trebbiano and Malvasia, dwarf all others in terms of quantity. Trebbiano, in fact, can lay claim to being Italy's most widely planted white grape. This popularity has more to do with its high yields and resistance to disease than to any intrinsically high level of quality. It tends to produce neutral wines with high acidity, factors which in France make it popular for use in Cognac, where, under the name Ugni Blanc, it accounts for 95 per cent of the area under vine.

If the French see it as being fit only for distillation, how does it come to be so widely planted in Central Italy? It would be nice to be able to report that its popularity is merely a relic of an age that saw quantity as of greater consequence than quality, but this would hardly explain the fact that more people seem to be turning to it today for its ability to churn out vast amounts of wine, suffering little by way of dilution in the process. True, some of the more quality conscious producers despise it, with Franco Bernabei merely regarding it as an excellent base for vinegar, but Trebbiano, like a poor novelist slated by academics, remains popular with the general public.

It is at its most popular in its Tuscan homeland. The move towards more Sangiovese in Chianti left the producers with a surplus of white grapes. Though white wines have traditionally been of little importance in Chianti, some producers reasoned that a more modern approach would increase quality and enhance any chance of success. To a certain extent, they have been proved correct. A group of large producers, led by Antinori, Frescobaldi and Ruffino, banded together in the late seventies to develop and market a wine called Galestro. The modern vinification techniques that these producers brought to the production process gave a light, clean and fresh wine, low in alcohol (10.5°) and completely different from previous Tuscan white wines. It has proved successful, in Italy at least, and the Chianti Classico Consorzio have followed suit with their Bianco della Lega, similarly based on Trebbiano. Like Galestro, it is, at best, a fresh and pleasant dry white wine, but no amount of modern vinification can compensate for the dogged neutrality of the Trebbiano grape.

Neither Galestro nor Bianco della Lega have yet been granted DOC, but most Tuscan DOCs for white wines are also blends, with Trebbiano being the predominant grape. Some of the better known examples include Bianco Vergine Valdichiana, Val d'Arbia, Montescudaio and Montecarlo, the latter being greatly helped by the inclusion of up to 40 per cent Sémillon, Pinot Grigio, Sauvignon and Roussanne.

Much better known, as we move south into Umbria, is Orvieto. From the area surrounding the beautiful town of that name, it was traditionally an *abboccato* wine (medium sweet), but is now more often made dry. Even

Above: *The vineyards in the foreground yield to the stunning hilltop village of Orvieto. The wine is now more often seen as a dry white of some distinction. Certain single vineyard versions of considerable quality make this a wine to watch.*

Below: *A couple of large, ripe bunches of Trebbiano Toscano. Its high yields make it a favourite among growers, but its wines are generally neutral.*

10 years ago, it used to be indistinguishable from other Trebbiano-based wines of Central Italy, but a recent move by some producers to increase the proportion of varieties like Grechetto and Drupeggio has paid dividends. In the case of Luigi Bigi, one of the largest producers, they have also taken to bottling separately the wine from their Torricella vineyard, and it is probably the best Orvieto currently available. The success of this move to both better grape varieties and single vineyards in Orvieto will, it is to be hoped, show other producers that quality can be made to pay.

Although seen less and less these days, the Orvieto Abboccato can be worth searching out. Light and honeyed, it is never so sweet as to be cloying, and from people like Decugnano dei Barbi, it has an attractive "botrytis" character that gives it a certain interest. Also worth looking for is the Torgiano Bianco from Lungarotti. Called Torre di Giano, its relatively high proportion of Grechetto gives it a fullness of character that belies the fact that, by law, it needs to contain a minimum of 50 per cent Trebbiano.

There is no such saving grace for Est! Est!! Est!!!, which contains 80 per cent Trebbiano. Its strange name is derived from the story, true or not, of a zealous servant preceding his master, a dipsomaniacal Bishop, on the road to Rome. The servant's brief was to mark with "Est" (Latin for "It is") the walls of inns that dispensed good wines, thus enabling his Bishop to hit the flagon immediately upon his arrival. Such was the servant's thirst upon reaching the town of Montefiascone, located on the shores of Lake Bolsena, that his judgement became blurred, and he enthusiastically marked the wall of an inn three times. His boss concurred, and got no further on his journey to Rome, apparently spending the rest of his days reaffirming his servant's initial judgement.

Rather like a person who "dines out" on a particular story for a great length of time, the wines of Montefiascone lack the character that is needed to maintain our interest once the tale of the Bishop begins to pall. Fairly crisp and nutty when from producers like Mazziotti and Antinori, they are at least superior to Lazio's most widely seen Trebbiano, from Aprilia.

All the Trebbiano wines we have previously encountered have been from one of three clones: the Tuscan, the Romagnolan or the Giallo (yellow). When we move to the east coast, to the Abruzzi, the grape they call the Trebbiano there is in fact the Bombino Bianco. It is thought to be a native of southern neighbour Puglia, whence it is generally shipped north to be used as a base for Vermouth. At some point, however, the grape was transported to the Abruzzi, where it was adopted as their very own Trebbiano.

This means that producers of Trebbiano d'Abruzzo, a DOC as well as a grape, can use either the Bombino Bianco or the Trebbiano Toscano, or a mixture of both. Recently, according to influential writer Burton Anderson, the Tuscan clone has been gaining in popularity, largely because of its higher yields. This probably explains the neutrality of most wine sold as Trebbiano d'Abruzzo, although, as a rule, it is reliable and usually inexpensive.

From one producer, however, it is neither neutral nor inexpensive. Edoardo Valentini despises the Toscano clone, and uses only the Trebbiano d'Abruzzo. Through a careful selection of grapes, a traditional but controlled fermentation and a period of ageing prior to bottling, he turns out a wine of such richness and finesse that it can only confound those who approach it as a humble Trebbiano. A fine illustration of the importance of the producer's name on the label, it is, in my opinion, Italy's greatest dry white wine, easily capable of standing in the company of fine white burgundy, whose nutty, honeyed character it vaguely resembles.

Trebbiano, alas, only reaches these heights in the hands of Valentini, and only

Above: *Bottling the 1986 vintage at Colli di Catone. Apart from their Colle Gaio, their frosted bottle Frascati is the best wine of that denomination.*

then in the finest vintages. Malvasia, however, Central Italy's second most widely planted white grape, usually out-performs Trebbiano. Sadly, it is neglected by many producers who prefer the safety net provided by the higher yields of the Trebbiano.

On its own, as we have seen in Emilia-Romagna, the Malvasia can make delicious wines. Its one drawback is its tendency to oxidise quickly, but careful handling can overcome this problem and give a wine of tre-

mendous nuance and character. This is well exemplified by Avignonesi's Malvasia, which could stake a fair claim to being Tuscany's finest dry white wine. One of the few contenders for this title would be Torricella (no relation to Bigi's Orvieto), made in the best vintages by Ricasoli at their Chianti Classico estate. Rich and refined, its subtle character is greatly appreciated by the few who get to taste it.

But these are rare examples. Popular proof of the Malvasia's potential lies, of all places, in Frascati. The most popular wine of the Castelli Romani, the hills to the south of Rome, it has been, for several centuries, the great carafe wine of Roman *ristoranti*. It was traditionally slightly sweet (called "Cannellino"), a style to which the Malvasia grape is suited, but it is now more often seen as a soft, dry white wine of little or no character.

This can, in part, be attributed to a shift in fashion, but a quick look at the DOC regulations, and the permitted grape varieties, provides a fuller answer. Malvasia di Candia and/or Trebbiano Toscano must make up 70 per cent of the blend, the remaining 30 per cent being either Malvasia del Lazio or Greco. This is the theory. In practice, much of the Frascati on the market contains a higher proportion of Trebbiano, simply because, as we have seen, it is easier to grow and produces more. The wine, after all, sells well, largely because of its famous name, so, goes the general view, there is little need to restrict yields or grow difficult grape varieties.

Below: *Trebbiano grapes arriving by the tractorload at the Cantina Sociale di Ortona in the Abruzzi.*

This is not the way Antonio Pulcini sees it. His Colli di Catone Frascati is generally the best, especially the blend that goes into his frosted bottle, or "*bottiglia satinata*". This is 100 per cent Malvasia, and has more body, perfume and interest than any other Frascati that I have come across. It also has a slightly higher price, but this is more than justified by the higher quality.

Pulcini owns few vineyards, buying in most of the grapes to meet the growing demand for his wine. He is willing to pay a premium price for the best grapes, and the results are there for all to taste in his wines. In 1985, however, he decided to go one step further and produce a wine from his own Colle Gaio vineyard. Ideally situated on steep, southwest facing slopes, it contains only Malvasia. He reduced the yield to 25hl/ha (less than that for *grand cru* white burgundy), made a vigorous selection of the grapes (he refused to make any Colle Gaio in 1986), macerated the juice on the skins for 36 hours to obtain more flavour, and then fermented at a cool temperature.

The wine is outstanding. It has a pronounced perfume (from the high proportion of Malvasia del Lazio), is very concentrated and complex on the palate, and has astounded a number of people who had previously given up Frascati as a lost cause. Pulcini has redeemed Frascati, and has also displayed the importance of the Malvasia grape in the blend.

There are several other whites in the Castelli Romani that are made predominantly with Malvasia and some, like Velletri and Marino, can be good value alternatives to Frascati. Light in colour and dry and soft in flavour, they are often indistinguishable from the real thing – but substantially cheaper. Further east, in Molise, Malvasia lends a bit of aroma to the Trebbiano in Masseria di Majo Norante's Ramitello, an attractive modern white wine from this tiny region.

Malvasia and Trebbiano play a small supporting role in Verdicchio, the dry white wine from the Marches, the central section of the Adriatic coast, that is known more for its amphora shaped "Gina Lollobrigida" bottle than for its character. Verdicchio is the major grape (a minimum of 80 per cent), and the best known version comes from the Castelli di Jesi zone, although some people feel that the lesser known Matelica offers better quality.

Verdicchio dei Castelli di Jesi has, over the years, had its claim for acceptance as a "serious" white wine taken lightly, mainly because of the gimmicky bottle. La Lolla may have been a good way of attracting people's attention 30 years ago, but today most producers are searching for a way to project a new image. Many are now making single vineyard wines, some of which can be excellent, and Bucci have even tried, with some success, to put their wine in *barrique*. But the wood masks the best of the Verdicchio grape, the crisp, salty character that is ideally matched with a plate of seafood. Its crispness, nuttiness and compatibility with seafood have led some people to call it an Adriatic Muscadet, though this is perhaps unfair on it, for it has a higher level of consistency than its French counterpart.

Because of its fairly high natural acidity, Verdicchio makes a good sparkling wine. Though little of it is seen outside of the Marches, it is well worth a try if you are passing through. The same could be said of Bianchello del Metauro, Bianchello being the grape, and Metauro the valley in which it is grown. Crisp and lively, it can be a refresher in the summer sun in which the Adriatic coast basks.

Until the recent rise of Galestro, Vernaccia di San Gimignano was Tuscany's most famous dry white wine. Made from Vernaccia grapes grown around the beautiful hilltop town of San Gimignano, it has a long tradition, and was known in medieval London as Vernage. The name Vernaccia seems to be derived from the same Latin root as the word vernacular, so was simply the title appended to the most thriving local variety. It is only in the last decade or so that the traditional style of Vernaccia, golden in colour, rich and pleasantly oxidised in flavour with a distinct bitterness on the finish, has given way to a fresher, lighter and more modern style.

Unlike in other areas, however, where the application of modern winemaking practices has led to a uniformity of style, the character of the Vernaccia grape continues to shine through in these new-wave wines. Producers like Falchini and San Quirico have proven that you can have the best of both worlds, though for my money Teruzzi and Puthod's more traditional wines are superior, especially their oak aged *riserva*, Terre di Tufo. Though Galestro may have eclipsed it in popularity, Vernaccia remains the most interesting of the traditional Tuscan dry whites.

While the fame of the village of Montalcino now rests safely in the hands of Brunello, it once was based on its Moscato vines. Villa Banfi, the large American company responsible for the Riunite Lambrusco co-operative, have, with their recent move into Montalcino, re-introduced the vine and, because they could claim that it was traditional to the area, have been granted a DOC. Low in alcohol with a vibrant, perfumed character, Moscadello di Montalcino closely resembles Moscato d'Asti, and fully vindicates the amount of effort that Villa Banfi have put into re-establishing it.

Another ancient grape that has recently been dragged back from the brink of extinction is Umbria's Grechetto. Part of the Greco family, it has developed, over the centuries, a distinctly Umbrian character that sets it apart from the rest of this venerable clan. While high yields remained the foremost consideration in people's minds, the low-yielding Grechetto fell out of favour, only saved from dying out altogether by a few producers around the villages of Todi and Foligno.

The traditional style of Grechetto is luxuriantly rich with appley and nutty overtones. From producers like Vagniluca, Caprai and Fabbri, its deep coloured and characterful wines are among the best of Central Italy, surpassed only by the likes of Valentini's Trebbiano and Pulcini's Colle Gaio.

The promise it has long displayed has recently been recognised by other producers. The best Orvietos are those where the Trebbiano proportion has been reduced to allow for more Grechetto in the blend. Another Grechetto-based blend is Adanti's Bianco d'Arquata, with Malvasia, Trebbiano and Garganega in support. Concentrated and assertive in youth, it mellows and takes on a certain Burgundian richness after a couple of years in bottle.

A sign that its future seems assured is the way it has been taken up by people like Marchesi Antinori. Grown on their Castello della Sala estate in Umbria, it is blended with Chardonnay and fermented and aged in *barrique* for a short period. It is a striking wine, lent a particular Frenchness of style by the Chardonnay and *barrique*, but with its Italian provenance asserted by the Grechetto grape.

Pick of the Native Whites

────────────── **Best Producers** ──────────────

Frascati Colli di Catone, Colli di Tuscolo, C. S. di Monteporzio Catone, Fontana Candida, Gotto d'Oro, Villa Simone, C. S. di Montecompatri

Orvieto Antinori, Barberani, Barbi, Bigi, Decugnano dei Barbi, Dubini Locatelli, Papini, Le Velette

Trebbiano d'Abruzzo Casal Thaulero, Cornacchia, Illuminati, Pepe, Sant'Agnese, Cantina Tollo, Valentini

Verdicchio Bianchi, Brunoria, Bucci, Castelfiora, C. S. di Cupramontana, Fazi Battaglia, Garofoli, MecVini, Umani Ronchi, Zaccagnini

Vernaccia di San Gimignano Falchini, Fugnano, Guicciardini-Strozzi, Monte Oliveto, Pietrafitta, della Quercia, La Quercia di Racciano, Il Raccianello, San Quirico, Teruzzi & Puthod, La Torre, Vagnoni

────────────── **Vintages** ──────────────

1987, 1986 (few of the white wines of this zone improve with ageing).

The *barrique* also comes into play in Bigi's Marrano, 100 per cent Grechetto from the Orzalume vineyard. First produced in 1985, it is an excellent illustration of Grechetto's potential when handled properly. Though still in the early stages, the wine seems set to blossom with time. And, thanks to this renewed interest, so does the Grechetto grape.

Below: *Gianfranco Garofoli with a distinctive bottle of his Verdicchio dei Castelli di Jesi. He is standing in front of an old wooden press that dates from 1871; today, most Verdicchio is pressed with more modern equipment, and fermented at a cool temperature to give it its fresh, crisp character.*

The resurgence of Grechetto in Umbria has been matched by an increased interest in French grapes, notably Chardonnay, in Tuscany. Both are part of the growing belief in quality, and, in the latter instance, it is an interest motivated by the knowledge that good white wine can only ever be made from something other than the indigenous Trebbiano. The search for a replacement, however, has proved something of a Holy Grail.

Chardonnay was the first thought of many people. It has been planted in Tuscany for over a century, but was only brought into serious production by Frescobaldi in 1973. If Tignanello can lay claim to being the first of the new-style Tuscan reds, then the Pomino "Il Benefizio" of Frescobaldi can proudly take credit for being the prototype of the post-Trebbiano Tuscan white. A blend of 80 per cent Chardonnay with Pinot Bianco and Pinot Grigio, it is fermented and aged in *barrique* and acquires, with time, a distinctly Burgundian character. Early vintages were, in the New World fashion, heavily oaked, but both 1985 and 1986 have shown greater restraint and elegance.

The vineyards of Pomino, planted at an altitude of 400-700 metres, favour the production of white wine, and the zone was given a DOC in 1983. It was the first DOC granted that was based on Chardonnay and Pinot Bianco, and the appealing creamy character of the *normale* from Frescobaldi is always in the fore of Tuscan whites.

Where Frescobaldi led, others have followed. Pinot Bianco and Chardonnay are now firmly established in Tuscan viniculture, in many instances being used as a splash of colour to relieve the blank canvas of Trebbiano. The Bianco di Coltibuono, for instance, has improved markedly since the proportion of Chardonnay was raised to 40 per cent.

Others, having seen the effect that a dollop of Chardonnay can have on a blend, have gone all the way and are now making varietal wines of some distinction. The styles vary, from wines like Avignonesi's Il Marzocco and Villa Banfi's Fontanelle, fermented and aged in *barrique,* to those from Capezzana and Isole e Olena, crisp, fresh and non-oaked. Since the 1987 vintage, the latter two producers have been especially impressive. Paolo De Marchi of Isole e Olena feels that the key to their success resides in the cool night-time temperatures they get in the Autumn, during the last stages of ripening, at the altitude at which the grapes are grown. This not only preserves the grapes' acidity, but also favours the gradual development of an elegant and delicate varietal character.

Having reached the point where fine tuning rather than major overhaul is required to improve their red wines, Tuscan producers are now devoting more attention to their whites. And they now realise, probably for the first time, that certain sites, because of their high altitude, easterly or westerly aspect and well-drained soil, are ideal for the production of white wines. This has given them the belief

and confidence to predict that, within a decade, Tuscany may surpass Friuli as the home of Italy's finest dry white wines.

Chardonnay has fired the imagination of some producers, but Filippo Mazzei of Fonterutoli feels that the cool sites are best suited to the Sauvignon grape, and that it will produce the great Tuscan white wine. Others are experimenting with it, but as yet rival producers in Sancerre and New Zealand can still sleep soundly at night. Maurizio Castelli, though, with two hectares planted at Castello di Volpaia, did make a wine that was grassy and herbaceous, but he disliked its assertiveness and put it into *barrique* for seven months to temper it. The result, Torniello, is good, but is more akin to Californian Fumé Blanc than to Sancerre.

Other French varieties are being experimented with on a smaller scale. Alcero di Napoli of Castello dei Rampolla has blended Traminer with Chardonnay and Sauvignon, while Fontodi have employed the same grape in their delicately aromatic Meriggio. Castelli has planted some Sémillon from Château Yquem at Volpaia and in Orvieto, where he feels its susceptibility to botrytis will help to improve the *abboccato* style. And even the great German grape Riesling is making inroads, with Paolo De Marchi planting a small amount in a particularly cool site at Isole in the belief that it can produce a wine of similar perfume, depth and steeliness to the best of Collio, and perhaps even Alsace.

These are just a few examples of the constant experimentation with white wines in Tuscany. Unlike the red wines, though, they have yet to take a convincing form. Perhaps this is because white wine production has always been regarded as of secondary importance, or simply because, until recently, neither the requisite know-how nor the necessary raw materials have been available to make excellent white wines.

An attempt to impose some order on the chaos has been made through the Predicato system which was outlined in the section on the red Super Tuscans. Once again, Chardonnay, Predicato del Muschio, and Sauvignon, Predicato del Selvante, are the major grapes, making up a minimum of 80 per cent of each category. The same conditions regarding yield and the altitude at which the vines can be planted apply to whites as they did to the reds, but a similar confusion regarding nomenclature appears to exist. This is a problem that will continue to dog Tuscan whites until the authorities start to grant

Above: *Chardonnay grapes arriving at Lungarotti's cantina in Torgiano. He was one of the first producers in Central Italy to experiment with Chardonnay.*

DOCs for the better grape varieties. But while most Tuscan DOCs remain obscure and anonymous, something attributable to the prevalence of Trebbiano, few producers will be actively seeking a DOC for their better wines.

Either way, French grapes will stay in Tuscany. They have not made the same inroads into the rest of Central Italy, with the odd exception of Lungarotti's Chardonnay di Miralduolo and Antinori's Cervaro della Sala in Umbria, but they seem certain to be adopted by inspired winemakers before long. This will be a positive move if it results in the replacement of Trebbiano, but if imports are used in preference to native vines like Grechetto, Malvasia and even Trebbiano d'Abruzzo, then, by contrast, Italy will lose some of her great vinous treasures.

*B*ehind the whirl of activity and experimentation that characterises Tuscan viniculture, there lie some great traditional gems, sheltered from the modern world like monks in an abbey. In the case of Vin Santo, "holy wine", the analogy is apt. This amber-coloured nectar, usually sweet, though some producers insist that the drier style is the true Vin Santo, was probably once used in religious ceremonies, but it has for a long time now been produced by each farm in the region simply for their own enjoyment.

Unlike Chianti, some of which was sold to merchants, all the Vin Santo remained on the farms. Its particular production methods facilitated this, as the quantities made are small and its oxidised style makes it less fragile than simple table wines. The result was that, as practices varied from farm to farm, there sprung up an amazing variety of styles, each claiming to be "true" Tuscan Vin Santo. This glorious confusion continues to reign today, and on the farms that adhere to traditional methods, there are many great Vin Santo produced. But it is an expensive process, and some people have attempted, unsuccessfully, to cut a few corners in an attempt to make a more affordable version.

The expense is incurred from the very outset, and mounts throughout the process. The grapes, usually Malvasia and Trebbiano, are picked normally, but are then laid on racks or, more traditionally, hung from rafters, to dry, in a similar manner to that used for Recioto della Valpolicella. The loss of liquid is greatest during the early stages, and this is when the weather is most important. It should be fairly warm, and above all dry, or else rot may set in, with a subsequent adverse effect on the quality of the wine.

Once this early stage has passed, the danger of rot is reduced. The grapes are crushed once they reach about 32°, usually at the end of January. The juice is then placed in "*caratelli*", the traditional barrels that usually have a capacity of about 50 litres. Added to the freshly crushed juice is a small amount of "*madre*" (or "mother"), a thick black sludge that consists of the lees from the previous batch of Vin Santo. Certain producers, like Paolo de Marchi at Isole e Olena, feel that this "mother" is the most important element in the process, giving life (by way of yeasts and nutrients) and complexity to the wine.

Once the juice and *madre* are together in the cask, it is sealed with wax and the fermentation begins. The casks are traditionally kept in an attic, next to the roof, and feel the full effect of the seasonal extremes in temperature. Fermentation proceeds slowly at first, because of the cold winter temperatures, but becomes tumultuous during the hot summer months. It continues like this

for a couple of years, and by the third year the seal is ready, at some farms, to be broken, and the wine bottled. Other producers, like Avignonesi and Isole e Olena, leave the wines in cask for a further one to three years, during which time they become more concentrated. The wines are removed from the *caratelli* in December and placed in demijohns (at Isole e Olena, at least) for another six months before being bottled. The *madre* is removed from the casks while they are cleaned, in preparation for the new wine, when the process begins again.

There are numerous variations on this theme. This process is used at Isole e Olena, producers of one of the best Vin Santo. Avignonesi employ a similar method, but use Grechetto grapes rather than Trebbiano and leave their wines in cask for six years. So great is the evaporation during this period that of the 45 litres of wine they place in cask, only 15 litres of Vin Santo are produced. But the result is one of the most glorious wines in the world, concentrated, nutty and complex, with an indescribably long finish. It is one of the world's great sweet wines, bearing comparison with Yquem, the great German wines and some of the Australian Liqueur Muscats.

Few match Avignonesi, though, just as Yquem stands alone in Sauternes, but there are many Vin Santo that are honest examples, less complex than the greatest but easier to drink. They make excellent aperitifs if your preference is for sweet wines, though the alcoholic weight (often exceeding 15°) of some makes them ideal after dinner wines.

Pick of Vin Santo

Best Producers Avignonesi, Isole e Olena

Very Good Badia a Coltibuono, Villa di Capezzana, Castello di Volpaia, Frescobaldi, Villa di Vetrice, Felsina Berardenga, Castell'in Villa, Giovanni Cappelli, Antinori, Monte Vertine, Pagliarese, Selvapiana, Castellau, Brolio.

Note on Producers There are, to be sure, many other good producers whose wines I have not tasted. But there are also a number of wines labelled as Vin Santo that bear little or no relation to the real thing. Beware of crude and cheap imitations, in other words.

Slowly sipped with a hard almond biscuit, "*cantuccini*", they evoke Tuscany as no other wine, even Chianti, can. At their best, they remain probably the supreme expression of Tuscan viniculture.

Below: "Caratelli" *of Vin Santo maturing away in the cellars at Fattoria Selvapiana. The wines ferment and are aged in these sealed casks for anything from 3-6 years before being bottled.*

Key to map
1 San Severo.
2 Falerno.
3 Solopaca.
4 Greco di Tufo.
5 Taurasi.
6 Vesuvio.
7 Vulture.
8 Castel del Monte.
9 Copertino.
10 Alezio.
11 Pollino.
12 Cirò.
13 Donnici.
14 Savuto.
15 Melissa.
16 Lamezia.
17 Sant' Anna di Isola
     Capo Rizzuto.

The South of Italy, generally known as the Mezzogiorno (literally "midday", as with the south of France, which is called the Midi), consists of four regions: Campania, Puglia, Basilicata and Calabria. Though northerners will tell you that it begins once you leave Rome, it is generally held to start when you cross a line that stretches from the Gulf of Gaeta in the west to the Gargano Massif in the east.

Northerners are quite content to view the South as a whole. To them, it is a poverty stricken, barren sweep of land, baking under a hot, southern sun and peopled by work-shy, indolent natives. Lifting aside the veil of prejudice reveals a different type of South, a zone of diverse peoples and landscapes, rich in natural beauty and history, though still poor and backward in many places.

The South bears many traces of the Greek civilisation that was established on its shores almost 3,000 years ago. The Greeks were as much a civilising influence in the South as the Etruscans were in the North, this part of Italy becoming known as Magna Graecia. Their civilisation flourished, and men like Pythagoras, Aeschylus and Archimedes, prevailing influences on Western thought, came to be associated with it. But by the beginning of the second century BC, a long period of decline was ended by Roman invasion, and the South was not to reach such intellectual heights again.

Crumbling Greek ruins rising out of the Calabrian coast are haunting reminders of those great days. Today, Calabria, along with Basilicata, is the poorest of Italy's regions. Agriculture is the age-old way of earning a living, but the young, unwilling to work the land for a pittance, have emigrated in droves to the cities of the north. There is little industry to keep them at home, and what little there is seems poorly, and even corruptly, managed.

Campania, its name taken from the volcanic plains beyond Naples, is more affluent.

Above: *In the foreground vines and citrus trees vie for space on the steep, terraced Campanian slopes. In the background is Amalfi. The beauty of the coastline south of Naples is stunning, and the generally undistinguished local wines do little to distract your attention from the view.*

The magic of the Bay of Naples, guarded by the islands of Capri and Ischia, still acts as a siren, luring thousands of tourists here each summer; today, its beauty is tame and benevolent. Naples, though, remains a hellish city, industrial and corrupt, but beyond the city boundaries, the countryside is beautiful if undeniably stark.

On the eastern side of the Apennines, Puglia, the South's most affluent region, strides ahead. From its rugged and mountainous northern stretches to the hot Salento peninsula of the south, its agriculture is adapting to modern ways, and tourism and industry, especially in Bari, Taranto and Brindisi, is thriving. The coast may lack the primal beauty of Calabria, but the natives will gladly exchange that for the assurance of a decent standard of living.

The sluggish pace of the Southern economy has long been mirrored by the progress of the winemaking industry. While wines from the rest of Italy have risen to international prominence, those from the South, with a few notable exceptions, have lagged behind. Producers have all the natural and technological attributes needed to make fine wine, but lack the will to make the sacrifices that are required for quality.

The wines of the South are as diverse as the people and the land. A rich seam of Aglianico runs from Campania through to Basilicata, but the outcrops of quality are few and far between. Calabria, the top of the Italian boot, is dominated by the Gaglioppo and Greco grapes, while in the east, Puglia's thriving economy is matched by a wealth of native grapes, from the Negroamaro in Salento through the Uva di Troia in the hot, central plains to the Montepulciano in the mountains that stretch to the northern border with Molise.

In the field of wine, the South is rich in raw materials. But a crucial element in the alchemist's art, in the transformation of a base raw material like grapes into something as valuable as fine wine, is the dedication and mastery of the artist. Unfortunately, too many of the South's winemakers lack this dedication. Perhaps they have grown soft through the generous subsidies provided by the Cassa del Mezzogiorno, the government organisation charged with revitalising the South's economy, for they have everything else at hand to make wines of real class.

The great, bubbling geyser of indifferent wine that gushes out of the South cannot be allowed to submerge the trickle of fine wine that dedicated producers are turning out. Their numbers are increasing yearly, a sign that before long, the Mezzogiorno may fulfil the expectations it has long promised, but seldom achieved.

The South's great red grape is the Aglianico, arguably the only one that can be spoken of in the same breath as the Nebbiolo, Sangiovese and Montepulciano. But whereas the greatness of that trio is amply confirmed by a multitude of impressive names to which they are linked, the Aglianico can only point to a handful of notable wines as evidence that it is worthy of inclusion in such noble company.

It is probably Italy's oldest known grape variety. The Greeks are credited with introducing it to Basilicata, where its success prompted them to call Italy "Enotria Tellus", or the land of vines. From Basilicata, the vine spread through the rest of Magna Graecia, the southern part of Italy that extended from Naples to Sicily. It became known as the *Vitis hellenica* (vine of the Greeks), and this was eventually corrupted to its present form, Aglianico.

It is a late ripening variety that thrives in volcanic soils on cool, hillside sites. These are the conditions found in the hills surrounding Monte Vulture, an extinct volcano in northern Basilicata where the Greeks first established their colonies. On the cooler, higher reaching slopes, in the area around Rionero and Barile, the vine is planted at an altitude of 750 metres above sea level. Trained in a bush system and propped up by

Below: *Donato d'Angelo standing with his uncle midst the Aglianico vines planted on the slopes of Monte Vulture, an extinct volcano. This ancient vine was brought to Italy by the Greeks.*

three converging canes, the Aglianico excels here as nowhere else.

This was officially ratified in 1971, when DOC was granted for Aglianico del Vulture. The zone extends down the slopes to the plains, where the Aglianico gives higher yields and broad, baked wines of little distinction. From the low bearing vines on the slopes, however, where the cooler climate (as cool as Northern Italy) provides a longer

growing season, with the vintage seldom beginning before the end of October, the Aglianico produces ripe, finely balanced grapes that can, with skill, be transformed into deep coloured and intense yet elegant wines of great quality.

This, unfortunately, happens all too rarely. There is little shortage of skill or technical expertise, but what is lacking is the will to make quality wines. Few producers, it seems, can plan low yields, a careful selection of the grapes and care during vinification and ageing into their production process. This, it is agreed, is because they have little incentive to produce quality, as the price they receive for their wines is too low to enable them to make the necessary sacrifices.

One producer, though, has shown that it can be done. Fratelli D'Angelo have for some years now been the leading producers in the zone. But while their wines have always been good, fine, strapping expressions of the Aglianico, even they have had difficulty selling their wine at the price they have had to charge. An improvement in their wines since the beginning of the 1980s, though, which has seen a move away from extended barrel ageing and a consequent decrease in the level of volatile acidity (which particularly marred their 1977 *riserva*), has enabled them to begin selling their wines in England, America, Germany and even the north of Italy at prices that, given the quality, are ridiculously cheap, but given the zone, are vertiginously high.

Winemaker Donato D'Angelo buys only the best grapes, and only makes an Aglianico in the finest of years. He macerates on the skins for 8-10 days, racks the wine twice before the end of January to ensure that it does not pick up any off-flavours from dead yeasts and then transfers it, at the beginning

Above: *Donato d'Angelo tasting his 1985 Aglianico from* barrique. *Though* barriques *are not so widely used in the South, d'Angelo's wines benefit from their short stint in small oak.*

of February, to 50 hectolitre *botti*, where it stays for 18 months to two years. The result is a tightly knit, intense wine of great power and finesse. Of recent vintages, both the 1982 and 1985 have been outstanding.

Here, as elsewhere in Italy, the *barrique* is creeping into the cellars. D'Angelo's 1982 *normale* (which sports a tan label, while his *riserva* has a yellow label) had the distinctive sweet, vanilla scented tannins of the *barrique* woven into the dense fabric of the Aglianico, but by 1985, he obviously felt confident enough to release a stunning, *barrique*-aged wine called Canneto. It is thoroughly modern, but also provides ample evidence of Aglianico's greatness.

Until recently, the finest wine made with Aglianico was considered to be Taurasi. Although the DOC discipline permits up to 30 per cent of Piedirosso and/or Barbera, the best Taurasi, that produced by Mastroberardino, is made solely with Aglianico. Grown at an altitude of between 450 and 750 metres in the cool Irpinian hills south of Benevento in Campania, Taurasi is tough and chewy when young, and often unattractive. Indeed, Mastroberardino's wines from the early 1980s often had a distinctly unpleasant lactic or sour-milk character in their youth, but they seem to throw this off as they age and open out. With a minimum of three years ageing (four for *riserva*) stipulated by law, one of which must be in oak or chestnut *botti*, they certainly have plenty of time to shrug off their youthful, gangly character.

Mastroberardino's reputation was made with his great 1968 *riserva,* but nothing since then has, in my experience, aspired to these heights. While D'Angelo's growing reputation has spurred him on to greater things, the plaudits that Mastroberardino has received have only served to help him maintain his previous level. And as Taurasi's claim to fame rests as squarely on Mastroberardino's shoulders as Vulture's does on those of D'Angelo, a certain forward movement on the part of the Campanian winery will be necessary to close the gap that D'Angelo has opened.

Aglianico is widely diffused throughout the rest of Campania and Basilicata, but it is seldom seen in the other regions of the south. A recent DOC has been granted for it in the Taburno hills, close to Taurasi, while elsewhere in Campania it is part of the blend that goes to make up Falerno (the Falernum of Roman renown) and is made into a delicate dry *rosato* by Mastroberardino called Lacrimarosa d'Irpinia. Just as none of these Campanian versions rank with Taurasi, so does little from Basilicata come close to matching Aglianico del Vulture, though that from the Colli Lucani in the eastern part of this region has an attractively robust character that, while not up to D'Angelo's standards, can equal some of the other wines produced in the DOC zone.

Aglianico holds sway in Basilicata, but its primacy, in numbers if not in quality, is challenged in Campania by the native Piedirosso. Also known as the Per'e Palummo, it makes sound, fairly full wines in Ischia (where it is blended with Guarnaccia and Barbera) and the other beautiful island that flanks the Bay of Naples, Capri. Despite being the predominant part of the blend in Vesuvio Rosso DOC,

Above: *Grapes from these Gaglioppo vines go into the production of Cirò. A wine of great antiquity, it is today a hefty red with a certain interest.*

and an important constituent of Solopaca DOC (a light and pleasant red, with Aglianico and Sangiovese augmenting the Piedirosso's presence), the best wines from this grape are probably two *vini da tavola.* It is made as a varietal on Ischia by D'Ambra, the island's best producer, and is blended with Aglianico and Merlot to make Ravello, a fairly hefty but elegant red from the Amalfi coast.

Moving south into the toe of the Italian boot, Calabria, we come into the fiefdom of the Gaglioppo grape. It is usually blended with other grapes, local ones like the Greco Nero and Bianco, the Nerello Cappuccio and Nerello Mascalese, as well as the ubiquitous Trebbiano Toscano.

The most famous wine made from the Gaglioppo is Cirò rosso, of which it makes up

Below: *Vines near Ravello, on the Amalfi coast. The red, white and* rosato *wines produced there are the finest from this part of Campania.*

95 per cent of the blend, the other 5 per cent being Greco Bianco and Trebbiano. Produced on the eastern, Ionian coast of Calabria, Cirò trades, to a certain extent, on its great antiquity. It is said to be a direct descendant of Cremissa, a chalice of which was granted to winning athletes in the ancient Olympics. It is not recorded what the vanquished were offered, but the tradition lingers to this day, with Italian Olympians receiving Cirò as an accompaniment to their meals.

It is a muscular wine with a hefty 13.5° of alcohol and a fairly rich, round and tarry character. In the past, this tarriness was held to blend well with Nebbiolo, so much Cirò found its way to Alba, where it was used to soften the rough edges of Barolo and Barbaresco, and to give a little fruit to wines that had become eviscerated through spending too long in cask. From certain producers though, particularly Librandi, Cirò is quite capable of standing on its own as a full, honest wine with little pretension to greatness. There is also a decent, full-bodied *rosato* produced from the same grapes.

The lighter, fresher style of Gaglioppo is produced due west of Cirò around Donnici. The DOC zone is situated south of Cosenza and inland from the Tyrrhenian coast, and here the Gaglioppo is leavened with Greco Nero and up to 20 per cent of white grapes.

South of Donnici is the DOC zone for Savuto, where Gaglioppo (up to 45 per cent) is blended with Greco Nero, Sangiovese and other red grapes, as well as a maximum of 25 per cent of the white Malvasia and Pecorino grapes. The wine takes its name from the Savuto river, which rises in the Sila mountains and wends its way south-west before meeting the Mediterranean at Camporra S. Giovanni. Though not as full-blooded as Cirò, Savuto has more depth and elegance than Donnici, something it derives from the steep slopes on which the vines are planted, at an altitude of between 80 and 180 metres, in the river valley. The best Savuto is probably that of Giovanni Odoardi, a doctor who produces wine as a hobby. With his livelihood guaranteed by the hospital, he can afford to indulge in luxuries like low yields and single vineyard wines, both of which are rare in the south.

Of the other Gaglioppo-based wines, Lamezia, grown around the town of S. Eufemia Lamezia in western Calabria, is a light, refreshing red, while Pollino in the north, fuller and more serious, and Sant'-Anna di Isola Capo Rizzuto, a region in the east, are the major DOCs.

No single grape in Puglia enjoys the virtual monopoly that the Gaglioppo does in Calabria. Here, several grapes have carved up the zone, asserting their territorial rights and combining to produce vast quantities of wine, most of which has traditionally been shipped north for blending.

In the south, in the Salento peninsula, the Negroamaro plays the leading rôle, often ably supported by the Malvasia Nera. The former is, as its name suggests (it literally translates as "bitter black"), a source of dark, bitterly tannic red wines while the latter lends a distinctive perfume and a soft, sweet texture to the blend. The wines were often shipped north for blending, where their colour and strength boosted a number of pallid wines, especially Chianti. The Malvasia, in particular, would develop an attractive scent with age, and it was this perfume that Maurizio Castelli found in a number of old wines from the venerable merchants that prompted him to plant the grape on an estate at Castellare.

Today, however, the wines are less in demand for blending. When the vines were trained low, in a bush system, the grapes achieved higher sugar levels, but now, as they are trained high, in the *tendone* system, yields have increased and alcohol has decreased. Unfortunately, higher yields, though responsible for lighter wines, have robbed them of concentration and any elegance they once displayed. The result is, except in rare cases, wines that are hard and unbalanced.

The best wines of Salento tend to be *vini da tavola* from respected producers. Giuseppe Calò's Portulano, Zecca's Donna Marzia rosso and Cosimo Taurino's Notarpanaro rosso are all fine examples of what these two grapes can achieve. The latter producer also makes an excellent Rosso di Brindisi *riserva* called Patriglione that vies with the best of Salento's reds. Other DOCs include the delightfully named Squinzano, the rapidly improving Alezio, and Copertino and Salice Salentino. In the case of the latter two, the wines from the best producers need time to shed the tannic bitterness of the grape, but open out after seven to ten years to show considerable class.

Despite their quality, a strong case could be made for declaring the dry *rosati* of Salento as the best wines from these two grapes. They combine the delicacy of the style with a southern strength and a great depth of flavour, giving them an extra dimension that few other rosés have. Most of the DOCs cover this style, but a number of producers also make a Rosato del Salento. Perhaps the best is Calò's Rosa del Golfo, though Leone De Castris's Five Roses certainly rivals it for renown.

The other great blending grape of the South is the Primitivo. Besides the dark, strong, rich and spicy wines it produces in southern Puglia, one of its progeny is thought to be California's Zinfandel, taken there, no doubt, by an emigrant some generations ago. Back home, a couple of Primitivo's wines are worth singling out. One is the recent DOC at Gioia del Colle on the Adriatic coast south of Bari, where it produces strapping, assertive wines, while the other is Primitivo di Manduria, a splendidly individual creation from the Salento peninsula. It comes in a variety of styles, from dry or *amabile* at 13.5° to a *Dolce naturale* at 16° and a couple of fortified versions, the

liquoroso Dolce naturale at 17.5° and the *liquoroso secco* at 18°. Not widely seen, they are worth searching out for interest's sake alone.

Leaving the Salento peninsula and moving north, the slightly cooler climate, especially in the hilly interior, lends itself better to the Uva di Troia and, to a lesser extent, Bombino Nero grapes. Wines like the colourfully named Cacc'e Mmitte di Lucera, and Rosso Barletta and Rosso Canosa, have about two-thirds of Uva di Troia, the rest comprising Montepulciano, Sangiovese and myriad other grapes. They are seldom of anything more than local interest, though further north, Rosso di Cerignola, a blend of Uva di Troia and Negroamaro, is one of the better of these mid-Puglian wines.

The Bombino Nero comes into its own in Castel del Monte *rosato*, dry and moderately full but not up to the standard of quality found in the Salento *rosati*. The *rosso*, predominantly Uva di Troia, is round, rich and vaguely interesting. By far and away the best wine that I have tasted from Castel del Monte is Rivera's *riserva* Il Falcone. Brimful of power and elegance, its class derives from the fact that it contains much more Montepulciano than is legally allowed.

Until recently, one of the better of the Uva di Troia based wines was Torre Quarto, similar in style to Rosso di Cerignola with Negroamaro and Malbec in the blend. In what seemed on paper a promising development, Torre Quarto recently replaced the Malbec element with Montepulciano, but seem to have also geared themselves to the production of a lighter style, for recent vintages are fresh, soft and pleasant but wholly lacking in

Above: A "trullo" near Locorotondo in Puglia. Similar to the "nuraghi" of Sardinia, they are the ancient and typical dwellings of this part of Italy.

the class and character that used to be evident in the wines.

In the north of Puglia, as we approach the border with Molise, the Montepulciano moves to centre stage. The only DOC is in San Severo, where the wines at their best, from producers like D'Alfonso Del Sordo, have the plummy ripeness of fruit that characterise this great grape, while never quite matching what the Abruzzi can produce.

The ancient Aleatico straddles these little fiefdoms, being produced throughout Puglia in two styles. The *Dolce naturale* is sweet, luscious and warming, while the fortified *liquoroso* is, at 16°, the stronger and richer of the two. Though seldom seen abroad, they are worth trying if you come across them in Puglia.

The French grapes have been slower to take hold in the Mezzogiorno, perhaps because experimentation proceeds at a more languorous pace under the hot, southern sun. The leader in this field has always been Attilio Simonini, whose wines, sold under the Favonio label, are made from grapes like Cabernet Franc and Pinot Nero.

Based in northern Puglia, near Foggia, his vines are grown on the hot, baked Capitanata plain, the name Favonio deriving from the warm wind that blows out of Africa over the flat, Puglian landscape. Given the conditions, it is surprising that anything creditable can possibly emerge. Great heat, after all, is the enemy of fine wine, and there can be little doubt that, despite its Mediterranean provenance, the vine gives of its best in cooler, more northerly climates.

The Cabernet Franc and Pinot Nero are particularly noted for wines from more northerly climes, so the success that Simonini has had is all the more surprising. Both are of good quality, though they betray their southern provenance by a loosely knit and rather soft finish, despite Simonini's efforts to retain acidity by picking early. The Puglian sun is a fierce combuster of acids, and picking early seems to give the Cabernet Franc its strikingly herbaceous and assertive character. The Pinot is more delicate, if slightly confected, and surprisingly enjoyable.

A more recent convert to French varieties in the south is Giovanni Odoardi in Calabria. In addition to the vines he has for use in Savuto, he has planted Cabernet Sauvignon and Cabernet Franc in several of his more favoured sites since 1983. The young vines are only beginning to come into production, although the Cabernet Sauvignon from his Vigna Pian della Corte vineyard already comprises 10 per cent of the blend, with 40 per cent Gaglioppo, 35 per cent Sangiovese and 15 per cent Montepulciano. Early results are promising, and, as his Vigna Scavina and Vigna Garrone are also planted with Cabernet, the potential looks favourable.

Despite the excitement that such experimentation brings to those of us weary of the poor quality of many southern reds, the question must be raised as to whether the likes of Simonini and Odoardi should instead be turning their attention to native grapes. The world of wine is, after all, awash with good to excellent Cabernet, but we are rarely granted glimpses of what vines like Gaglioppo, Aglianico and Negroamaro can achieve given an unswerving pursuit of quality by the producer. That people like D'Angelo, Rivera and Calò can succeed indicates that the way is open if only producers would strive to follow it.

Both Simonini and Odoardi are pursuing similar experiments with white grapes. The latter has planted Chardonnay, Sauvignon and Traminer Aromatico, all of which should come into production around 1990, while the former's fresh varietal versions of Pinot Bianco and Chardonnay are the precursors of many of today's modern southern whites.

Some, like Rivera, based at Andria, inland from Trani, are turning out crisp varietal versions of Pinot Bianco and Sauvignon that combine freshness and character. And Rivera's neighbour at Andria, Tenuta di Torrebianco, a new operation owned by northern *spumante* producer Gancia, have used the cooler climate to great effect to produce an astonishing Chardonnay called Preludio N° 1. It has better depth, balance and varietal character than many a more northerly example of this grape, and if others in the south can harness this potential, by matching the right grapes with the best sites and microclimates rather than blindly following a discredited tradition, then the future for white wines will be bright.

Once again, though, the wisdom of a wholesale conversion from native to French white grapes depends on whether more can be extracted from the former than has previously been the case. As with the native red grapes, the south is home to an array of local curiosities, some of which have great potential, as well as others of national renown.

In terms of quality, the leading grape is the Greco. As its name implies, it is of Greek origin, and has, since the days of Magna Graecia, been planted throughout the South, and even as far north as Umbria, where it is known as the Grechetto. It is usually named after the locality in which it is grown, and its

Above: *Carlo Mastroberardino with Greco grapes. This vine is probably the South's best native white grape.*

styles range from angular and dry to a sweet yet delicate white of amazing complexity.

Campania is home to the best known dry Greco, grown in the same Irpinian hills as Taurasi, around the village of Tufo. The best producer of Greco di Tufo is undoubtedly Mastroberardino, whose single vineyard version, Vignadangelo, is dry, elegant and worthy of admiration, if a little difficult to embrace wholeheartedly. The other producer of note here is Struzziero.

Little of the other commercially significant Greco-based wine of Campania is seen abroad, simply because most Capri *bianco* is drunk by the tourists who have made this island their own. A blend of up to 50 per cent Greco with Falanghina and Biancolella, it is pleasant enough to sip while your senses are

Red Grapes: DOC Zones and Best Producers

Aglianico

An ancient grape of Greek origin, found largely in Campania and Basilicata and producing some of the best red wines of southern Italy.

Basilicata

Aglianico del Vulture From producers like D'Angelo, this is the finest wine from this grape. Deep coloured, chunky and powerful, with a good capacity for ageing. D'Angelo, Paternoster, Sasso.

Aglianico dei Colli Lucani From eastern Basilicata, close to the border with Puglia. Seldom seen outside the region and rarely a match for that from Vulture.

Campania

Taurasi Rivals Vulture for the title of best Aglianico, though up to 30 per cent Piedirosso is permitted in the blend. From Mastroberardino, it needs age. Mastroberardino, Struzziero.

Taburno A recent DOC that remains an unknown quantity to all but the locals.

Falerno From around the town of Mondragone, also noted for the quality of its *buffalo mozzarella*. Made largely from Aglianico with some Piedirosso. Moio and Villa Matilde are the producers of note.

Gaglioppo

Calabria

Cirò A full red and *rosato*, from 95 per cent Gaglioppo. Caruso, Ippolito, Librandi, San Francesco.

Donnici A lighter style, with Gaglioppo comprising at least 50 per cent of the blend. Bozzo and the Cantina Sociale are the two producers of note.

Pollino Must be made from a minimum of 60 per cent Gaglioppo. Medium depth and quality, with moderate ageing potential. C.S. Vini del Pollino.

Sant'Anna di Isola Capo Rizzuto From up to 60 per cent Gaglioppo, light and, at best, fresh, though seldom seen.

Savuto Rivals Cirò as the best wine from this grape, which must comprise at least 30 per cent of the blend, with a host of others, including Greco Nero and Sangiovese making up the rest. Odoardi is the best producer here.

Negroamaro

Usually blended with the Malvasia Nera in southern Puglia.

Puglia

Alezio Up to 80 per cent Negroamaro in the full red and delicate yet muscular *rosato*, the latter of which ranks with Italy's best. Calò, Coppola.

Brindisi A red and *rosato* from 70 per cent Negroamaro. Taurino excels.

Copertino Red and *rosato* from 70 per cent Negroamaro, grown north of Alezio.

Leverano Another of Salento's Negroamaro/Malvasia Nera DOC blends. Conti Zecca is the most noted producer.

Salice Salentino Probably the best Negroamaro-based red, plus a decent *rosato*. De Castris, Taurino.

Squinzano From the area between Salice Salentino and Brindisi, a good red and *rosato* are produced much in the mould of the rest of Salento's reds. Strippoli, Valletta.

Uva di Troia

Blended with Sangiovese and Montepulciano in central and northern Puglia.

Puglia

Cacc'e Mmitte di Lucera From up to 60 per cent Uva di Troia grown in the north of the region. Seldom distinguished. C.S. Svevo Lucera.

Castel del Monte The red is from up to 65 per cent Uva di Troia, the *rosato* from Bombino Nero. Rich, soft and distinctively Puglian, it is generally regarded as one of the better reds of the region. Bruno, C.S. Locorotondo, Rivera, Strippoli.

Rosso Barletta Seldom of anything more than local interest. C.S. Barletta, Picardi, Strippoli.

Rosso Canosa Adjacent to, but inland from, Barletta, and rarely more distinguished.

Rosso di Cerignola The best of this latter trio from northern Puglia. Torre Quarto, though *vinò da tavola*, is the best wine of the zone.

---

distracted by the beauty of Capri.

Most of Calabria's white wines are based on Greco. The use of temperature control during fermentation has resulted in a change of style, from the rather dull wines of a decade or so ago to fresher and more delicate versions that bring out to a greater degree the grape's character. Of the DOC wines, both Cirò *bianco* and Melissa are of interest, especially the former which, because it contains at least 90 per cent Greco, as against the 75 per cent found in the latter, has greater depth. On the east coast, south of Catanzaro, Squillace and Lametino are two *vini da tavola* of more than local curiosity that are based on Greco.

Calabria's (and Italy's) most convincing example of Greco is the sweet version produced on the south-east coast at Bianco. From semi-dried grapes, it is sweet and usually quite strong (between 15-17° of alcohol), but is totally unlike the rest of the south's luscious and mouthfilling wines made from raisined grapes, in that it is not oxidised or raisiny in flavour.

The version to look for here is that from Umberto Ceratti. It has such a striking, elusive and fragile scent of peel and flowers mingled with its rich yet finely balanced fruit that it once stopped the conversation at a table of ten people from various sectors of the London wine trade. Nick Belfrage had brought a bottle back from Italy while researching his book *Life Beyond Lambrusco,* and we had grudgingly agreed that it should replace 1975 Château Rieussec as the sweet wine at the end of the meal. When it was poured, though, any thoughts of the marvellous Sauternes were dispelled by the brilliance of Ceratti's Greco di Gerace (as it was called before DOC was granted). It is a great wine deserving wider recognition.

A small amount of Greco is found in Puglia, but here it is used in blends with Malvasia to produce the likes of Gravina, a dry white from the west of the region, near the border with Basilicata. Like Greco, the Malvasia is a pan-southern variety. In Campania and Puglia, it is blended with Trebbiano to produce Solopaca and Leverano, though neither rises much above the ordinary. At Leverano, though, the vino da tavola of Conti Zecca, Donna Marzia, is made exclusively with Malvasia, and shows the quality this fine grape can achieve with care. In Basilicata, Malvasia is planted on Mt Vulture, where it produces decent sweet and slightly sparkling wines that never rise to the quality level set by the red Aglianico.

Trebbiano is not native to the South, but the Toscano clone was imported in the sixties because of its vigour, and it has been gaining ground since. Though it is DOC in Gioia del Colle in Puglia, and is blended with Bombino Bianco in San Severo, much of what is produced, from high yielding vines trained high in the *tendone* system, is shipped north for

blending. Indeed, the same could be said for Bombino Bianco, large quantities of which are produced to supply Vermouth houses with a base for their product, and producers of German "quality" wines and Sekt with a base metal that, they feel, can be easily transformed into gold. Unfortunately for them, Bombino Bianco resembles the great Riesling as much as their illegal blending resembles alchemy, but the clamour for Liebfraumilch has ensured a market in the north for the wines it produces.

In contrast to the neutrality of much of the production from Trebbiano and Bombino Bianco, the Moscato produces wines

---

White Grapes: DOC Zones and Best Producers

Greco
Of Greek origin. Capable of producing high quality dry and sweet white wines.

————Campania————
Greco di Tufo Dry and nutty. Mastroberardino, Struzziero.
Capri For drinking "in situ". De Rosa.

————Calabria————
Cirò Bianco Not as distinguished as the red, though much improved in recent years.
Greco di Bianco Sweet, strong and stunning. Ceratti excels.
Lametino The white (*secco* or *amabile*), non-DOC wine from Lamezia. Blended with Malvasia.
Melissa Made predominantly with Greco, it is light and dry.

throughout the south that are perfumed and characterful. Moscato di Trani, from the area surrounding the town of the same name on Puglia's Adriatic coast, has a rich amber colour and a luscious, honeyed and scented fruit. It comes in two styles, a *Dolce naturale* with 15° alcohol, and a fortified *liquoroso*, which must have at least 18° of alcohol. It rivals the great Sicilian versions as one of the south's best examples of this grape. Others are made in this style, especially in Calabria, but little matches the best of Trani, while in Basilicata, a lighter, sparkling version is produced in Vulture.

The great rival for Trani's crown is a Moscato produced in Calabria by Giovanni Odoardi. Though he claims it has been made in the family since 1400, it was only made commercially available in 1986. Called Valeo, it is made from Zibibbo grapes (Moscato di Alexandria) and another, local clone of Moscato. It is fermented in small barrels and aged, for three to four months, in slightly larger, five hectolitre casks. Amber in colour, it is delicately scented, the direct aroma of the grape muted and honed by its spell in oak. On the palate, it is rich but surprisingly dry, with great length and delicacy. As less than 150 cases are produced annually, little is seen on the market, and its great quality should ensure a constant demand.

Of the local curiosities, the Fiano is the best known, mostly because of the wine that Mastroberardino produces from grapes

Above: *Trebbiano vines at San Severo in northern Puglia. The Montepulciano grape is also planted there, where it produces wines of great appeal.*

grown at Avellino. An ancient vine, it was known to the Romans as Apianum, because of the allure its ripe grapes held for bees. Mastroberardino's Fiano di Avellino from their Vignadora vineyard is the most celebrated, largely because it is so characterful. It certainly has great concentration, but its perfume, which is variously described as being reminiscent of hazelnuts or sweaty salami, is the reason why people come to love or hate it.

While Fiano's fame slowly spreads, the two grapes found in Ischia *bianco*, Biancolella and Forastera, are not yet household names. The *normale*, crisp and pleasant, contains a higher percentage of Forestera, while the *superiore*, fuller with more character, has an extra degree of alcohol and a larger proportion of Biancolella.

In Puglia, the Verdeca is perhaps the most important of an obscure roll-call of grapes. Its finest manifestation is Giuseppe Calò's crisp and fresh Bolina, but it also combines with Bianco d'Alessano in Locorotondo and Martina Franca. Other grapes, like Coda di Volpe, Asprino and Pampanuto are found in certain parts of the south, but they deliver as little now as they promise for the future.

THE ISLANDS

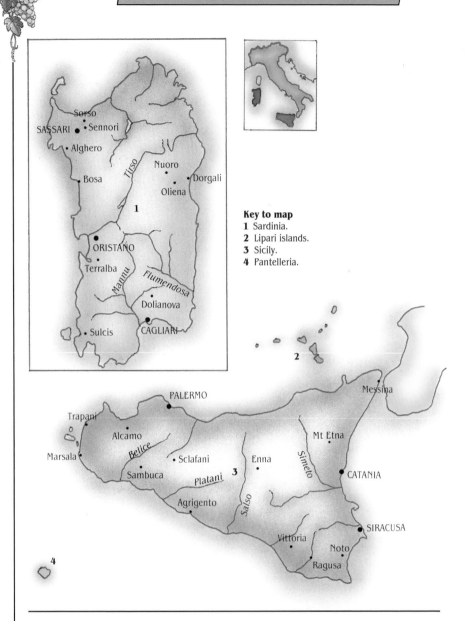

Key to map
1 Sardinia.
2 Lipari islands.
3 Sicily.
4 Pantelleria.

taly, jutting out into the Mediterranean as it does, has relatively few islands. Of those, the major ones, Sicily and Sardinia, are large enough to have developed a distinct and separate culture, while others, like Ischia and Capri, have remained linked with, and dependent upon, the mainland.

The insular mentality that can lead to such classic English newspaper headlines as "Fog in Channel–Europe cut off" is strongly in evidence in both Sicily and Sardinia. They are, respectively, the first and second largest islands in the Mediterranean. Links between the two can be established by certain topographical similarities, both having ruggedly mountainous interiors ringed by a thin strip of beautiful coastline, but their two cultures are strikingly different.

This is largely because of the stamp left by various invaders over the centuries. Sicily has been occupied by numerous foreigners since the Greeks made it part of Magna Graecia in the 8th century BC. They were succeeded by the Barbarians, who in turn were supplanted by the Saracens. The Normans replaced the Saracens in the 11th century, and were followed by the forces of the Anjou and Bourbon Kings of Naples, whose reign was ended by Garibaldi in the 19th century.

Greek temples at Agrigento and a theatre at Siracusa, Roman bridges and vestiges of Saracen architecture, and the Norman bequest of fair hair and blue eyes to some of the population are living reminders of the island's history. Since the end of the Second World War, Sicily has enjoyed a large degree of autonomy, and the island's economy has moved from medieval to modern proportions within the space of a couple of generations. Industry has moved in, but agriculture, aided by the blazing Mediterranean sun and a rich volcanic soil, remains an essential element of the economy. Olives and their thick, strong oil, pungent herbs and superb garlic, vividly

Above: *Harvesting in the vineyards at Vittoria in south-eastern Sicily. Their wine, Cerasuolo di Vittoria, is a light, quaffable red of some distinction.*

coloured and brilliantly flavoured vegetables are all part of Sicily's bounty. In addition, the waters around the coast yield a great range of seafood, all of which is simply prepared throughout the island's restaurants.

Sicily numbers several smaller and related islands among its possessions. Off the north-east coast are the Lipari, or Aeolian, islands of volcanic origin. Once believed to be the home of Aeolus, God of the Winds, their rugged, volcanic beauty, set in a brilliantly blue sea, serves as a refuge for those wishing to escape the pressures of the twentieth century. And off the south-west coast, closer to Africa than to Italy, is Pantelleria, famed for its capers and sweet, rich Moscato wines.

Sardinia, despite an equally tumultuous history, remains more isolated, and more enigmatic, than Sicily. Cretans are thought to have been the first to colonise the island, after which Romans, Pisans, Genoese and Spaniards took turns in lording it over the natives. The Sards, though, absorbed little from these outsiders, with the bulk of the population remaining in the wild and isolated mountains of the interior, scraping a living by tending their sheep. The cuisine is robust and distinctive, while their haunting folk music, seemingly unchanged for centuries (pan pipes remain an essential instrument), is beautiful to listen to.

Both islands have been transformed by the rapid developments of the post-War years. This is as true of the wines as it is of the economy and the way of life. Once noted for strong, powerful reds and oxidised (whether intentionally or not) whites, as well as the oddities like Marsala of Sicily or Vernaccia di Oristano in Sardinia, the islands' wines have been transformed by the efforts and energies of a few outstandingly tireless individuals.

Ezio Rivella led first the firm of Corvo and then Sicily along the path to modern wine-making, and other Piemontese have followed the same route, building upon the strong base he established. Sella e Mosca, Sardinia's largest private winery, has been the subject of the sincerest form of flattery, imitation, by a number of the island's co-operative wineries after it led the way in the early seventies with a fresher and lighter style of wines.

The industry on both islands is dominated by co-operatives, with several large private concerns, like Corvo and Regaleali, or the odd brilliant individual like Marco De Bartoli or Contini, adding a certain flourish. The quality of the wines from the co-ops varies according to the skill of the winemaker and the strength of the director. Unfortunately, the political demands are such that the quality of the wine is often the least important of the director's considerations.

Politics have greatly hindered the transformation of the bulk of islands' wines, as has inertia, both on the part of the grower and the authorities. The former, secure in their knowledge that the Cantine Sociali will take their grapes regardless of quality, have pushed yields to the upper limits, or have left the grapes on the vines long past the point when they should have been harvested, simply to increase sugar levels. The latter have exacerbated the situation by paying farmers for potential alcohol rather than quality, and by propping up, with healthy injections of cash (liberally dispensed by the EEC) incompetent, and sometimes even corrupt, operations.

In an ideal world, a co-operative would be closely involved with work in the vineyard, advising farmers on what to grow and where and how to plant and train their vines, and when to harvest their grapes. At the winery, the grapes would be sorted not according to potential alcohol but to their quality, health and sugar/acid balance. The best would be vinified separately, at a controlled temperature in stainless steel tanks, and there could even be a provision for the separate vinification of favoured vineyard sites belonging to farmers who cannot do this themselves.

The aim of a co-operative should be to improve the individual member's lot by providing technical expertise, and help with sales and marketing. By improving the quality of the collective product, a higher price could be asked, thus generating more revenue that could in turn be redistributed to the members. There are good co-operatives, like Dolianova in Sardinia and Sambuca in Sicily, but too often political considerations, inertia and shortsightedness combine to produce a wine that is virtually unsaleable, and which must instead be drained off into the European wine lake.

That there is a great wealth of raw materials waiting to be transformed into wines of real interest is evident by the quality of some of the better wines that have emerged. This is especially the case in Sicily. Surprisingly, given the popular conception of full, southern reds, Sicily produces more white than red wine. The leading red variety, in terms of production, is the Calabrese, also known as the Nero d'Avola. It is grown throughout the island, often being blended with Nerello Mascalese and Perricone. The latter, also called Pignatello, is, according to some producers, merely the local name for Barbera.

The only DOC in which Nero d'Avola figures prominently is Cerasuolo di Vittoria, a fresh, youthful red from the area around Ragusa, a town in the south-east corner of the island. Probably because of the Nero d'Avola element, it is held by some authorities to be a likely candidate for ageing, but different approaches to production and the inclusion of lighter grapes like Frappato (up to 40 per cent), have conspired to make most of what is produced light, fresh and attractive when young. Good producers include Carlo di Modico, Coria and Giudice.

Nero d'Avola also lends style to some of Sicily's better *vini da tavola*. Eloro di Casale (produced at Noto, not far from Ragusa), Faustus (from the northern coast, just east of Palermo) and, from the south, Steri (made near Agrigento by Giuseppe Camilleri) and, of course, Regaleali and Corvo, are, though different in style, all established as the island's leading red wines. Newer labels, like Giacomo Rallo's Donnafugata, Terre di Ginestra and the Cellaro from C.S. di Sambuca in Sicilia, are all fine examples of Sicily's fresh, modern reds.

The style varies as much according to the

Above: *Crushing grapes at the Cantina Sociale La Vittoria in south-east Sicily to make an attractive light red.*

Above: *These flasks in the laboratory at the "Cantina Sperimentale di Noto" are signs of increasing research into what training systems and grape varieties are best suited to particular sites. The work augurs well for the future.*

gives a wine of good depth, further to the north and east, around Messina, it is the major component in the finer Faro *rosso*. Though it gives red wines of good colour, it seems that the Nerello Mascalese could soon come to rival the Negroamaro and Sangiovese as the source of Italy's finest *rosati*. It lends structure and depth to those from Cellaro and Donnafugata, and more experience should result in better wines.

Sardinia's reds are similarly based on three major grape varieties, but they are almost always produced as varietals. Cannonau, a Spanish import (the Garnacha, or the Grenache, France's second most widely planted variety), has been grown on the island for at least two centuries, and is fully acclimatised to Sardinian conditions. As in Spain and France, its hallmarks are a full, honest fruit and a hefty whack of alcohol.

It comes in a variety of styles, from soft and generous to sweet and fortified. The DOC zone covers the whole island, and the discipline stipulates that the wine must have a minimum of 13.5° alcohol (15° for *superiore*). Many producers opt out of DOC in order to make a lighter style of Cannonau. One of the most impressive and distinctive Cannonaus is the sweet Anghelu Ruju of Sella e Mosca, made from partially dried grapes. With up to 18° of alcohol, it has a deep garnet colour, a spiced raspberry type of fruit on the nose and a rich, sweet and powerful fruit on the palate that puts one in mind of port, both for its texture and potency.

Sardinia's other widely grown red grape of Spanish origin is the Monica. The Monica di Sardegna DOC produces moderately full and decent quaffing wines, while the zone centred around Cagliari, on the south of the island, is home to stronger, sweeter and sometimes even fortified wines.

producer's preference as it does to factors like soil, climate and *uvaggio*. At Regaleali, for instance, their *rosso*, following the prevailing fashion, has become lighter over the last few years, but their flagship red, Rosso del Conte (probably Sicily's best red), has remained as full and beefy as before. They use only late picked Perricone and Nero d'Avola grapes to get a deep coloured, broadly flavoured and robust wine that ages for up to a decade and more.

Nerello Mascalese constitutes 80 per cent of the blend for Etna *rosso*, grown on the eastern slopes of the volcano. While here it

Amidst the sea of Monica and Cannonau, in the south-west corner of Sardinia, is a small island of Carignano. Once again, it is Spanish in origin, but, as Carignan, is now France's most widely planted red grape variety. The DOC zone is centred on Sulcis, and in addition to a good *rosato*, a generously proportioned red is produced.

The white grapes of the islands offer greater diversity, both in numbers and in styles. This wealth makes it all the more depressing that over half of Sicily's total production comes from a mere two varieties, the Catarratto and Trebbiano Toscano, that are both capable of making sparkling mineral water seem lively and characterful.

The Catarratto covers 40 per cent of the island's surface that is under vine, but it is receding in importance. It is being replaced by the Trebbiano, a sturdier, higher yielding but no less boring vine. The former is found in Bianco Alcamo and Etna *bianco*, and is blended with Trebbiano to produce the delicious Cellaro *bianco*. Here, a careful selection of grapes grown on slopes reaching up to 700 metres, followed by scrupulous control during vinification and a rigid selection policy (they bottle only 5 per cent of what they produce) shows that even these two grapes, when handled carefully, can produce something of interest.

The low yielding Inzolia is, along with Marsala's Grillo, the best white grape of Sicily. Though prone to oxidation, it can, when vinified with care, give a wine of great delicacy and character. It is used in Corvo's Colombo Platino, and in Regaleali *bianco*, two of Sicily's finest white wines. The latter also contains some Sauvignon in the blend (up to a third), while their Nozze d'Oro, originally released to commemorate the owner's, Conte Tasca d'Almerita, fiftieth wedding anniversary, has a much higher proportion of Sauvignon, and is easily Sicily's finest dry white.

The Domaschina is a Sicilian native that has been showing promise in the hands of several producers. The introduction of temperature control during fermentation has enabled them to retain its delicate flavours, and to discover nuances that were not previously evident. De Bartoli reckons it has the potential to become Sicily's Chardonnay, and his version, Baglio Samperi, and the one from Donnafugata, both indicate that they are at least proceeding down the right path.

As with Sicily, almost all of Sardinia's white grapes are native to the island, or have been there long enough to have been granted honorary native status. The Vermentino falls into this latter category. It is a different grape from Liguria's Vermentino, being instead, like the grape of the same name grown on neighbouring Corsica, a Malvasia, probably imported from Spain several centuries ago.

It is widely grown, and accounts for some of Sardinia's more interesting white wines. It has traditionally been produced as a deep coloured, powerful and soft wine, especially in the northern Gallura DOC zone, but with the new technology, producers are discover-

ing that they can make a lighter and more delicate style that not only sells better, but is also quite delicious. Vermentino is produced as a *vino da tavola* throughout the island, but the best wines generally come from the north, with the trend in styles following the same pattern as the DOC zone.

Nuragus is Sardinia's most widely planted grape variety, but it lacks the intrinsic interest of Vermentino. Said to have been brought to Sardinia by the Phoenicians, it is named after the ancient conical stone fortress houses, the "*nuraghi*", that are dotted about the island. Nuragus is DOC in Cagliari's Campidano plain, where it produces soft, fresh wines that are, at best, pleasant.

The Torbato, another variety of Spanish origin, is in contrast probably Sardinia's finest white grape, but very little is produced. Sella e Mosca make the only commercial version that I know of from grapes grown at Alghero on the island's north-west coast.

Right: A row of "botti" in Sella e Mosca's cantina, long the pacesetters in quality wine in Sardinia.

Pick of Sardinia

Cannonau
Widely grown and produced in a variety of styles. Must have 13.5° of alcohol to be DOC.

Cannonau di Sardegna Can be red, *rosato*, of varying strengths, sweet, dry and fortified. Better producers include C.S. di Dorgali, C.S. Dolianova, C.S. Sorso-Sennori, Sella e Mosca. Other Cannonaus include a *passito* from the Consorzio per la Frutticoltura at Villasor and Anghelu Ruju from Sella e Mosca; Cannonau di Dorgali; Cannonau Capo Ferrato from C.S. Castiadio; Cannonau di Alghero and Cannonau del Parteolla.

Monica
Monica di Sardegna Good if less versatile than Cannonau. C.S. del Campidano, C.S. Dolianova, C.S. Marmilla, Zedda Piras.
Monica di Cagliari C.S. di Villacidro, Zedda Piras.

Malvasia
DOC di Bosa Dry, sweet, fortified, occasionally exquisite and usually expensive. Mercedes Cau Secchi, Donchessa, Deriu Mocci.
DOC di Cagliari Also dry, sweet and fortified, but the grape does not carry itself with the same distinction here. C.S. di Serramanna, C.S. Dolianova, C.S. Marmilla, Zedda Piras.
Planargia Grown around Bosa, and similar in style to the DOC wines, but a *vino da tavola*. C.S. della Planargia, Vigna Murapiscados.

Moscato
DOC di Cagliari Sweet and fortified versions. The Cantine Sociali at Dolianova and Marmilla both produce good versions.
DOC di Sardegna A Sardinian version of Asti. C.S. Gallura.
DOC di Sorso-Sennori Sweet, rich, scented and quite rare. The Cantina Sociale is the major producer.

Their *cru* Terre Bianche is especially fine, its ripe, broad, biscuity and slightly nutty fruit cut by a crisp acidity on the finish making it resemble nothing more than a very good *sur lie* Muscadet.

Of the two other native varieties of note, the Nasco and Vernaccia, the former is grown alongside the Nuragus on Cagliari's Campidano plain, where it is DOC for wines of varying degrees of sweetness and strength. It is usually seen as a dry, strong (14° alcohol) aperitif type wine, although it is also made in a fortified style, and it can be sweet in either category. The Vernaccia (not related to the Tuscan or any other Vernaccia) di Oristano is Sardinia's most famous, and quite possibly best, wine. Though unfortified, it naturally reaches at least 15° of alcohol after several years of cask ageing, and, as it develops a *flor* during this time, it acquires something of the character of an old sherry. There is also a sweet and fortified style, but the classiest is

definitely the dry, with the *riserva*, which takes on an extra dimension after at least four years cask ageing, being the epitome of this style.

Before the advent of stainless steel and temperature controlled fermentation, the producer working under the hot Mediterranean sun was often wiser to induce oxidation intentionally, to produce a gently oxidised wine rather than to attempt to make a lighter table wine, which would oxidise in any case. The result has been a number of wines, from Marsala to Anghelu Ruju to Vernaccia di Oristano, where the sun's heat has been harnessed to make wines of strength, rather than fought against in an attempt to produce lighter table wines.

Some of the great glories of the islands are produced in this style, from the two grapes, Malvasia and Moscato, that Sicily and Sardinia have in common. Their perfume is retained but accentuated and amplified, often simply by the way the grapes are dried in order to produce the exquisite *passito* wines.

Sardinia is home to most of the Malvasia found in the islands. The Malvasia di Sardegna is held to be a distinct clone, and is DOC in two zones. On the west of the island, south of Alghero, there is a zone centred on the Planargia hills around the town of Bosa. Malvasia di Bosa is much sought after for its finely scented, rich and complex character, but little is seen outside the zone. It can be either dry or sweet, and can be fortified. While the dry wines are best sipped on their own, the sweeter versions are usually served at the end of the meal. The fortified style has more immediate appeal, but seems to lack the finesse of the lighter version, whether *secco* or *dolce*.

A few producers in this area step outside the DOC discipline to produce a *vino da tavola* from the Malvasia. Often called Malvasia di Planargia, it is usually dry and youthful (not being aged for the two years required by

Above: *This newly installed refrigeration equipment at a co-operative in Sicily is necessary if the temperature is to be controlled during fermentation.*

Below: *These Moscato grapes, drying in the sun on Pantelleria, will be used in the island's great "passito" wines.*

Pick of Sicily

DOC Wines

Bianco Alcamo Baronati Normanni-Rallo, Pellegrino, Rapitalà, Rincione.
Cerasuolo di Vittoria Coria, Giudice, di Modico.
Etna Vignaioli Etnei, Linguaglossa, Villagrande.
Malvasia delle Lipari Hauner
Moscato di Pantelleria De Bartoli, Cantina Sociale (Tanit)

Non-DOC Wines

Cellaro A good red, white and *rosato* from the hills surrounding the Saracen town of Sambuca in south-west Sicily.
Cerdese *Rosso, rosato* and *bianco* produced by Fontanarossa.
Corvo An excellent range from the Duca di Salaparuta.
Donnafugata A recent venture by Giacomo Rallo that has been successful.
Eloro di Casale A distinguished red produced by Modica di San Giovanni.
Faustus Three styles from Giuseppe Mazzetti's Azienda Grotta.
Regaleali One of the island's top estates, presided over by the Conte Tasca d'Almerita and his family. Their Rosso del Conte and Nozze d'Oro stand out.
Rincione A good red, white and *rosato* from the Alcamo zone.
Steri Characterful wines, especially the red *riserva*, from Giuseppe Camilleri.
Terre di Ginestra A decent white and better than average red from the province of Palermo.

Though a Moscato di Pantelleria *naturale* and *liquoroso* are both produced, the best and most widely seen wine is the Moscato Passito. The grapes are picked at the end of August, and are laid out on mats to dry under the blazing sun. The hotter the sun the better at this stage, for the more rapid the "*appassimento*", the better the quality of the resulting wine. The grapes are turned over half way through, rather like a grilling steak, to ensure that the other side gets done as well.

The *appassimento* lasts for about three weeks, and at the end of this period the grapes, an unedifying brown colour, are crushed and fermented. The wines usually reach about 14° of alcohol, and are sweet and raisined. The biggest producer, the co-operative, sell their Moscato Passito under the name of Tanit and, though sound, it suffers by comparison with the version from Marco De Bartoli. Called Bukkuram, its heady perfume and intense flavour makes it one of Italy's great sweet wines.

The other Sicilian Moscato of renown comes from a producer who, like De Bartoli, is wholly committed to the concept of quality. Giuseppe Coria produces his sweet and delicately scented Moscato di Villa Fontane from lightly dried grapes grown near Vittoria, west of Siracusa. While De Bartoli's version is best caught in the first flush of youth, within a year or two of the vintage, Coria's is less impressive while young, but it can age for anything up to eight to ten years in bottle.

Compared with these two fine versions, Sardinia's three DOC Moscati are somewhat dull and plodding. Two of the zones, Cagliari and Sorso-Sennori (on the north-western coast) produce deep coloured, strongly scented and luscious wines of some distinction, while a recent DOC for Moscato di Sardegna aims for the production of a lighter, sparkling wine somewhat in the mould of Asti Spumante. No doubt it will find favour with the many Piemontese that visit the island each summer, but it has some way to go before rivalling Asti, either for quality or success in the export markets.

While the heat is used to amplify the scent of these aromatic grapes, there is another style of wine that harnesses the sun and transforms its potentially negative character into something beneficial. In Sardinia, we have already seen grapes like Nasco and Vernaccia that produce wines in this style, but Sicily is perhaps better known for its dry and oxidised wines.

These are from grapes that we have already met, the Grillo, Inzolia and Catarratto, but the method of production plays just as important a rôle in determining the style and quality of the wine. The wine is deliberately oxidised and aged in cask for a varying number of years, sometimes in a solera system. Among the better examples of this style are Corvo's Stravecchio di Sicilia, Coria's Stravecchio Siciliano and, of course, at its driest and best, Marsala, to which we shall now turn our attention.

law), though the version from the Cantina Sociale della Planargia is, intriguingly, *spumante* and *demisec*. Perfumed and charming, it is best drunk young.

The other DOC zone for Malvasia is found further south, in the popular Campidano plain. There are the same four styles as are found in Bosa, but here the wines lack the intensity, charm and finesse of their northern counterpart.

Sicily's only significant contribution to fine Malvasia comes, in fact, from the Lipari islands. Malvasia delle Lipari is always sweet and scented, but can also be made in a *passito* style (from dried grapes) or *liquoroso* (fortified). The best producer by far is the Swiss expatriate Carlo Hauner, an architect by profession who visited the islands as a tourist and decided to stay. His wines are intense yet delicate, with a pure scent of dried apricots and a rich, sweet fruit on the palate that finishes clean and long.

The Sicilians' preference for Moscato manifests itself in a number of fine wines from around the island. Though DOC in Noto and Siracusa, in the south-eastern corner of the island, little of either is seen. The finely perfumed Moscato Bianco is stipulated in both zones, but in Pantelleria, an island south-west of Sicily, the Moscato di Alexandria is used to produce a wine that is much more widely seen than either of those from the mainland.

The grape is known as the Zibibbo on Pantelleria, apparently after Africa's Cape Zibib, from whence it was brought to the island.

*O*n the western coast of Sicily lies the small and affluent port town of Marsala. It has a faintly African air, a gentle pace of life and what would seem to be a disproportionate number of statues of Garibaldi. This is because, as every Italian schoolchild knows, it was at Marsala that Garibaldi landed in 1860 at the beginning of the Expedition of the Thousand, which freed Sicily, Naples and the rest of the South from the rule of the Bourbons, and eventually led to the unification of Italy.

Its name derives from Marsah el Allah (Port of God), which is what the Saracens called it when they rebuilt it in the tenth century, giving it the African look it retains to this day. The wine that takes its name from the town was "invented" by an English merchant called John Woodhouse in 1773. Woodhouse came to know and like the strong, dry and oxidised wines of this part of Western Sicily, wines that were probably similar in style to the sherry that was being produced at the time, and he decided that he could make a market for them in England.

Woodhouse, probably drawing upon the English experience in the Iberian peninsula, fortified the wine in order to preserve it for the long journey back to Liverpool. His initial hunch proved correct as Marsala grew in popularity, and by the turn of the nineteenth century, Woodhouse was, according to the writer Bruno Roncarati, supplying Nelson's fleet with his "new" wine.

As sales increased, other merchants joined Woodhouse in shipping the wine to England, and in establishing premises and a small English colony in Marsala. A number of styles proliferated, as many as there were

producers, no doubt, but this did nothing to diminish the esteem in which it was held by the Victorians, both for its sweet and tangy flavour and its versatility in the kitchen.

The great heights it reached in the nineteenth century are sadly mirrored by the

Marsala DOC Regulations

Colour

"Ambra" (amber) Found under the Fine and Superiore styles, each of which must, by law, contain at least one per cent of *"mosto cotto"*. This stipulation makes this colour the least exciting of the three.

"Oro" (gold) Generally the finest, and also found under the Fine and Superiore styles. The use of *"mosto cotto"* is forbidden in the production of this colour.

"Rubino" (ruby) A new addition to the discipline. Made under the Fine and Superiore styles from Pignatello, Calabrese and Nerello Mascalese grapes. The use of *"mosto cotto"* is forbidden.

Sweetness

"Secco" (dry) Sweetness applies only to the Fine and Superiore styles, with dry indicating that there is less than 40 grams per litre of sugar in the wine.

"Semisecco" (semi-dry) This has between 40 and 100 grams per litre of sugar.

"Dolce" (sweet) This has over 100 grams per litre of sugar.

Styles

Marsala Fine Must be aged for at least one year, and have a minimum of 17 per cent of alcohol.

Marsala Superiore Must be aged for at least two years, and have a minimum of 18 per cent of alcohol.

Marsala Superiore Riserva 18 per cent alcohol, but four years of ageing.

Marsala Vergine Must have 18 per cent alcohol, and be aged in cask for at least five years. Must be unsweetened, so the use of *"mosto cotto"*, *"concentrato"* or *"sifone"* is prohibited. Marsala Vergine must be sold only in bottle.

Marsala Vergine Riserva or Stravecchio Has the same requirements as Marsala Vergine, but must be aged for at least 10 years.

Above: *Marco De Bartoli, pictured here with a glass of his Vigna La Miccia, has set himself the task of restoring the fortunes of Marsala.*

depths it has managed to plumb in our own century. Once one of the world's great fortified wines, it has declined from being a wine that could stand alongside sherry, port and madeira to one that provokes mirth if you dare include it in such illustrious company today. At the end of World War II, it seemed in its death throes, destined to become little more than a footnote to the history of wine. By the 1970s, Marsala had become a byword for sweet, sticky and fortified wines that were flavoured with anything from eggs to chocolate or bananas.

Today, the Marsalese are left wondering where they went wrong, and how they can restore their wine to its former glory. Most agree, sadly if reluctantly, that their grandparents ruined Marsala by following the industrial, rather than the potable path, and allowing it to become a flavoured concoction that was used for cooking rather than a wine for drinking. But when it comes to curing the industrial malaise that has settled over the industry, few have the energy or creativity to know where to begin.

They could, of course, begin in the vineyard. The grapes used for Marsala are Grillo, Inzolia and Catarratto. The first of this trio, the Grillo, was the original grape of Marsala, and is still viewed as the best. It is low yielding but reaches a high degree of ripeness and gives body and structure to the wine. Grillo, in fact, can produce wines that, when fermented to dryness, end up with as much as 16-18° of natural alcohol.

Of the other two grapes, the Inzolia is prized for the perfume it lends to the wine, while the Catarratto, a high yielding vine that produces fairly neutral wines, gives little to the final blend of quality Marsala. Its vigour, though, ensures that it is the most widely planted vine, for low bearers have little to offer to a wine that is sold at the lowest possible price.

It seems likely that Marsala was originally dry, but sweetened to satisfy the English market. Of the three ways used to sweeten Marsala, only one, "*sifone*", can claim to have the interests of quality in mind. *Sifone*, or "*mistella*", is produced by adding grape brandy to unfermented grape must. The resulting product is much finer, and gives a degree of sweetness that meshes with the wine, highlighting rather than masking its delicate flavours.

The production of *sifone* is, unfortunately, an expensive process, so cheaper Marsala relies upon the use of "*concentrato*", concentrated grape must, or "*mosto cotto*", boiled grape must, reduced to give a caramelly, cooked product, to add sweetness to the wine. In most cases, this sweetness is necessary, not to enhance flavours but to mask defects in the wines.

The DOC for Marsala is a contorted, ambiguous law that does little to provide any impetus for quality. The whole ugly edifice is constructed of compromises and concessions, almost all of which favour the industrial producers. The wines are classified according to colour (gold, amber and ruby), sweetness (dry, semi-dry and sweet) and style.

There are three basic styles of Marsala. The first, Marsala Fine, must have 17° of alcohol and be aged for one year before release, and it must be sweetened. It is usually anything but fine, being a cheap and rather nasty travesty of the name Marsala. The next style, Marsala Superiore, simply has an extra degree of alcohol and an additional year's ageing, and can be dry or sweet, depending on the style of the house. This was, and probably still is, the most popular style for drinking, being to Marsala what cream sherry is to Jerez. The Marsala Superiore Riserva, aged for four years, should be more elegant and concentrated than the younger wine.

The third style is unsweetened, and is known as Vergine. It must have 18° of alcohol and a minimum of five years' ageing (ten years for the Riserva or Stravecchio). These wines are dry and nuanced, and from the best producers, simply superb. They are wines to sip and marvel at, and, though highly individual, they are comparable to, in terms of breed and finesse, a very fine and dry old Amontillado.

Some producers use a solera system to make their Vergine, while others simply leave them in cask, on ullage, for a number of years, and refresh them with a bit of young wine prior to bottling. Or perhaps I should say "used to", for no firms that I know of are prepared, in the current market, to invest the money necessary to produce an old Vergine, and few have any stocks of the older wines that go into this product.

One of the few producers who continued to produce a great Vergine was Rallo, but they have unfortunately gone out of business. It is sad, wandering around their cavernous *cantina*, tasting the small amount of exquisite old wine they have left in cask, to realise that the world cares little about what happens to this once great company. Indeed, even the Marsala industry is more curious than concerned about the future of Rallo.

One man who cares passionately about Marsala is Marco De Bartoli. He detests the industrial product, and is determined not only to halt the demise of Marsala, but also to prove to a doubting world that Marsala can be, indeed is, a great wine.

Born into the Marsala trade, he knows and remembers the great wines of the past. After leaving university, he worked for the companies that his parents were involved with, Pellegrino and Mirabella. He became increasingly dissatisfied with the state of the Marsala trade, and frustrated at the indifference that the Marsalese displayed towards its decline. Knowing that nobody was laying wine down any more, he started, during the 1970s, to buy up stocks of old wines from the cellars of various families that he knew in the area. In 1980, he severed his contact with the trade and set up on his own at a small property that had belonged to his mother at Samperi, just outside Marsala. It was an acrimonious break, not only with the trade, but also with his family, who opposed what they viewed as a foolish venture.

Though De Bartoli made the break with a certain amount of fanfare, it was essentially a foolish move. Who after all, however outstanding the quality, would be prepared to invest more than the cost of a bottle of top quality Amontillado sherry in a little known wine that did not even call itself Marsala?

Fortunately for De Bartoli, he had his family's money behind him, as well as extraordinary reserves of energy within.

Using Grillo and Inzolia, he ages the wines in something of a solera system to produce a dry, unfortified Marsala-type wine called Vecchio Samperi. It is, says De Bartoli, the way

Below: *The large stocks that a Marsala producer must hold are difficult to finance when the wine is sold so cheaply.*

Above: *De Bartoli's Vecchio Samperi, seen here ageing in cask, is a dry, unfortified (and hence, not Marsala) wine of great character.*

Marsala was made before the English arrived and started sweetening and fortifying it. Because it is unfortified, he cannot call it Marsala, even though, because of various factors like the use of ripe grapes from low-yielding Grillo vines and the evaporation and concentration that occurs during the protracted ageing in cask, it naturally achieves 16-17° of alcohol.

He bottles a 10, 20 and 30 year old Vecchio Samperi. The youngest combines a dry, nutty and candied fruit that is wonderfully complex yet full of youthful vigour. As you move through the older wines, they get more intense and nuanced, taking on various shades of flavour that delight the palate. All are outstanding, and one sip of either, preferably at the end of a meal with a piece of strong cheese or a few nuts, is enough to convince anybody of the great heights that Marsala is capable of reaching.

In addition to a fresher, aperitif-style wine called Josephine Doré, which is drawn off the Vecchio Samperi solera after three years, De Bartoli now makes a couple of wines that bear the name of Marsala. They are, like the rest of his stable, thoroughbreds through and through. The first, called Marsala Superiore, is a 20 year old wine sweetened with *mistella,* and though it lacks the shades of flavour found in the drier Vecchio Samperi, it is wonderfully rich and characterful. His newest creation is a delicately perfumed and cool fermented wine made from Inzolia and Grillo grapes grown in his La Miccia vineyard. As if to display his contempt for the DOC discipline, De Bartoli has made it so that it is entitled to be called Marsala Superiore.

The De Bartoli wines have not only put Marsala back on the map of quality wine, but they have also shown the direction in which salvation lies for the rest of the Marsala producers. But unless the Marsala DOC is revamped, so that it is principally concerned with quality, then Samperi will remain a glorious but lonely outpost of quality in Western Sicily.

*I*NDEX

Names of wines, grape varieties, vineyards, and producers are indexed. The numerals in *italics* refer to illustrations.

Bibliography

Burton Anderson, *Vino*, Little, Brown and Company, Boston, 1980.

Burton Anderson, *The Mitchell Beazley Pocket Guide to Italian Wines*, Mitchell Beazley, London, 1982, revised edition 1987.

Nicolas Belfrage, *Life Beyond Lambrusco*, Sidgwick & Jackson, London, 1985

Michael Garner and Paul Merritt, *The Wines of Alba*, Bodley Head, London, to be published 1990.

Jancis Robinson, *Vines, Grapes and Wines*, Mitchell Beazley, London, 1986.

Luigi Veronelli, *Catologo Veronelli dei Vini d'Italia*, Giorgio Mondadori, Milan, revised edition 1989.

Vini d'Italia, Le Guide del Gambero Rosso, 1989.

Sheldon and Pauline Wasserman, *The Noble Red Wines of Italy*, New Century, 1985.

Picture Credits

Other than the illustrations listed below, all the photographs reproduced in this book were taken as a special commission by Michael Rock of Cephas Picture Library, Walton-on-Thames, Surrey. The publisher would like to thank him and his wife, Annie, for their special contribution to this book. Thanks are also due to Maureen Ashley M.W., and the many wine producers and importers who also supplied illustrations and sample labels for inclusion. The photographs are here credited by page number.

Maureen Ashley: 145, 147 both, 150 both, 153.
Fattoria Barbi: 96/7.
G. Belloni & Co. Ltd: 104.
Italian Wine Agencies: 149.
Martini & Rossi: 50.
Carlo Pellegrino & C: 154/5.
Leonildo Pieropan: 72.
Cantine Coop. Riunite: 88, 89.